THE
GAINSAYERS

A Converted Anti-Mormon Responds To Critics of the LDS Church

GAINSAYERS
Those who. . .
oppose or deny
speak or act against
contradict
dispute or declare false

Darrick T. Evenson

Third Printing: June, 1998

International Standard Book Number:
0-88290-338-1

Horizon Publishers' Catalog and Order Number:
1023

Printed and distributed
in the United States of America by

Horizon
Publishers
& Distributors, Incorporated

Mailing Address:
P.O. Box 490
Bountiful, Utah 84011-0490

Street Address:
50 South 500 West
Bountiful, Utah 84010

Local Phone: (801) 295-9451
WATS (toll free): 1 (800) 453-0812
FAX: (801) 295-0196

E-mail: horizonp@burgoyne.com
Internet: http:// www.horizonpublishers.com

Table of Contents

5

8. Answering Anti-Mormon Objections: The "Truth Will Prevail" Dialogue 167

1

Who's On
the Lord's Side?

The Anti-Mormon Battle Cry: "They're Stealing Your People"

"They're *stealing* your people!!! They *must* be stopped!!!"[1] Those are the words of J. Edward Decker, International Director for Saints Alive/Ex-Mormons for Jesus, in a form letter addressed to pastors across the United States and elsewhere. He was pitching a film called "The Godmakers" which, along with the book by the same name, purports to be "A Shocking Expose of What the Mormon Church REALLY Believes"! The film has been shown and reshown around the country to packed and overflowing audiences, usually at "born-again" Christian churches. The book is claimed by adversaries of The Church of Jesus Christ of Latter-day Saints to be on the Christian best-seller list, and that Christian book stores can't keep the item in stock. Along with the book and film there are dozens of other books and tracts purporting to be exposes of the Church.

It is claimed that there are thousands of Ex-Mormons for Jesus who have left the LDS Church and are now attempting to minister to the Mormons about the "true" Jesus. Where "The Godmakers" is being shown, paid advertisements announce the upcoming showing of the film and plead with Latter-day Saints to "use their free agency" to see the film.

Being myself a onetime anti-Mormon, and now a returned missionary for The Church of Jesus Christ of Latter-day Saints, I feel a need to set the record straight. I was once deceived into believing the reports and railing accusations of the anti-LDS movement, but after literally thousands of hours of research, and many, many hours on my knees, I came back to the Latter-day Saint fold and now proclaim with the Saints that Jesus is the Christ, our Savior, and Joseph Smith was His Prophet for this dispensation.

As one who was carefully trained in anti-Mormon "witnessing techniques" and doctrinal approaches, I am able to share insights concerning the anti-Mormon movement with Latter-day Saints so they'll know how to respond when they're confronted by anti-Mormon propaganda and antagonists. I was not, in any way or fashion, commissioned by the LDS Church to write this book; it is entirely my own undertaking. I trust that it will be perceived as a valuable contribution to Latter-day Saint literature.

The LDS Church Uses Extensive Missionary Efforts to Overcome Anti-Mormon Propaganda

Anti-Mormon adversaries like to depict themselves as the underdogs in what they describe as a battle against a Satanic and powerful force called the Mormon Church.

The *gainsayers* of today are well organized and financed. They're using modern media presentations and up-to-date marketing and public relations methodologies to further their work. They extend their outreach far beyond their own membership, drawing support and assistance from many Christian churches who show their films, provide audiences for their speakers, and echo their propaganda. They're agressive and rapidly expanding their outreach.

In reality, when compared to the cumulative size of the many churches of today's Christendom, the LDS Church is like a molehill next to a mountain, similar to the ancient Christian Church next to the many followers of Moses (the churches of the Pharisees, Sadducees, Hemerobaptists, Herodians, Boethusians, Masabothians, etc.).

But Jesus commanded His disciples to preach His gospel to all nations, in spite of the relatively small size of the Church:

> Then the eleven disciples went away into Galilee, into a mountain where Jesus had appointed them.
>
> And when they saw him, they worshipped him: but some doubted.
>
> And Jesus came and spake unto them, saying, All power is given unto me in heaven and in earth.
>
> Go ye therefore, and *teach all nations, baptizing them* in the name of the Father, and of the Son, and of the Holy Ghost:

> Teaching them to observe all things whatsoever I have
> commanded you: and, lo, I am with you alway, even unto
> the end of the world. Amen. (Matthew 28:16-20)

The Saints of the Most High try to live up to this commandment of their Master. They send out missionaries by the thousands and tens of thousands every year with the good news that God has sent His Only Beloved Son, in whom there is no sin, to be a final sacrifice for the sins of the world, and that He has set up his latter-day Kingdom as foretold by the prophets since the world began. LDS missionaries are mostly young men and women who willingly give 1½ to 2 years of their lives, and their life's savings, because they love the Lord and His gospel. They want to share this good news with the rest of the world.

Anti-Mormon Portrayals of LDS Missionaries

But how do anti-Mormon adversaries portray these young men and women who voluntarily serve their Lord, without charge, and sometimes endure many hardships and labor even in peril of life and limb? According to an anti-LDS tract called "Here They Come...30,000 of Them: Mormon Missionaries":

> They are persistent—truthless—deceitful.[2]

According to Ed Decker, of Saints Alive/Ex-Mormons for Jesus:

> The Mormon missionary presents himself to you as a
> member of the Christian flock....His appearance, his
> countenance, his speech all say, "Hi, I'm a sheep just like
> you. I look like you, I smell like you, I say baa like you,
> so I must be a sheep just like you." What you can't see
> is that under the surface, a wolfskin lurks.[3]

Anti-Mormons Not Motivated by Love for Latter-day Saints

Anti-Mormon activists often assert that they love the Mormons, and that love is the motivating force behind their actions. But do you really think they love the Mormons?

The Church of Jesus Christ of Latter-day Saints is repeatedly presented by anti-Mormon adversaries in their literature and discussions as a Satanic institution. They spread many false and slanted reports about the Church. Their anti-Mormon propaganda frequently utilizes numerous "yellow journalism" techniques of deception to mislead the perceptions of those who read it. They militantly preach against the Church in their meetings.

They do all they can to dissuade people from listening to Latter-day Saint missionaries.

Are these acts of love? Certainly not! And for anti-Mormons to assert that love is their motivating force is pure sham. Their actions speak louder than their words.

The Basic Issue: Who's On The Lord's Side?

The purpose of this book is to get at the basic issues of the controversy. If what members of the anti-LDS movement are saying is not true (and it isn't!), then those who heed their message have everything to lose if they accept their report. LDS Church members and investigators who are led astray by anti-Mormon claims lose access to the Savior's redeeming grace if they turn away from the benefits of His atonement and from the ordinances the Lord authorized: baptism, receipt of the gift of the Holy Ghost, priesthood ordination, and sacred temple ordinances. To reject the Church is to reject the gospel, and to reject His gospel is to reject the Savior, our Lord Jesus Christ. And Jesus said, "I am the way, the truth, and the life: *no man cometh unto the Father, but by me.*" (John 14:6) So, we come to life and truth when we come to the Lord. Therefore, we must ask ourselves: Who's on the Lord's side?

The Author's Conversion to The Church of Jesus Christ of Latter-day Saints

I accepted the Lord as my personal Savior when I was fifteen. I had been praying fervently to God that he would show me the way to the truth because at that tender age I needed reassurances about God's plan for me; I really didn't know it.

When I was eighteen, I was invited to services of The Church of Jesus Christ of Latter-day Saints. I went, and I was impressed. I had read somewhat about Mormons before, and I greatly admired them. Those from my Protestant church who had led me to repeat their mouth confession of Christ had told me I that I had been saved for all time, *but I didn't see the fruits of the Spirit in them.* On the other hand, as I became acquainted with the Latter-day Saints, I found that the Mormons had what I felt were the fruits of true religion. The Latter-day Saints seemed to have a certain glow about them, a certain happiness and fulfillment that I just didn't have, no matter how many times I went up to be saved by my mouth confession.

I went to my New Testament and began to read about Christ in the scriptures. I would stay up late at night and far into the morning reading and praying, trying to grasp whatever it was that the Saints had.

Finally, after considerable study and preparation, I was baptized into The Church of Jesus Christ of Latter-day Saints, and shortly thereafter, after more prayer and study, I received a personal testimony that Jesus truly was the Christ, and that Joseph Smith was His Prophet. My testimony came like a warm waterfall and it filled my heart with the burning of the Spirit which testified to me of the truthfulness of the gospel and of the Church.

What I felt on that occasion was very similar to that which the two disciples reported when they met and spoke with the risen Lord on the road to Emmaus:

> And they drew nigh unto the village, whither they went: and he made as though he would have gone further.
>
> But they constrained him, saying, Abide with us: for it is toward evening, and the day is far spent. And he went in to tarry with them.
>
> And it came to pass, as he sat at meat with them, he took bread, and blessed it, and brake, and gave to them.
>
> And their eyes were opened, and they knew him; and he vanished out of their sight.
>
> And they said one to another, *Did not our heart burn within us, while he talked with us by the way, and while he opened to us the scriptures?* (Luke 24:28-32)

My conversion was accompanied with tears of joy as I received the burning of the Spirit. My life was changed, and I had never known the kind of happiness that I experienced in those few months right after my conversion.

A Turning Point: Duped by Anti-Mormon Literature

But several months later, an incident changed the course of my life. I wanted to learn all I could about the gospel, so I went to buy some Church books at a local Christian bookstore. Satan has a history of preying upon the innocent, and at that time in my spiritual adolescence I was very naive about the things of man and the things of the devil. I walked into the Christian bookstore and I heard the ringing of cash registers and some Christian rock music being played in the background. I was innocently in search of some books written by Latter-day Saints about the gospel and other Church-related subjects.

After walking around for a few minutes I found a complete section of books with pictures of the Salt Lake Temple on them. But I stopped in my tracks when I saw that they were shelved in the "Cult/Occult" section of the bookstore.

As I picked up the largest book, something told me to put it back down, but curiosity got the best of me and I began reading it. I read through anti-Mormon books that day in the bookstore for more than three hours. A darkness seemed to cover my mind, like dark clouds that mar a beautiful day. I had walked into that bookstore a joyful person, but I walked out sad, confused, and embittered.

The authors of those books asserted that I had been deceived by the Mormons and that the Church and its leaders were guilty of fraud and deception. I was told in those books that the burning of the bosom which accompanies many testimonies was a Satanic feeling that could not be trusted, and that I should rely solely on the evidence that they were to present to me. And those authors told me I was not to pray, because Satan could influence the answers one received through prayer.

In my consternation, I immediately went inactive from the Church. I told my family and friends that I would find out the truth no matter how long it took. Those anti-Mormon books so influenced and embittered me that I even told my family that I would "Spit Mormonism out of my mouth!"

I quit school and began to gather anti-Mormon literature. I had somewhat of a savings (I had planned to use it for my mission) and I was living at home, so I could devote all of my time to get to the bottom of the controversy those books had raised in my mind. The "evidence" those books presented seemed to me to be devastating in its indictments against the LDS Church, and I decided that I wanted to join myself with others who I was told had encountered similar experiences in "finding the truth about Mormonism."

I decided that if I wanted to fully understand the arguments I was encountering, I needed to know as much as I could about the doctrines, histories, and theologies of the different churches. I began to study those things at great length. I also began to spend my waking hours studying LDS Church history and doctrine, as well as those of the other churches of Christendom.

Indoctrination at the Melodyland Christian Center

About this time I was terribly confused; I really didn't know who to believe. I did some traveling, and I got a chance to meet some real ex-Mormons. I went down to southern California and started to attend a Bible class at Melodyland Christian Center in Anaheim.

For a number of months I attended the class given by Reverend Walter R. Martin, who is regarded in Protestant circles as a foremost authority on what they call "the cults." In his class I was taught more about how to witness to cultists, especially to Mormons. I was forcefully taught that Mormonism was a non-Christian cult, and that it was a responsibility of the Body of Christ to "win their souls to Christ."

As the weeks went by, I also was taught some pretty wild things about the Mormons. I was told that the Mormon leaders talked about Christ just to deceive the Mormons and the public. I was told that the Mormons themselves were 'dupes.' I found that they were constantly mocked and ridiculed by the anti-Mormons. I was told that the Mormon Jesus was a "different" Jesus than the "Biblical" Jesus; that in the Latter-day Saints secret temple rituals there was much immorality; that the Mormon Church was an evil and invisible empire striving and conspiring to take over the United States government.

I also was told that in the Washington D.C. Temple there was an exact replica of the Presidential oval office, and when the Mormon church takes over the U.S. government by force, the prophet will rule from that exact replica. (I could never figure out why he needed an exact replica. Why couldn't he use the White House oval office? Or why couldn't he build his exact replica in Salt Lake City and reign from there?) I was told other things so lurid that they can't be repeated here.

Somehow, the assertions made to me by anti-Mormon writers and teachers, that Mormons weren't Christians, did not hold true to what I felt when I talked directly to Latter-day Saints. I could still remember how much the Mormons talked about Jesus, and the beautiful testimonies of Him they frequently bore. So my personal logic shifted and I began to rationalize the things the anti-Mormons had told me, mixing it with my own personal experiences and observations. I concluded, somehow, that the leaders of the LDS Church alone weren't Christian, rather than all the Latter-day Saints, and I rationalized that those leaders had somehow duped the Church members. But then I began to read the beautiful testimonies and witnesses of the Savior which the Mormon leaders had shared and taught—testimonies that rivaled anything else that I had seen and heard, all coming from the General Authorities of the Church.

Many other things were taught as witnessing techniques that were either halftruths or just outright lies. That bothered me quite a bit, but I passed over the problem at that time.

While in southern California I also spent much of my time at several of the theological seminary libraries, and at Latter-day Saint Institute libraries as well. The further I searched, the more the railing accusations of anti-Mormon adversaries began to fall. When I found their first lie, their first misrepresentation, that should have been enough to tell me that I had been deceived by the anti-Mormons, but I wasn't ready to accept that yet. I was determined to get at the truth on all points.

Most Ex-Mormons for Jesus Have Never Been Mormons

One day, while working in an "Ex-Mormons for Jesus" booth, I worked along side a young man named Dan. My conversation with him began a change in my perception of the "Ex-Mormons" movement. I happened to ask Dan how long he had been a Mormon. "Oh, I was never a Mormon," Dan replied, "but I've studied Mormonism for years!"

I began to ask every Ex-Mormon for Jesus behind that booth how long he had been a member of the Church. To my surprise, not one had ever been a Latter-day Saint! One woman replied that her sister was a Mormon. One man replied that his uncle was a Mormon. I asked Dan if it was honest to say they were Ex-Mormons for Jesus. He said, "That's the name of our ministry, and we do have ex-Mormons—they usually form the hierarchy, and we do try to have at least *one ex-Mormon at each event*, but the ministry is growing and we sometimes get overbooked!"

I was rather upset, and I was determined to speak with the leaders of the ministry in order to set things straight. I was beginning to feel that it wasn't ethical to use lies in order to destroy what they thought was a lie; it didn't make sense to me.

When I began to study the anti-Mormon literature more deeply, I began to notice a curious thing: some authors would contradict the conclusions or theories of other authors. How could this be, I thought to myself. I also noticed that some of the things the anti-Mormons were saying just didn't ring true. At first I thought that the authors who wrote against the Mormon Church just made a few honest mistakes. As time went by and my studies continued, I came to realize that these weren't "honest" mistakes.

An Anti-Mormon's Claim to LDS Experience: an Example of Authority Fabrication

While working in the anti-LDS movement, I also observed several instances in which anti-Mormons tried to fabricate or exaggerate their Mormon backgrounds. They would attempt to establish that they somehow held stature or prominence among the Latter-day Saints before leaving the LDS Church. For instance, while at Melodyland I met Gene. According to what he told me, he had been a pastor in the Calvary Chapel Church. He told me that at a certain point in his life he began to rebel against God, and he decided to become a Mormon. He said that the LDS Church asked him to give firesides on how he renounced Christianity and the Bible and how he became a "Book of Mormon-believing Mormon." He said that the Mormon leaders were so impressed with him that they told him that he was destined to be an apostle. He said that the Church even went so far as to commission him to be the "anti-anti-Mormon" for southern California. (There is no such thing.)

Gene told me that he read all the information the LDS Church gave him to refute the anti-Mormons, but he alleged that when he checked it with anti-LDS literature and the original sources, he discovered that what the anti-Mormons were saying was true, and that the LDS Church had lied to him.

Soon afterwards, Gene said, he went to his LDS Bishop with a hypothetical situation that I'll recreate here:

Gene: Bishop, what if the Savior Jesus was on one side of you and told you to do something, and the living prophet was on the other side of you and told you to do the very opposite—whom would you follow?

Bishop: The living prophet, of course!

Gene said that was the straw that broke the camel's back for him, so he began his ministry to Mormons to lead them to the "real" Jesus. I found his tale a bit hard to believe, but I could see how many uninformed Protestants would believe it without a question.

I decided to check his story. I discovered that Gene had been ordained in the LDS Church to the priesthood calling of Elder, but that he held no position of leadership responsibility within the LDS Church. He was not an "ordained pastor" in any way. I had a chance to speak with Gene's LDS bishop. When I told him what Gene said that he, the Bishop, had told him, the Bishop roared with laughter. He told me that Gene had indeed given some firesides at his own request, but that Gene was beginning to tell people how he would change things as soon as he became an Apostle. The idea about becoming an Apostle was Gene's, no one else's.

It was when Gene had begun to tell people that he was to become an apostle, and what changes he would make, that he was called in and lovingly advised to follow the admonitions of the Savior that "Whosoever shall exalt himself shall be abased; and he that shall humble himself shall be exalted." (Matthew 23:12) Some other things were wrong in Gene's life that the Bishop couldn't share with me.

The Bishop also told me what actually happened in that dialogue Gene had described, which I shall reproduce here:

Gene: Bishop, here's a hypothetical situation. Let's say that Jesus was on one side of you and told you to do something, and the living prophet was on the other side of you and told you to do something very opposite than what Jesus told you—whom would you follow?

Bishop: A living prophet would never tell me to do anything opposite from Jesus!

Gene: Okay, let's say that an angel of light, or a demon, is pretending to be Jesus—whom would you follow?

Bishop: Well, if that was a demon and not Jesus then I'd follow the living prophet, of course!

I contacted the man Gene said commissioned him to be the "anti-anti-Mormon" for southern California, a Stake President. He told me that there was no such office, and observed that if there ever were such a position it would certainly be given to someone much more qualified than a new convert.

Needless to say, my discoveries about Gene did not increase my admiration for him, nor my confidence in the anti-Mormon precepts he tried to teach me. And it helped me to understand an interesting phenomenon in the "Ex-Mormons" movement—those who actually were Latter-day Saints for a time feel a strong need to embellish their depictions of their former LDS stature, making it appear that they previously held significant positions in the LDS general Church hierarchy.

Return to the Church

As the months went by, I met with other leaders of the anti-LDS movement, and I found more, many more, of the same types of things I have already described. I found them increasingly repugnant, and felt more and more that their conduct was the very opposite of true Christian behavior. It also became increasingly clear to me that their deceptive teachings and half-truths were the very antithesis of the gospel of Jesus Christ.

Through my research, their anti-Mormon claims and assertions fell, one by one, until I was on my knees again, in tears, returning to my God and Savior, in whom I should have placed my faith in the first place.

I regained my testimony of the Gospel and Church of Jesus Christ, and the joy I had known during that brief period following my baptism began to return to me again. I was back among the Saints of the Most High, and I rejoiced in their companionship.

When the call came, I served a mission in California, often-times running into sincere people who innocently believed the reports of these adversaries of the Lord's work. It was obvious that their mischief was widespread.

Many Others Once Deceived by the Gainsayers
Have Returned to the Church

I am not the only one who has been deceived by the *gainsayers* and then come back to the fold, by any means. There are many others like me who have left them after discovering the true nature of their methods, messages and motives.

I found some of my answers from Latter-day Saint books and articles which answer anti-LDS claims. These things can be found in Church libraries and Institutes of Religion. I also discovered that if one will check the statements, claims, and credentials of most of the outspoken anti-Mormon adversaries, he will eventually discover just who is telling the truth and who is opposing the Lord's work. Mostly, I discovered the truth observing the lives of the Saints themselves.

Anti-Mormon organizations attempt to recruit "born-again" Christians from various Protestant churches. Though many of these recruits are good people who sincerely believe that they are "saving the souls" of the Mormons, I found that the spirit of love and true Christian service doesn't linger long with them once they join the anti-Mormon movement. There is a spirit of hatred, mockery and ridicule among their leaders which soon rubs off onto the new recruits. The "bad apple at the bottom of the barrel" syndrome is quite apparent. The love new recruits claim they are showing towards the Mormons soon evaporates as they begin to function under their organization's leadership and methodology.

Would One Go to Judas to Ask About Christ?

I have often wondered why the Gentile Christian world accepts the stories told by those people who call themselves Ex-Mormons for Jesus and naively assumes those people will tell them the *truth* about the Latter-day Saints. Why don't they ask the Saints themselves?

Would one go to Judas to ask about Christ? Would one expect a Pharisee who opposed Jesus of Nazareth to give him a fair view of Christianity? Would one expect a Nazi to give an unbiased report of the Jewish people and their aims?

Would one expect a member of the Ku Klux Klan to give a reliable report of the black people? Would one expect a communist leader to clearly describe the workings and aims of the free-enterprise system?

The *gainsayers* assert that what they are saying is true because they themselves were there—they had been Mormons. This, in itself, is a falsehood—the majority of Ex-Mormons for Jesus have never been Mormons. (Along this line of reasoning, not ours but theirs, perhaps Latter-day Saints should use former "born-again" Christians to interpret the Protestant concepts of Christianity for the outside world.)

This is from a news article by Michael D'Antonio about ex-born-again Christians who are starting groups:

GROUP AIDS THOSE EXITING
FUNDAMENTALIST RELIGIONS

It wasn't easy for Bill Jackson to get out. During the years he struggled to withdraw from Christian fundamentalism, he found himself praying absentmindedly. Bible verses popped in and out of his head. And when a friend was killed in an auto crash, he thought it was God's retribution.

"I was depressed and very hung up for years," he recalls. "I found myself praying when I didn't intend to, and feeling like I was always backsliding or influenced by the devil." Although it came along too late for him, Jackson says a new group, Fundamentalists Anonymous, will help others with a transition "that took me five years to make by myself." Jackson is one of the first members of the new Fundamentalists Anonymous. It is intended to ease the social and psychological trauma suffered by those who leave strict fundamentalist churches.

"It's inevitable that something like this would come about," says David Bromley, a sociologist who specializes in religion. "There are support groups for former Mormons, ex-priests, alcoholics, virtually everything. Now, because the growth rates have been high for years, it would make sense that there would be people coming out of the fundamentalist churches and looking for something like this." More than 100 one-time fundamentalists have responded to a small newspaper ad for Fundamentalists Anonymous, and the group is already working with members in Chicago and Los Angeles.[4]

The only difference between being an ex-Mormon and being an "ex" anything else is that you can make a profit being an ex-Mormon, even making it a full-time occupation! Why? Because so many people are curious to know what the Latter-day Saints believe.

Some People Want to Hear The Prosecutor's Case, but Not the Case for the Defense

I've often wondered why those seeking information about the Mormons don't just go to the Saints to find out what the Saints believe. The Latter-day Saints will tell them and show them for *free*. They even have books that quote what their enemies say about them, but in those same books the anti-Mormon accusations are refuted.

So, if anyone wants to ask the Latter-day Saints what they believe, the Saints are more than happy to tell them. And if anyone wants to know what the anti-Mormons are saying, the Saints will show them what the anti's are saying in books that weigh both sides of the argument. An offering plate won't be passed in front of them, and the Saints won't ask for love offerings or send them a price list! The Saints especially welcome people who have read the book and seen the film "The God Makers" to find out the *rest* of the story. Yet it seems that some people are content to hear only the "prosecution's" case, witnesses and evidence, without hearing the case for the defense.

The same mockery of justice occurred to a young man from Galilee who was accused of sedition, magic, and treason. Because the prosecution had the cards already stacked, the easily swayed crowd yelled, "Crucify him! Crucify him!" That young man was the Son of God!

Why Opposition? The World Hates the Things of God

Every year there are hundreds of thousands of people who become Latter-day Saints. The majority of those converts who are adults previously were active in one or another of the various Christian churches. More than a few of them were ministers and pastors. At times people who become Latter-day Saints are shunned by their non-LDS families, lose their jobs, or are in other ways harasssed because of their decision. As the Master has said:

> I am come to set a man at variance against his father, and the daughter against her mother, and the daughter-in-law against her mother-in-law.
> *And a man's foes shall be they of his own household.*
> (Matthew 10:35-36)

And also,

> *Ye shall be betrayed* both by parents, and brethren, and kinsfolks, and friends; and some you shall they cause to be put to death.
> *And ye shall be hated of all men for my name's sake.*
> (Luke 21:16-17)

It isn't that individuals call these persecutions down upon themselves when they join the Lord's church. This enmity is forced upon them by a world which hates them without really knowing the reason. Why? Our Redeemer said:

> If the world hate you, ye know that it hated me before it hated you.
> If ye were of the world, the world would love his own: but because ye are not of the world, but I have chosen you out of the world, therefore the world hateth you.

Remember the word that I said unto you, The servant is not greater than his lord. If they have persecuted me, they will also persecute you; if they have kept my saying, they will keep yours also.

But all these things will they do unto you for my name's sake, because they know not him that sent me. (John 15:18-21)

Christ's Church Was Considered a Cult by Other Sects in New Testament Times

At the time the Savior was upon the earth, there were a number of different churches and religious sects among the people of Palestine. Most of them claimed to be "orthodox" and "historic" Israel. They all claimed that they believed in the *Tanahk* (Hebrew: Bible)—what we now call the Old Testament. They all held different opinions of various religious doctrines, and their ministers and scholars (scribes) would argue and debate over their differing interpretations. The ministers of those churches were trained in the different scriptural academies which were much like the theological seminaries of today.

Some of the churches, especially the Pharisees, claimed to believe totally in the Hebrew scriptures, but also had a rather large oral tradition as well. Other churches, like the Sadducees, claimed the Old Testament as their sole authority without any traditions. Because there were no more prophets to correctly interpret the scriptures, the churches turned to their own understanding. And since one man's opinion could differ from another's, there sprung up many different sects who claimed to believe in the Messiah (*Christ*) who was to come, and in the scriptures (*Tanahk*). They all regarded themselves as Messianists, or followers of the expected Messiah.

Not all the sects were accepted on equal ground, however. There were a few groups that differed so radically from what was referred to as orthodox and historic that the larger churches put them under the designation of being *Minim* (Hebrew: Cultists). These sects included the Cutheans (the church of the Samaritans), the Essenes, the Ananites, the Isunians, and the *Nazarenes* (the followers of Jesus of Nazareth).

So the Nazarenes, called by the Gentiles "Christians" and by themselves "Saints," were classed among the cults in their day by the orthodox churches. The Nazarenes were very different from all the rest of the churches because the rest of the churches believed that God's revealed word was found only in the scriptures (Old Testament), and that when the scriptures ended, that ended God's revelation to man. In contrast, the Nazarenes believed that God continued to reveal His will to man through prophets and through His only Begotten Son, Jesus.

"Cult"—A Word Meaning "You're Different than We Are"

What's the dictionary definition of the word *cult*? The word simply means "a system of religious worship." Every church, then, is a cult, just as every church is a *sect* (definition: "a group of people having the same principles, beliefs, or opinions").

But in recent years, the word-usage tendency among mainline, large church denominations has been to use the word *cult* to mean "a religious organization with beliefs which are distinctly different from the beliefs of the mainline groups." The tendency is for large groups to consider their beliefs to be "orthodox," and to regard smaller organizations with differing beliefs as "cults."

That's what the mainliners of Christ's day did. The Pharisees and Sadducees regarded Jesus and His followers as a cult. And that's what the mainliners do today: they regard Jesus and His followers—the Latter-day Saints—as a cult.

And there's nothing "bad" about being a "cult"—*it's just a term the big guys use to tell the little guys "You're different than we are."*

Why Mainline Churches Won't Call Their Opponents "Christians" or "Saints"

I often used to wonder why the other ancient sects did not call the disciples of Jesus "Christians" as the Gentiles called them, or the "Saints," as they themselves were known to each other. I found that the term *Christian* was a Greek term that, when translated into Hebrew or Aramaic, means *Messianist*, a term that the orthodox sects reserved for themselves. In other words, the Pharisees and Sadducees—the mainline churches in Palestine during the mortal ministry of Jesus—believed that they themselves were the true followers of a christ who had not yet appeared, and *the mainliners thought that the Nazarenes believed in a false Christ (Jesus of Nazareth) and in a false prophet (John the Baptist).*

They didn't refer to the Saints as "Saints" because that was the scriptural term used by God for the people of God, and the apostate sects of Israel certainly did not want to call the Nazarenes the people of God!

The parallel holds true, today. The mainline churches do their best to reserve the term "Christian" for themselves. They're not about to use either the term "Christian" or "Saint" in reference to the Latter-day Saints. Anti-Mormons *gainsayers* go a step further, doing their best to spread the belief that Mormons are not "Christians."

Christ's New Testament Church
Founded on Revelation and Prophets

God had promised through the prophets that He would send a great prophet to open up the dispensation of the meridian of time, and prepare Israel for the coming Messiah (*Christ*). All the other churches thought that the ministering of angels was a thing of the past, but God sent angels to Zacharias and his wife Elisabeth informing them that they would have a son who would be a prophet of the Highest. Another who received an angelic visit was Miriam, or Mary, who was betrothed to Joseph. Both Mary and Joseph were descendants of King David. The Angel Gabriel had told Mary that she was to be with child, and that she was to be the mother of the Son of God.

God sent His great prophet to prepare the way in the desert, as a voice crying in the wilderness, "Prepare ye the way of the Lord, make his paths straight." (Mark 1:3). His prophet was sent to lead Israel out of her apostasy, and to prepare her for the coming of the Lord Himself. This prophet was John, he who was called John the Baptist. The Lord said of him:

> Among those that are born of women there is not a
> greater prophet than John the Baptist: but he that is least
> in the kingdom of God is greater than he. (Luke 7:28)

In this passage Jesus was saying that John was a great prophet—that there had never been any prophet who was greater, but that He Himself was greater than John.

Modern Mainline Churches Like the Pharisees of Christ's Day

I remember on my mission receiving a flyer at my door about an upcoming anti-Mormon lecture being delivered at the local "born-again" church. My companion and I soon found ourselves in conversation with two "born-again" men in their mid-30's. The men did their best to witness to us; they gave several typical anti-Mormon techniques a try, and asked all the "pat" questions.

When they began to compare the Mormons with the hypocritical Pharisees of old, I told them that I couldn't understand their reasoning. I reminded them that the Pharisees didn't believe in living prophets, and that the Pharisees rejected the prophet John the Baptist. When I had said that, they both looked at me, then at each other, and laughed. One said, "Sure the Pharisees believed in living prophets, but John the Baptist wasn't any prophet!" I then quoted to them the Savior's words found in Luke 7:28

(see above). One of them scratched his head while looking to the other and said, "Was John the Baptist a prophet?"

Modern mainline Christian churches are just like the Pharisees: they reject the reality of modern revelation and believe that God doesn't speak through prophets today. And like the ancient Pharisees, they believe that the canon of scripture is closed.

Modern Mainliner Opposition Similar To That Used Against Christ In New Testament Times

In the days of Jesus, many of the common people believed that John was a prophet sent by God, but the ministers of the sects did not. They taught that God had completed His revelation with the close of the Old Testament and that no more prophets would come or be needed. Why did they teach that? The answer is obvious. Because they didn't have any living prophets among them, and had not had prophets among them for hundreds of years.

When the Lord Jesus began His mortal ministry, the very first thing He did was to be baptized by His Prophet John. The leaders of the other sects did not believe in Jesus because, among other things, He went to John. The leaders of those sects believed that John was a false prophet.

Because the prophet John and Jesus Christ were taking away members from their flocks, the religious leaders banded together to stop Jesus and John by spreading lies and rumors against the two of them. Jesus was aware of their falsehoods and criticisms, and made references to them in His teachings. He said:

> John came neither eating nor drinking, and *they say, He hath a devil.*
>
> The Son of man came eating and drinking, and *they say, Behold, a man gluttonous, and a wine-bibber, a friend of publicans and sinners.* But wisdom is justified of her children. (Matthew 11:18-19)

That was not the end. Through the use of more lies, false accusations, and false witnesses, the ministers succeeded in opposing John and Christ till they finally brought about their deaths. Of course, Jesus gave up His life voluntarily as a sacrifice for sin. Yet the Master was constantly harassed by those who opposed Him; they tirelessly sought to bring accusations against Him. And when nothing legitimate could be found with which to accuse Him, they set up false witnesses to lie and distort the truth.

Ancient Mainline Churches Had "Cult Fighters" Too

The leaders of the other sects believed that Jesus of Nazareth and His Prophet John were "stealing their people," and they conspired together in an effort to stop them. The churches chose certain men, usually religious leaders themselves, who made it their life's work to be cult fighters. One very famous cult fighter was Saul of Tarsus, a prominent Pharisee, who was very zealous in his persecution of the most dangerous "cult" of all—the *Nazarenes*.

Why did Saul of Tarsus persecute the Nazarenes? Because the Nazarenes were one of the "cults." They believed in such "unorthodox" things as the ministering of angels, living prophets and apostles, continuous revelation, and that Jesus was truly the Messiah. All these things set the Nazarenes at variance with the other churches, including the other "cults." The anti-Nazarene movement proclaimed that John was a *false prophet* and that Jesus was a *different Christ* from the true Messiah who was to come.

Saul of Tarsus succeeded in persecuting many of the Saints, but God had a plan for him. On the road from Jerusalem to Damascus, Saul had a vision:

> And Saul, yet breathing out threatenings and slaughter against the disciples of the Lord, went unto the high priest,
>
> And desired of him letters to Damascus to the synagogues, that if he found any of this way, whether they were men or women, he might bring them bound unto Jerusalem.
>
> And as he journeyed, he came near Damascus: and suddenly there shined round about him a light from heaven:
>
> And he fell to the earth, and heard a voice saying unto him, *Saul, Saul, why persecutest thou me?*
>
> And he said, Who art thou, Lord? And the Lord said, *I am Jesus whom thou persecutest*: it is hard for thee to kick against the pricks.
>
> And he trembling and astonished said, Lord, what will thou have me to do? And the Lord said unto him, Arise, and go into the city, and it shall be told thee what thou must do.
>
> And the men which journeyed with him stood speechless, hearing a voice, but seeing no man.

And Saul arose from the earth; and when his eyes were opened, he saw no man: but they led him by the hand, and brought him into Damascus.

And he was three days without sight, and neither did he eat nor drink.

And there was a certain disciple at Damascus, named Ananias; and to him said the Lord in a vision, Ananias. And he said, Behold, I am here, Lord.

And the Lord said unto him, Arise, and go into the street which is called Strait, and enquire in the house of Judas for one called Saul, of Tarsus: for behold, he prayeth,

And hath seen in a vision a man named Ananias coming in, and putting his hand on him, that he might receive his sight.

Then Ananias answered, Lord, *I have heard by many of this man, how much evil he hath done to thy saints at Jerusalem:*

And here he hath authority from the chief priests to bind all that call on thy name.

But the Lord said unto him, Go thy way: for he is a chosen vessel unto me, to bear my name before the Gentiles, and kings, and the children of Israel:

For I will shew him how great things he must suffer for my name's sake.

And Ananias went his way, and entered into the house; and putting his hands on him said, Brother Saul, the Lord, even Jesus, that appeared unto thee in the way as thou camest, hath sent me, that thou mightest receive thy sight, and be filled with the Holy Ghost.

And immediately there fell from his eyes as it had been scales: and he received sight forthwith, and arose, and was baptized.

And when he had received meat, he was strengthened. Then was Saul certain days with the disciples which were at Damascus.

And straightway he preached Christ in the synagogues, that He is the son of God.

But all that heard him were amazed, and said; Is not this *he that destroyed them which called on his name in*

*Jerusalem, and came hither for that intent, that he might
bring them bound unto the chief priests?*

But Saul increased the more in strength, and confounded
the Jews which dwelt at Damascus, proving that this is the
very Christ.

And after that many days were fulfilled, the Jews took
counsel to kill him. (Acts 9:1-23)

No doubt in the eyes of the ministers of the other churches, Saul had
become a traitor and joined the cultists. Saul, now as a despised Nazarene,
began, in the eyes of those ministers, to *steal their people—he had to be
stopped!* What did they say about Saul (who by this time had changed his
name to Paul)?

For we have found this man a pestilent fellow, and a
mover of sedition among all the Jews throughout the world,
and a ringleader of the sect of the Nazarenes. (Acts 24:5)

Previously, when he had been a "cult fighter" against the Nazarenes,
Paul was trusted without question by the ministers. He had great power
and influence, and he could easily persecute the Nazarenes (Christians),
and even jail them with false witnesses and invented evidence. Yet Paul
sacrificed his position, his power and influence, his occupation, his freedom,
the praise of the world, and ultimately his life because he learned from
his vision who truly was on the Lord's side! But did he really sacrifice
much? In return for all his mortal suffering he found the eternal truth that
conquers death.

Before Paul's death he went to Rome, and there he preached of Jesus
in the synagogues. Paul showed the people from the scriptures that Jesus
was the Christ, and that John was His Prophet who was sent to prepare
the way. But by this time the evil reports of the anti-Nazarene *gainsayers*
had reached Rome and tainted the perception of those to whom he preached.
They said, "As concerning this sect, *we know that everywhere it is spoken
against*." (Acts 28:22)

This passage shows the extent of the defamation campaign waged against
the early Christian church by its enemies. Even in Rome, a continent away
from Palestine, the Church was held in disdain as a result of the negative
publicity generated by its enemies. John was called a false prophet and
Jesus a false Messiah. Both were accused of being in league with the devil.

Ancient Anti-Nazarenes Used Wild
Accusations and False Witnesses Freely

Even before, during Christ's mortal ministry, these accusations were forcefully voiced. When Jesus cast out demons, the anti-Nazarene adversaries said He did it through the power of *"the chief of the devils."* (Luke 11:15) When people began to heed God and reject the doctrines of men, the ministers of the other churches became enraged and spoke openly against Jesus:

> And there was much murmuring among the people concerning Him: for some said, He is a good man: others said, Nay; but He *deceiveth the people....*
> Then came the officers to the chief priests and Pharisees; and they said unto them, Why have ye not brought Him?
> The officers answered, Never man spake like this man.
> Then answered them the Pharisees, *Are ye also deceived?* (John 7:12, 45-47)

As the common people of Palestine began to see the miracles of Jesus and hear His words, they began to flock to Him. Unlike the learned scribes and Pharisees who received their knowledge through their religious schools, the common people recognized that He indeed was the Light to whom they should look, the Messiah! In contrast, the cult fighters believed Jesus was false and that He was stealing their people. He had to be stopped! Unable to find legitimate evidence against Him, they opposed Him with falsehoods:

> Now the chief priests, and elders, and all the council, sought *false witness* against Jesus, to put him to death;
> But found none: yea, *though many false witnesses came,* yet found they none. At the last came *two false witnesses,*
> And said, This fellow said, I am able to destroy the temple of God, and to build it in three days. (Matthew 26:59-61)

In the case of Stephen the gainsayers did the very same thing; they used false witnesses against the Saints:

> Then they suborned men, which said, We have heard him speak blasphemous words against Moses, and against God.

And they stirred up the people, and the elders, and the scribes, and came upon him, and caught him, and brought him to the council,

And *set up false witnesses,* which said, This man ceaseth not to speak blasphemous words against this holy place, and the law:

For we have heard him say, that this Jesus of Nazareth shall destroy this place, and shall change the customs which Moses delivered us. (Acts 6:11‑14)

The anti-Nazarenes had *lied,* but in their minds the truth had to be exaggerated because the Nazarenes were *stealing their people* and they were determined that the Nazarenes *must be stopped!*

In the next chapter I'll compare the anti-Nazarene movement of the first few centuries and the anti-Mormon movement of today. I know assuredly that Jesus is the Christ, and I do not know of a people who love Jesus more dearly than the Latter-day Saints. If you don't believe me, talk to the Saints themselves and discover what I have said is true.

To the Saints, honest seekers of truth, who are reading this let me say that today's persecution against the Saints is just another sign that you have the true Gospel of Jesus Christ. The Master Himself said:

Blessed are they which are persecuted for righteousness' sake: for theirs is the kingdom of heaven.

Blessed are ye, when *men shall revile you, and persecute you, and shall say all manner of evil against you falsely, for my sake.*

Rejoice, and be exceeding glad: for great is your reward in heaven: for so persecuted they the prophets which were before you. (Matthew 5:10‑12)

2

Satan's Counter-mission: Ancient and Modern Parallels

Modern Anti-Mormons Use the Same Techniques as Those Who Fought Against Christ's Church in New Testament Times

"Mormonism: Christian or Cult?"[1] That is the question anti-Mormon leaders say they've answered. And their answer, of course, is cult. They also pose the query, "Is Mormonism Christian?" Naturally, the *gainsayers* answer in the negative, asserting their view that Mormonism is opposed to Christianity and Christianity is opposed to Mormonism.

Similarly, ancient adversaries must have asked questions like "Nazarenism: Messianist or Cult?" or "Is Nazarenism Messianic?" If you had lived in the days of the ancient apostles, you could have posed these questions while they were in hot debate. If you had asked the ministers of the various churches in Palestine if the Nazarenes were Messianists, they would have responded, "Certainly not." But if you had asked the leaders of the Nazarenes, the apostles and prophets of Jesus, you would have received a completely different answer: an affirmative response.

A parallel situation exists today. If you could ask the ministers of various mainline Protestant churches in America if the Mormons are Christians, they would tell you, "Certainly not." But if you could ask the leaders of the Mormons, the apostles and prophets of Jesus, you would receive a completely different answer: a reply strongly in the affirmative.

During my many months of seeking the true answer to the question "Who's on the Lord's side?" I discovered an important truth: that *the ancient anti-Nazarene movement and the modern anti-Mormon movement parallel each other in a startling way.* In ancient times the adversaries of Jesus and his prophet John the Baptist proclaimed that they, themselves, were the defenders of the orthodox and historic Messianic faith, and that the Saints, the followers of Jesus of Nazareth, believed in a different Christ from the "true" Messiah in whom they believed. Likewise, modern adversaries of Jesus and his prophet, Joseph Smith, proclaim that they, themselves, are the defenders of the orthodox and historic Christian faith, and that the Latter-day Saints believe in a different Christ than the "true" Jesus in whom they believe.

The "Nazarenes": Ancient Nickname for the Followers of Jesus Christ

Before even beginning to answer the question, "Mormonism: Christian or Cult?", there is a need to define terms. It is known that the mainline churches in the days of Jesus and His prophet John were *apostate*, meaning that even though they claimed to believe in the scriptures, and many of their members worshipped the god which their churches taught with sincerity, they were not churches which God Himself had established.

Because they didn't believe in living prophets, they rejected John the Baptist. Later, they crucified the very Jehovah whom they praised in the streets and in the synagogues, though they didn't recognize that Jesus of Nazareth was that divine being.

They did not refer to the followers of Jesus of Nazareth as "Saints" because that was the scriptural term for the people of God. They did not call the followers of Jesus "Christians" because in their own tongue that is what the apostate mainline churches *called themselves.* The term *Christian* is the Greek word for the Hebrew term used to designate one who believed in the coming Messiah, or *Christ.* Instead, they called the followers of Jesus *Nazarenes*, and Jewish scholars even today consider ancient Christianity "more correctly Nazarenism."[2]

The Ancient Decision: Treat Christ's Church as a "Cult"

Soon after the Prophet John Zacariah (John the Baptist) came on the scene, the apostate churches banded together against him, regarding him as a false prophet. The history of their persecutions of his followers and of the followers of Jesus is well documented. The leaders of the apostate churches gave the followers of Jesus the "Nazarene" nickname and decided to appoint certain men to oppose the Nazarenes everywhere. These appointed men were "cult fighters."

It was recognized by those conspiring men that in order to deceive the public more fully, they couldn't persecute the Nazarenes by themselves because it might draw sympathy to Jesus's cause. Those people may well have recognized that the Saints had been persecuted in all previous ages, and they may have realized that this could be a sign that the despised Nazarenes were in fact the true Messianists. In the face of this dilemma, the accusers came up with a brilliant plan—they would fight against all the cults, but they would declare to the people that the Nazarenes were the most dangerous cult of all.

When the apostles of Jesus were called before the Sanhedrin, they boldly bore their testimonies of Christ, and their enemies in turn sought to kill them. Yet, the great Jewish scholar Gamaliel knew that if the Nazarene's apostles were to be killed it would just add fuel to the fire. Their martyrdom would only cause the Nazarene movement to grow. Gamaliel had a brilliant plan, and it worked:

> Then stood there up one in the council, a Pharisee, named Gamaliel, a doctor of the law, had in reputation among all the people, and commanded to put the apostles forth a little space;
>
> And said unto them, Ye men of Israel, take heed to yourselves what ye intend to do as touching these men.
>
> For before these days rose up Theudas, boasting himself to be somebody; to whom a number of men, about four hundred, joined themselves: who was slain; and all, as many as obeyed him, were scattered, and brought to nought.
>
> After this man rose up Judas of Galilee in the days of the taxing, and drew away much people after him: he also perished; and all, even as many as obeyed him, were dispersed.
>
> And now I say unto you, Refrain from these men, and *let them alone*: for *if this counsel or this work be of men, it will come to nought*:
>
> *But if it be of God, ye cannot overthrow it; lest haply ye be found even to fight against God.* (Acts 5:34-39)

Thus, the ancient Jews placed the Nazarenes among the cults. According to one Christian historian:

This new Jewish-Christian party in the eyes of the religious leaders of the time was, at the worst, simply regarded as guilty of *minuth* (cultism), namely, a variety of Jewish heresy, or rather, Jewish sectarianism....Early passages in the Talmud still contain hostile references to the *minim* (cults), among whom were numbered the Jewish Christians....[3]

Justin Martyr's "Dialogue with Trypho," A Defense of the Early Christian Church

The Latter-day Saints believe that Jesus Christ is their Savior and Redeemer. They also believe that Joseph Smith, the first prophet of the Church in this dispensation, was like John the Baptist: a forerunner called to prepare the way for the Lord. I have described already from the Scriptures how the apostate churches during the time of Christ did not believe in John, the prophet of God, nor in the Christ who was baptized by him.

In those months that I sought for the truth, I discovered among the writings of scholars and the translated remnants of the ancient Christians and ancient anti-Nazarenes, a fuller picture of the anti-Christ movement which is mentioned only briefly and sporadically in the Bible.

I remember reading an ancient Christian work called "Dialogue with Trypho," in which the Christian apologist Justin Martyr (surnamed Martyr posthumously) defends his belief that Jesus is truly the Messiah against the accusations of Trypho (a member of one of the churches of apostate Israel) and his companions.

The book states in the beginning that when Justin expressed his belief in Jesus to Trypho and his companions, they rejected his testimony and tried to witness to him. When Justin attempted to teach them the first principles of the Gospel he was met with laughter and ridicule from Trypho's companions. According to Trypho and his companions, they knew all about who this fellow from Nazareth really was. Trypho said to Justin, "Surely this man (Jesus) has deceived you!"

Justin, however, was not at all surprised to have been witnessed to in such a manner. Trypho and his companions were raised, no doubt, as God-fearing, scripture-believing Messianists. It became evident, as I read the book, that all these men were familiar with the anti-Nazarene accusations of the day.

Justin was seen by them as a Nazarene—a cultist, and was looked upon by the companions of Trypho in contemptuous amusement, the same way many modern *gainsayers* view the Saints. However, Trypho had a concern, a sincere one, about Justin, and wanted to show him the error of his ways. Justin was seen by Trypho and his companions as someone who was sincere, yet deceived!

Very often, and this happened to me numerous times while I served my mission, people who had been deceived by anti-Mormon adversaries would glory and boast in themselves that they knew all about Mormonism. I found that this meant, of course, that they knew next to nothing about the Church, but had read some anti-LDS literature.

When we explained the Gospel to them they would typically disregard what we tried to teach them. Instead of listening, they would laugh and make fun of us. This same thing happened to the Savior. When Jesus came into the ruler's house, and saw the minstrels and the people making a noise,

> He said unto them, Give place: for the maid is not dead, but sleepeth. *And they laughed him to scorn*. (Matthew 9:24)

Jesus also foresaw that such mockery would be thrust upon His Saints, and He spoke a prophetic warning against those who deride, ridicule and mock: "Woe unto you that laugh now! for ye shall mourn and weep." (Luke 6:25)

Justin understood why those men had laughed at him and had ridiculed and mocked his beliefs. To Trypho Justin said:

> You Jews have sent chosen men into every part of the empire...proclaiming, "A godless and *libertine heresy* has arisen from a certain Jesus, a Galilean magician. We had him crucified, but his disciples came and stole him by night from the tomb where he had been put when taken down from the cross, and they deceive people, saying that he has risen from the dead and ascended to heaven." You slander Jesus, saying that he taught those godless and unholy things that you report to every race of men in your attacks against those who confess Christ as both their own Teacher and the Son of God.[4]

What Justin recognized was that the churches of Mosaidom had together formed a *counter-mission* to combat the work of true Israel—the Church of Jesus Christ.

Satan's Objective in All Dispensations:
to Oppose Christ's Church

It is the work of Satan to counter and oppose (*gainsay*) the mission of the Church *in any age*. What was true in the former days is also true in the latter.

Many of the accusations and criticisms leveled against the Latter-day Saints are exact parallels of the charges leveled against the Saints who followed Jesus of Nazareth in the meredian of time. Whether they have been consciously copied by modern gainsayers or whether they have been inspired by the same evil being who inspired them in Jesus's day is not known. But the fact remains, that anti-Mormon adversaries make many of the same accusations against Mormondom that were asserted by critics of the Nazarenes in Jesus's day.

In ancient times, Justin undoubtedly knew that Trypho and his companions had heard many untruths about the Nazarenes (the "Saints" or true "Christians"). They could have received instruction on how to witness to the cultists, of which the Nazarenes were said to be the most dangerous.

Trypho and his companions no doubt had heard from their ministers or local cult fighters that the Nazarenes were a sincere but yet a deceived people. No doubt Trypho and his companion had been told that the Nazarenes were corrupt and evil; that their Messiah was a false one; that their prophets were false prophets; that their scriptures (which would become the New Testament) were false additions to the holy word of God, and that unless the Nazarenes would turn away from their delusion it was clear that there would be no hope for them.

Justin and Trypho contended for hours, both using the scriptures freely. Justin used them to show that in Jesus came the fulfillment of prophecy in reference to the coming Messiah. Trypho used the scriptures to assert that there were doctrinal errors among the Nazarenes as well as warnings against false prophets.

Justin told Trypho that chosen men were sent from Jerusalem "through all the land to tell that *a godless heresy* of the Christians had sprung up, and to publish those things which all they who knew us not speak against us."

After quoting Isaiah, Justin told Trypho, "Accordingly, *you displayed great zeal in publishing throughout the land bitter and dark and unjust things* against the only blameless and righteous Light sent by God." Trypho responded by saying, "These and such like scriptures, sir, compel us to wait for Him who, as Son of man, receives from the Ancient of Days the everlasting kingdom. But this so-called Christ of yours was dishonorable and inglorious, so much so that *the last curse contained in the law of God fell on him, for he was crucified*!"

Trypho claimed that the New Testament was contradictory, and said to Justin, "And you, having accepted a groundless report, *invent a Christ for yourselves*, and for his sake are inconsiderately perishing." Justin then explained to Trypho and his followers that they were the ones who were being persuaded by "teachers who do not understand the Scriptures" and that the followers of Jesus "have not been deceived."

Throughout the book, Justin continued to give his testimony and teach, or to try to teach the Gospel, but Trypho continued to try to convince Justin that he was unwarily involved in a cult, and that Jesus of Nazareth was a false Messiah, a "different Christ" from the scriptural Christ. In the end Trypho informed Justin that he had been somewhat misinformed about the Nazarenes but that he could find no need for Jesus. Both men walked away with their prior convictions, but Trypho, to be sure, was a bit more enlightened.[5]

I have wondered what the fate of Trypho was. Did he die in anticipation of the very Messiah that he rejected? I believe Trypho rejected Jesus as the true Christ, and rejected the Nazarenes as the true Messianists, because the anti-Nazarenes (truly the anti-Christs) of his day convinced him earlier in life, through the use of lies, half-truths, and trumped-up evidences, that John the Baptist was a false prophet, and that the man Jesus was an evil magician who had deceived the people into believing he was the Christ. How very sad!

Justin's fate is well known. Like many of the Saints of the Most High before and after him, Justin sealed his testimony of the Savior with his own blood. As it was in former days, so it is in the latter days!

Ancient Jewish Efforts to Combat Early Christianity

Like Justin, modern Latter-day Saint witnesses have been ridiculed, threatened, mocked, and assaulted. But their labors have not been for naught because they have brought many of the elect out of Babylon, and have counted it as worthy to suffer for Christ's name (see Acts 5:41).

According to the eminent Christian historian and scholar, Dr. Adolf Von Harnack:

> The Jews sought to extirpate the Palestinian churches and to silence the Christian missionaries. They hampered every step of Paul's work among the Gentiles; they cursed Christians in their synagogues; they stirred up the masses and the authorities in every country against him; systematically and officially they scattered and broadcast

> horrible charges against the Christians which played an
> important part in the persecution as early as the reign of
> Trajan; they started calumnies against Jesus; they provided
> heathen opponents of Christianity with literary ammunition;
> unless the evidence is misleading, they instigated the
> Neronic outburst against the Christians.[6]

What Dr. Harnack meant by "the Jews" were those Jews who opposed the Nazarenes, not all Jews, for the Master Himself was a Jew, as were all of His apostles.

The churches of Mosaidom did not remain passive in the face of the challenge with which the Church or true Israel confronted them. The Gospel of Jesus Christ was a direct threat to the traditions of orthodox Messianity. Even in the earliest periods after the Lord sent out His missionaries two-by-two to all the world, when the other churches were not yet unduly pressured by the growth of the new faith, arguments were formulated to combat the claims of the Nazarenes.[7]

In like manner, the many books, articles, and tracts about Joseph Smith, the Latter-day Saint Church, the Book of Mormon, etc., which came from opposing parties, were full of distortions, half-truths, out-right lies, and other forms of misinformation. They were put forth to deceive in a manner similar to what occurred in New Testament times.

Ancient Anti-Christian Writings Had Little Historical Value

According to Joseph Kausner, an eminent Jewish scholar and historian who was an authority on the religious situation in the time of Jesus and Paul, the anti-Nazarene (anti-Christian) writings of the ancient *gainsayers* had "little historical value, since they partake rather of the nature of vituperation and polemic against the founder of a hated religion, rather than objective accounts of historical value."[8]

Ancient Cult Fighters and Authorities on the Cults

Some noted divines made it their life's work to be authorities on the cults. Rabbi *Solomon ben Issac* was a popularly acclaimed authority on the cults. According to his adherents, he supported himself and his family by growing grapes so as not to misuse the Torah by earning bread from it. His commentary on the Bible (which was used as sort of a "cult reference guide") mentions "Jeshu the Nazarene" four times, mostly as a "magician and perverter of the people."[9]

The first tract containing extensive quotations from what was to become the New Testament was in Hebrew. It was "Wars of the Lord," by *Rabbi*

Jacob ben Reuben. Its admitted goal was to "disarm the Christians (Nazarenes) wherever possible, and to persuade them of the truth of Judaism."[10]

Another popular cult fighter was the *Rabbi Simeon ben Azzai*. Just as modern *gainsayers* delight in attempting to present what they regard as "devastating" evidences against the LDS faith, so as a foe of Jesus and his prophet John did Simeon ben Azzai become highly excited when he found in Jerusalem, then lying in ruins, a Jewish document which referred to "Jesus of Nazareth" as "a bastard son of a married woman." This "find" was valuable enough for Ben Azzai to communicate it to his pupils, who for their part were not slack in giving the discovery a wider circulation.[11] Simeon ben Azzai must have been an instructor on the cults at his academy.

Rabbi Joseph Kimchi wrote in his book called "Book of the Covenant" a model disputation between a Nazarene and an orthodox Messianist in which the Messianist refutes the incarnation and Jesus's claim to be the Messiah, all on scriptural grounds.[12] Kimchi's son, *Rabbi David Kimchi*, wrote a counter-mission book called "Answer to the Christians." In this work he attempts to dismantle allegorized "foreshadowings of Christ." What about the scriptural messianic prophecies which were fulfilled by Jesus of Nazareth? Well, Kimchi reports in boldness after a "careful study" of the "evidence," that in Jesus "not one had been fulfilled."[13]

Ancient Anti-Christian Propaganda Attempted to Negate New Testament Scripture

A significant portion of ancient counter-mission propaganda was dedicated to the denigration and defamation of the New Testament. A classic example of such defamation is the parody of the Gospels called "Sefer Toledoth Yeshu" (The Life of Jesus). This book had been written at the time of the Gospels, and was very popular among the various churches who rejected Jesus and His apostles. In this work, the miracles attributed to Jesus are explained away, and Jesus Himself is not regarded as the Son of God, but as the illegitimate offspring of Mary and a Roman soldier. Other criticisms were made which asserted that the Gospels contradicted each other.

Similarly, some counter-mission writers repeated accusations already recorded in the New Testament, namely, that Jesus was not the Messiah because He could not save Himself (Mark 15:29-32), and that the disappearance of Jesus's body was the result of chicanery, and not a miracle (Matthew 28:11-15). A few early *gainsayers* also noted that a number of verses from the Hebrew Bible were incorrectly quoted in the New Testament. For example, they compared Deuteronomy 6:5 with Mark 12:30 and Luke 10:27. How could Jesus be the Messiah, the *gainsayers* asked, if Jesus and

His disciples were ignorant of verses that even the youngest child would know?[14]

Another popular anti-Nazarene book was "Nizzahon Vetus" (Book of Polemic), a book intended to expose the heresies of all the cults, the Nazarenes being among them.[15] Not only did the *gainsayers* try to refute all the prophecies of Jesus in "Nizzahon Vetus," but they asserted that God had warned man against Jesus in scripture:

> ...the reason for God's concern was that he foresaw that
> Jesus would attempt to mislead the world by saying he is
> God, and so the Holy One, blessed be he, decided that
> it would be better that men should die so that Jesus could
> be hanged without having eaten from the tree of life and
> all the world know that he is not God.[16]

The book goes on to say that Jesus admitted to being a sinner.

Another great cult fighter was the *Rabbi Abbahu*, who was "a great opponent of all *Minim* (cultists), and especially of Christians."[17] Rabbi Abbahu was a cult fighter in the true sense: while he said he was opposed to all cults, he exerted most of his energy against the Nazarenes.

The ancient anti-Christs used mockery as a means to an end. Jesus, in His lifetime, as Luke 2:48, 51 shows, was regarded as the actual son of Joseph. But when, at Pentecost, the preaching of the Apostles proclaimed that Jesus was the Son of God, then the counter-missionaries took hold of this divine truth and attempted to make a mockery out of it. They said:

> Since God has no son, while Jesus, as the Nazarenes
> themselves admit, is not Joseph's son, it follows that he
> was born out of wedlock.[18]

According to the ancient mythmakers, the husband of the mother of Jesus was Paphos (Joseph) ben Yehudah; His mother was Miriam (Mary), the "women's hairdresser." They called her *S'tath da* (adulteress).[19]

The counter-missionaries in the days of Christ and His ancient apostles and prophets were highly organized, and they had some of their most prominent men, usually ministers, serving as cult fighters. Other cult fighters, besides those listed above, were *Rabbi Johana ben Zakhai* (A.D. 80-90), *Rabbi Samuel the Lesser*, and *Rabbi Tarphon* (A.D. 90-130). Scripture academies were often the focal points and headquarters for such cult- fighting activity. The academy at Sura, for instance, was well known for its cult-fighting activities around A.D. 354-374.

About A.D. 95 there came *Gamaliel*. His life's work was based on personal determination "that factions should not increase in Israel." He personally assisted in controverting and converting Nazarenes into ex-Nazarenes all over Palestine.[20]

Pliny's Investigation of Charges
Against the Early Christian Church

What happened to the ex-Nazarenes who became converted back to orthodox Messianity by the ancient *gainsayers*? The answer to that question was recorded by Pliny, an ancient Roman governor of the province of Bithynia and an historian. He was called, in the autumn of A. D. 112, to investigate claims and charges against the Christians. The Saints (or Nazarenes) were being accused of all manner of crimes. According to Pliny:

> These accusations spread (as is usually the case) from
> the mere fact that the matter was being investigated, and
> several forms of mischief came to light.[21]

A large number of people were accused in an anonymous pamphlet. Many proclaimed that, according to Pliny, "they had once been Christians but had given this up in some cases three, in others as much as twenty, years before."[22] According to a modern historian:

> These former Christians claimed that theirs had been
> a religious cult, the whole of whose guilt consisted in the
> habit of its adherents to meet on a fixed day before it was
> light, when they sang in alternate verses a hymn to Christ,
> as a god, and bound themselves by a solemn oath not to
> do wicked deeds, but never to commit fraud, theft or
> adultery, bear false witness, as well as other crimes."[23]

Through the work of the anti-Nazarenes many were deceived, and were convinced by the power of the *gainsayers'* lies that they had been in a religious cult!

Early Gainsayers Did Great Harm to the Ancient Church

Were the anti-Christs of former days successful? Unfortunately, in many places they were. From the scattered evidence which now can be traced, it appears that in the thirty to forty years after the fall of Jerusalem, the Christians in Palestine become a despised and dwindling sect, and many members left the Church.[24] Among these ex-Nazarenes were certain individuals who chose to witness against their former brethren.

In the Latin work "Martyrium Pionii," of the late third or early fourth century, the Christian apologist Pionius recounts his clash with the *gainsayers* of his day. Having noted that some of his fellow Saints had been invited to synagogues and had in other ways been exposed to counter-mission propaganda, the martyr alluded to a particular accusation which claimed that Jesus was but a man and died a despicable violent death as a criminal. After refuting this charge, using arguments of unequal force (Jesus departed of his own free will, no one ever heard of the world being full of the followers of a criminal, etc), Pionius attributed a further intriguing statement to those counter-missionaries with whom he came into contact: that many of the false statements and accounts about Jesus and His Saints could be traced to apostates—ex-Nazarenes who were, according to the martyr Pionius, "lawless people, whose testimony cannot be believed."[25]

The *gainsayers* of the former days saw it as their calling to challenge the messengers of the true Christ. They admonished their followers to "Be diligent in the study of the Torah in order to answer a heretic and question him."[26] To such men, the ancient Christians (or Nazarenes as they were called) were not only cultists—they were revolutionaries who were planning to overthrow the Roman government. The *gainsayers* repeatedly accused the ancient Saints of being "a vast invisible empire conspiring against the state."[27]

As it was in the former days, so it is in the latter day! In the former days, believers were called the Nazarenes; in the latter days, they are called Mormons.

In the former days the Nazarenes were persecuted and killed because they believed in an unaccepted prophet and a different Christ. Likewise, in the latter days the Mormons have been persecuted and killed because they believe in a prophet who also is rejected by the world, and a Jesus who is different from the being described in most "Christian" creeds.

In the former days, the Nazarenes were categorized by their detractors as being among the other cults: the Cutheans, Essenes, Isunians, Therapeutae, etc. In the latter days the Mormons are regarded by "mainline" churches as being among the other cults: the Adventists, Jehovahs Witnesses, Freemasons, Christian Science, etc.

In the former days, ministers called cult fighters united with ex-Nazarenes to use any means possible to counter the mission of the Church. In the latter days ministers call cult fighters have united with ex-Mormons to use any means possible to counter the mission of the Church.

It is the work of Satan to deceive mankind into believing the truth is a lie, and his lie is the truth. Satan has not changed his tactics, and history has truly repeated itself! Jesus the Christ, the Sinless One, had a definite opinion about those who thought themselves to be the true Messianists, but who actually opposed the religion of God:

O generation of vipers, how can ye, being evil, speak good things? for out of the abundance of the heart the mouth speaketh.

A good man out of the good treasure of the heart bringeth forth good things: and *an evil man out of the evil treasure bringeth forth evil things....*

Ye serpents, ye generation of vipers, *how can ye escape the damnation of hell?*

Wherefore, behold, I send unto you prophets, and wise men, and scribes: and some of them ye shall kill and crucify; and some of them shall ye scourge in your synagogues, and persecute them from city to city. (Matthew 12:34-35; 23:33-34)

Other Anti-Mormon Charges Are Parallels of Ancient Anti-Nazarene Accusations

It has been repeatedly demonstrated in this chapter that accusations made by modern *gainsayers* against the Latter-day Saints are mere repetitions of attacks made against the early Christian Church. Satan repeats his tactics in all periods of time.

What are some other objections anti-Mormon adversaries raise against the Latter-day Saints which have parallels in the ancient anti-Nazarene movement? There are several. For instance, according to the *gainsayers*:

Mormonism is but another descendant or offshoot of the pagan mysteries in modern form that seeks to hide its true anti-Christian nature beneath the camouflage of professed Christianity and Biblical terminology.[28]

In a similar manner, the ancient anti-Nazarenes accused the early Christians of borrowing from the pagan cults, as is affirmed by Christian scholar and historian R. H. Fuller:

It was held that Christianity was essentially a plagiarization from the mystery cults. The myth of a dying and rising god, which was held to be basic to these cults, was transferred to Jesus of Nazareth. The Christian sacraments of baptism and the eucharist were held to be adaptations of the rites of these pagan cults.[29]

Another criticism leveled by anti-Mormon adversaries is the claim that Mormonism destroys and breaks up families. Again, this was an anti-Nazarene charge leveled against the Church in Jesus's day.

> Tampering with domestic relations was one of the earliest charges brought against the followers of Jesus.[30]

Yet another criticism with ancient parallels is the anti-Mormon claim that the LDS faith is really atheism. According to one of the *gainsayers*:

> Most Mormons are naively unaware of the fact that Mormonism is simply classical atheistic humanism deceptively packaged in pseudochristian terminology.[31]

Another anti-Mormon has stated that "Joseph Smith was a classical humanistic atheist."[32]

The anti-Nazarenes of ancient times made the same type of accusation about the early Christians:

> Because of the Christians' refusal to engage in the state religion they were sometimes described as "atheists". . .[33]

In yet another accusation, anti-Mormons have alleged that Joseph Smith was heavily involved in magic. According to the *gainsayers*:

> From early childhood he and his family had been dabbling in divination, necromancy, and various forms of ritual magic. Smith believed in and practiced occultism until his death. This is the secret foundation of the Mormon Church he established.[34]

The anti-Nazarenes of ancient times made a very similar accusation against Jesus:

> It is written in the Gospels that he was in Egypt for two years, and there he must have learned magic. . .[35]

The demonstration of parallels between the accusations of the ancient counter-missionaries and the modern ones could go on and on.

3

Man Can Attain Godhood: Ancient Evidence for Modern Mormon Doctrine

The Key Accusation of Anti-Mormons Based on a Twisting of the Temptation Account in Genesis

Attacks against Mormonism, like attacks against the ancient Nazarenes, have varied in content over the years. A relatively recent accusation devised by anti-Mormon adversaries is the assertion that the doctrine that man can attain Godhood is Satanic in origin rather than inspired of God. For instance, the foundation of both the recent book and film, "The God Makers," is the central accusation that Lucifer is "the original God Maker." The fundamental assertion of the "The God Makers" is that when the Serpent in the Garden of Eden offered the forbidden fruit to Eve, saying "ye shall be as gods, knowing good and evil," he lied. Both the film and the book hold that the Mormons have "called the Serpent's lie the truth" when they say that men can become gods.

That line of logic constitutes the foundation of recent anti-Mormon criticism against the Saints. It has become their cornerstone accusation, and the reason they have named their book and film "The God Makers." According to these modern *gainsayers*:

> Jesus called Satan a liar and the father of it i.e., the father of *the* lie. No greater lie could be conceived than that humans could become Gods. Eve was deceived by the Serpent's seductive offer to Godhood.[1]

And,

> It is astonishing how thoroughly Mormonism has embraced Satan's promise of godhood![2]

And also,

> Having accepted the fall of man as necessary and beneficial, both Mormonism and Paganism honor the lie that seduced Eve and avidly pursue the Godhood which the Serpent promised.[3]

While on my mission, a number of people told me that Mormons were very mistaken to view the Fall of Adam as a necessary step. They said they believed that God wanted Adam and Eve to live forever in the Garden.

I would respond, of course, by pointing out to them that Latter-day Saints don't believe that God made a mistake by placing the forbidden tree in the Garden, but rather that God foresaw that many would fall. That is why the Savior Jesus Christ is called the "Lamb slain from the foundation of the world" (Revelation 13:8).

Satan's Conversation with Eve: A Mixture of Truth and Falsehood

The Saints declare that *Satan did indeed lie* when "the serpent said unto the woman, Ye shall not surely die" (Genesis 3:4). But *he wasn't lying* when he said that "Ye shall be as gods, knowing good and evil" (Genesis 3:5). *God Himself says so* in the Bible:

> And the Lord God said, Behold, *the man is become as one of us, to know good and evil.* (Genesis 3:22)

With that key passage and the acceptance of the profound truth it presents, the entire anti-Mormon foundation of these modern *gainsayers* has fallen!

Was Lucifer promising Godhood to the woman? No! In his conversation with Eve, he was following his typical tactic of mixing truth with falsehood. He was telling her the *truth* when he told the woman that she would be *as*, or like, the gods in the respect that they know good and evil. But Lucifer *lied* when he said to the woman, "Ye shall not surely die."

The Bible states that:

> The Lord God commanded the man, saying, Of every
> tree of the garden thou mayest freely eat:
> But of the tree of the knowledge of good and evil, thou
> shalt not eat of it; for *in the day that thou eatest thereof
> thou shalt surely die.* (Genesis 2:16-17)

The Lord God told the man, Adam, not to eat of the fruit of the tree
of the knowledge of good and evil, presenting that instruction with the clear
alternative that if he did, he would surely die. Adam and Eve certainly
had a choice made available to them, else why would God allow a tree
like that to be in the Garden?

Lucifer, the serpent, not knowing God's plan, decided to try to deceive
Eve into partaking of the forbidden fruit, accurately promising her that
if she partook of it she would know good and evil as the gods do. Satan
did not promise the woman godhood, but rather made the truthful statement
that she would have knowledge of good and evil. The woman partook and
so did man.

In their effort to create a basis for opposition to the LDS Church, the
anti-Mormon critics have seriously distorted and maligned the simple truth
in this matter. All one needs to do is to carefully read the account of the
fall of Adam in the 3rd chapter of Genesis, and the entire anti-Mormon
foundation of logic that alleges that Mormons follow Satan is rubble!

Jesus Christ Persecuted for Being a God Maker

Why did the ministers of the other churches of his day hate Jesus so,
and what was their major accusation against Him? The Gospel according
to John says,

> Then the Jews took up stones again to stone him.
> Jesus answered them, Many good works have I shewed
> you from my Father; for which of those works do ye stone
> me?
> The Jews answered him, saying, For a good work we
> stone thee not; but for blasphemy; and because that thou,
> being a man, *maketh thyself God.* (John 10:31-33)

Jesus Christ was persecuted for being a *God maker!* Jesus did not deny
this, but responded:

> Is it not written in your law, I said, *Ye are gods?*
> If *he called them gods, unto whom the word of God came,*
> and the scripture cannot be broken;
> Say ye of him, whom the Father hath sanctified, and
> sent into the world, Thou blasphemest; because I said, *I
> am the Son of God?* (John 10:34-36)

Jesus was quoting Psalm 82:6: "I have said, *Ye are gods; and all of you
are children of the most High.*"

Early Christians Taught That Man Can Become a God

The doctrine that man can attain godhood was repeatedly taught by many
of the early Christian fathers. For instance, here is how the ancient Christians
interpreted Psalm 82:6. This is from *Jerome:*

> "I said: *You are gods, all of you sons of the Most High.*"
> Let Eunomius hear this, let Arius, who say that the Son
> of God is son in the same way we are. That *we are gods*
> is not so by nature, but *by grace.* "But to as many as receive
> him *he gave power of becoming sons of god.*" I made man
> for that purpose, that *from men they may become gods.*
> "I said: You are gods, all of you sons of the Most High."
> Imagine the grandeur of our dignity; *we are called gods
> and sons! I have made you gods* just as I made Moses a
> god to Pharaoh, so that *after you are gods, you may be
> made worthy to be sons of God.* Reflect upon the divine
> words: "With God there is no respecter of persons." God
> did not say: "I said, You are gods," you kings and princes;
> but "all" to whom I have given equally a body, soul, a
> spirit, *I have given equally divinity and adoption.* We are
> "all" born equals. Our humanity is of one of equality.
> "Yet like men you shall die." You see, therefore, that
> man will die. God does not die. Adam, too, as long as he
> obeyed the precept and *was a god*, did not die. After he
> tasted of the forbidden tree, however, he died immediately.
> In fact, God says to him: "The day you eat of it, you must
> die." The Hebrew has a better way of expressing this: "But
> you like Adam shall die." Just as Adam was cast out of
> the Garden of Eden, so, likewise, were we. "And shall fall
> like one of the princes." Since the Lord had said: "*all of
> you sons of the Most High,*" it is not possible to be the
> son of the Most High, unless He Himself is the Most High.

I said that all of you would be exalted as I am exalted.
But, you "shall fall like one of the princes." It is precisely
because we had been so elevated that we are said to have
fallen.[4]

Jerome also wrote,

"Give thanks to *the God of Gods.*" The prophet is
referring to those gods of whom it is written: I said: "*You
are gods*;" and again: "*God arises in the divine assembly.*"
They who cease to be mere men, abandon the ways of vice
and *are become perfect, are gods and the sons of the Most
High.*[5]

Tertullian wrote that:

If, indeed, you follow those who did not at the time
endure the Lord when showing Himself to be the Son of
God, because they would not believe Him to be the Lord,
then call to mind along with them the passage where it
is written, "I have said, *Ye are gods, and ye are children
of the Most High*;" and again, "*God standeth in the
congregation of gods*;" in order that, if *the Scripture has
not been afraid to designate as gods human beings, who
have become sons of God by faith*, you may be sure that
the same Scripture has with greater propriety conferred
the name of the Lord on the true and one-only Son of
God.[6]

According to Christian scholar G. L. Prestige, the ancient Christians
"taught that *the destiny of man was to become like God, and even to become
deified.*"[7]

Other ancient Christians also taught that men may become gods.
Athanasius, for instance, wrote that we are "*Sons and gods* by reason of
the Word within us."[8]

Irenaeus may justly be called the first Biblical theologian among the
ancient Christians. He was a disciple of the great Polycarp, who was a
direct disciple of John the Revelator. It was Irenaeus who was instrumental
in determining what gospel manuscripts should be combined into the New
Testament.[9] According to Irenaeus:

. . .While *man gradually advances and mounts towards
perfection*; that is, he approaches the eternal. The eternal
is perfect; and this is God. Man has first to come into being,

then to progress, and by progressing come to manhood, and having reached manhood to increase, and thus increasing to persevere, and *persevering to be glorified*, and thus see his Lord.[10]

And,

We were not made gods at our beginning, but first we were made men, *then, in the end, gods.*[11]

Also,

How then will any *be a god, if he has not first been made a man*? How can any *be perfect* when he has only lately been made man? How immortal, if he has not in his mortal nature obeyed his maker? For one's duty is first to observe the discipline of man and *thereafter to share in the glory of God.*[12]

And again,

Our Lord Jesus Christ, the Word of God, of his boundless love, became what we are that *he might make us what he himself is.*[13]

Clement of Alexandria wrote,

"To him who has shall be added;" knowledge to faith, love to knowledge, and love to inheritance. And this happens when a man depends on the Lord through faith, through knowledge, and through love, and *ascends with him to the place where God is*, the God and guardian of our faith and love, from whom knowledge is delivered to those who are fit for this privilege and who are selected because of their desire for fuller preparation and training; who are prepared to listen to what is told them, to discipline their lives, to make progress by careful observance of the law of righteousness. This knowledge leads them to the end, the endless final end; teaching of the life that is to be ours, *a life of conformity to God, with gods*, when we have been freed from all punishment, which we undergo as a result of our wrong-doings for our saving discipline. After thus being set free, *those who have been perfected are given their reward and their honours.* They have done with their purification, they have done with the rest of their service, though it be a holy service, with the holy; now they become pure in heart, and because of their close intimacy with the Lord there awaits them a restoration to eternal contemplation; and *they have received the title of "gods," since they are destined to be enthroned with other "gods" who are ranked next below the Saviour.*[14]

Origen wrote:

Everything which, without being "God-in-himself" is *deified by participation in his godhead*, should strictly *be called "God," not "the God."* The "firstborn of all creation," since he by being "with God" first gathered godhood to himself, is therefore in every way more honored than others besides himself, *who are "gods" of whom God is the God*, as it is said, *"God the Lord of gods spoke and called the world."* For it was through his ministry that *they became gods*, since he drew divinity from God *for them to be deified*, and of his kindness *generously shared it with them.* God, then, is the true God, and *those who through him are fashioned into gods are copies of the prototype.*[15]

He also wrote,

The Father, then, is proclaimed as the one true God; but *besides the true God are many who become gods by participating in God.*[16]

Thus it is evident that the early Christian fathers clearly understood, accepted, and taught the doctrine that man can attain godhood. And this broad pattern of quotations from numerous early writers is evidence that the doctrine was widely taught and embraced.

The Bible Teaches That Man Can Attain Godhood

What was the scriptural basis for their belief? The Bible teaches that God Himself has given power and dominion to man:

And God said, Let us make man in our image, after our likeness: and *let them have dominion* over the fish of the sea, and over the fowl of the air, and over the cattle, and *over all the earth,* and over every creeping thing that creepeth upon the earth. (Genesis 1:26)

The Bible repeatedly indicates that man has the potential to attain Godhood, ultimately obtaining all the qualities, powers, and attributes of the Lord Jesus Christ. For instance, it teaches,

> *Ye shall be holy*: for I the LORD your God am holy. (Leviticus 19:2)

And also:

> *What is man*, that thou art mindful of him? and the son of man, that thou visitest him?
> For thou hast made him a little lower than the angels, and *hast crowned him with glory and honour.*
> *Thou madest him to have dominion* over the works of thy hands; *thou hast put all things under his feet.* (Psalm 8:4-6)

And again:

> God standeth in the *congregation of the mighty*; he judgeth *among the gods....*
> *Ye are gods*; and *all of you are children of the most High.* (Psalm 82:1, 6)

And from the New Testament:

> *Be ye therefore perfect, even as your Father which is in heaven* is perfect. (Matthew 5:48)

Paul wrote:

> The Spirit itself beareth witness with our spirit, that *we are the children of God*:
> And if children, then *heirs; heirs of God, and joint-heirs with Christ*; if so be that we suffer with him, that we may be also *glorified together.* (Romans 8:16-17)

And also,

> Wherefore thou art no more a servant, but *a son*; and if a son, then *an heir of God through Christ.* (Galatians 4:7)

John the Revelator recorded the Lord's statement that:

> To him that *overcometh* will I grant to *sit with me in my throne*, even as I also overcame, and am set down with my Father in his throne. (Revelation 3:21)

God made Adam a god by giving him dominion over all the earth; He made Moses a god to Pharaoh, and He gave His firstbegotten Son His name as God. Psalm 2:7 says, "Thou art my Son; this day have I begotten thee." And Psalm 45:6 says, "Thy throne, O god, is for ever and ever: the sceptre of thy kingdom is a right sceptre."

So according to both the Bible and the writings of early Christians, those who take upon themselves the name of Christ and endure to the end shall become heirs of God and joint-heirs with Christ. They shall sit upon thrones and be kings and priests to God. But the ancient witnesses don't stop at that concept—they press on unequivocally to the highest level. According to both the Bible and the ancient Christians, the elect of god shall become gods!

Belief That Man Can Attain Godhood Not a Satanic Doctrine

In spite of the perverted doctrine set forth in "The God Makers" and other anti-Mormon diatribes, Lucifer has never offered Godhood to anyone. He hasn't the power to do so, nor does he have the desire, and there is absolutely no evidence to the contrary. In the Garden of Eden, Lucifer thought he was *spoiling* the plan of God by offering the fruit, but God knew what was to happen before it took place.

Lucifer *lied* when he said to the woman: "Ye shall not surely die." (Genesis 3:4) God said that if man partook of the tree of knowledge of good and evil he would surely die, but Satan said Ye shall *not* surely die. Satan lied in this portion of the enticement he offered Eve.

But Satan mixed fact and falsehood. When Satan said to the woman that the fruit of the tree would enable her to have a knowledge of good and evil, as the gods have that same knowledge, he was *not lying*.

It was God who created the tree and named it the tree of the knowledge of good and evil. When the man and the woman partook of the fruit of the tree of knowledge of good and evil, they did not become gods, but became able to know good from evil *as* the gods do:

> For God doth know that in the day ye eat thereof, then your eyes shall be opened, and *ye shall be as gods, knowing good and evil....*
>
> And the LORD God said, Behold, *the man is become as one of us, to know good and evil*: and now, lest he put forth his hand, and take also of the tree of life, and eat, and live for ever:

Therefore the LORD God sent him forth from the garden of Eden, to till the earth from whence he was taken.

So he drove out the man; and he placed at the east of the garden of Eden Cherubims, and a flaming sword which turned every way, to keep the way of the tree of life. (Genesis 3:4, 22-24)

God has offered man Godhood, but only through His Beloved Son, Jesus Christ. Lucifer offered no one Godhood, and lied when he told Eve that they wouldn't die. Adam and Eve did die, both physically and spiritually.

But Jesus gives man both *immortality*, which is freely given to all, and also *eternal life*, which is given only to those who obey Him. The Latter-day Saints believe, and the Bible testifies, that Godhood *is* Eternal Life, offered only through Jesus Christ.

Satan, on the other hand, caused man's bodily and spiritual death—the very opposite of Eternal Life. Lucifer, being opposed to God's plan of Eternal Life for His faithful sons and daughters, inspired the ministers and blind followers of the apostate churches in the days of Christ to reject Jesus. Because of Lucifer's promptings, the ministers chose to persecute Him because of what they regarded as a crime—because of him being a *God Maker*!

I cannot remember how many times, especially while I served my mission, I heard people say to me as they pointed their finger of accusation:

We're not saying you Mormons don't try to do good deeds, but you blaspheme God because you're only men and yet you say that you're able to become gods!

The answer to their accusation comes from the Savior Himself:

Is it not written in your law, *I said, Ye are gods*?
If *he called them gods, unto whom the word of God came*, and the scripture cannot be broken;
Say ye of him, whom the Father hath sanctified, and sent into the world, Thou blasphemest; because I said, I am the Son of God? (John 10:34-36)

The Concept That Lucifer Offered the Woman Godhood Is a False Anti-Mormon Fabrication

What is left of the false anti-Mormon dogma that Lucifer offered the woman Godhood, and that he lied in saying, "Ye shall be as gods, knowing good and evil" (rather than that he really lied in saying "Ye shall not surely die")? That false reading of scripture is the entire foundation of their accusation, and the reason they erroneously conclude that Mormons are a "Luciferian religion"!

There is nothing left! Their premise is completely without foundation.

False Approaches to Ascending to Heaven in Ancient Times

The Evil One is called by Jesus the father of lies. Satan has never offered Godhood to anyone. Instead, he has sought but failed to personally replace the true God in heaven, and to personally become the Most High, proclaiming that "I will ascend above the heights of the clouds; I will be like the most High."(Isaiah 14:14)

Because Satan rejected God's plan concerning how man could ascend to heaven (which all Christians claim they want to do), and sought his own way (as people do today when they reject and fight against God's plan), God cast him to earth. Lucifer rejected God's plan and fought against it, only to be defeated.

Similarly, men on earth in all dispensations have sought to ascend to heaven by other methods than God's way.

In ancient Babylon, men sought to ascend to heaven. But instead of listening to the seers whom God sent to lead them toward that goal, they arrogantly killed the prophets and built the great Tower of Babel. The Lord destroyed their tower and confounded their language.

In the days of the divided kingdom of Israel, many of God's people, the Israelites, were heavily influenced by the Babylonian religion. After returning to Palestine following their Babylonian captivity, the Israelites began to slay the prophets that God sent them, preferring to attempt to ascend to heaven their own way. The Lord confounded their understanding too. The sects grew up understanding their own speech, but the doctrines of any other sect were babel to them.

Then, in the meredian of time, God sent a great prophet, John the Baptist, to open a glorious new dispensation and prepare the way for the first advent of Christ. The sects opposed the truth in every way. When the plan of God was presented to them, first by the Prophet John, then by Jesus, and then by the apostles and prophets, they rebelled, as Lucifer did, and rejected it.

In the century following Jesus's death, his apostles and prophets were killed because they wanted to lead the people to heaven God's way, but the *gainsayers* that rejected them wanted their own way. The early Christian Church lapsed into apostasy and a new Babylon of apostate Christianity appeared. As before, the Lord confounded them, and the sects multiplied for many centuries, all understanding their own teachings, but the doctrines of other sects were babel to them.

Then God sent a great prophet, Joseph Smith, the prophet who restored the gospel in the latter days, to open a glorious dispensation and to prepare the way for the second advent of Christ.

Throughout most of the time of man, history has been a tale of two cities: Babylon and Zion.

"No God Besides Jehovah" Passage
a Condemnation of Idolatry

When Lucifer was cast to earth, he sought to try to deceive mankind into believing that he was God and that he should be worshipped. It is the work of Satan to attempt to deceive men into believing that the truth is a lie, and his lie the truth.

Occasionally anti-Mormons quote two verses of Isaiah that speak of there being no God comparable to the Lord Jehovah:

> Thus saith the LORD the King of Israel, and his redeemer the LORD of hosts: I am the first, and I am the last; and beside me there is no God....
>
> Is there a God beside me? yea, there is no God; I know not any. (Isaiah 44:6, 8)

After quoting these verses, they typically say, "So you see, Mormonism cannot be Christian because it places many gods beside the only true God!" Those who opposed the Savior and His apostles and prophets in the days of the New Testament Church, said the very same thing:

> Jesus Christ is not the Eternal; the Holy Ghost is not the Eternal; and we invite our Christian brethren to come to the point, and face the real issue, and tell us, if they can, how their idolatrous worship of other gods and another saviour than the Eternal alone can be reconciled with the many declarations made by the latter, that beside Himself there is no god, and no saviour, none like Him, and no one else?[17]

The truth is that the Saints of the Most High, whether they be the former-day Saints or latter-day Saints, do not place other gods beside the Eternal! God is the Most High God, and nothing in heaven or on earth equals Him.

The passages in Isaiah tell that the apostate pastors of the people were turning to idolatry, and regarding pagan gods, which were nothing but idols, as *equal* with the Lord Jehovah. They were placing idols alongside their worship of the LORD:

They that *make a graven image* are all of them vanity; and their delectable things shall not profit....

Who hath formed a god, or *molten a graven image* that is profitable for nothing?....

Assemble yourselves and come; draw near together, ye that are escaped of the nations: they have no knowledge that *set up the wood of their graven image, and pray unto a god that cannot save.*

Tell ye, and bring them near; yea, let them take counsel together: who hath declared this from ancient time? Who hath told it from that time? Have not I the LORD? And there is no God else beside me; a just God and a Saviour; there is none beside me. (Isaiah 44:9, 10, 20-21)

The Lord Jehovah declared that there was no Saviour other than Himself, and they that worshipped other gods, graven images along side of Him were really not worshipping Him.

The "Trinity" of Christian Creeds Taken from Pagan Babylonian Worship

A fundamentalist Christian scholar and author, the Reverend Alexander Hislop, wrote of this era:

So utterly idolatrous was the Babylonian recognition of the Divine unity, that Jehovah, the Living God, severely condemned His own people for giving any countenance to it: They that sanctify themselves, and purify themselves in the gardens, after the rites of the Only One, eating swine's flesh, and the abomination, and the mouse, shall be consumed together." (Isaiah lxvi. 17) *In the unity of that one and Only God of the Babylonians, there were three persons, and to symbolize that doctrine of the Trinity,* they employed, as the discoveries of Layard prove, the *equilateral triangle,* just as it is well known the Romish Church does at this day.[18]

They worshipped according to the Babylonian religion, and the Babylonians worshipped what they considered to be the Only God in a Trinity! What was their graven image that they used? The Reverend Hislop has written:

> That which is now called *the Christian cross was*
> *originally no Christian symbol at all, but the mystic Tau*
> *of the Chaldeans (Babylonians) and Egyptians.*[19]

When "born-again" Christians witness to Mormons about what they believe is the true nature of God, they use the equilateral triangle in an effort to prove that the Only God of their creeds is in a Trinity. What a paradox! The *gainsayers* attempt to condemn the Mormons with the very words (Isaiah 44:6, 8) with which the Lord Jehovah condemned His people, because the Israelites worshipped the Babylonian gods in a trinity with graven images. And the *gainsayers* are still worshipping the three-in-one Babylonian trinity against whom Jehovah was speaking.

The "Trinity" Is Not a Biblical Doctrine

Occasionally I have heard people assert that Mormons believe in a false God, or that their God is Lucifer (that misrepresentation of Mormon belief concocted by the *gainsayers*), and that the Trinity was a clear Biblical doctrine. "Born-again" Christians attempt to use verses such as the following in an effort to prove their Trinity theory to be Biblical: "I and my Father are one." (John 10:30)

Latter-day Saints respond, of course, that the oneness of God has to do with unity of purpose and objectives, not with physical substance. Jesus prayed to the Father: "Holy Father, keep through thine own name those whom thou hast given me, *that they may be one, as we are.*" (John 17:11) This passage would not make sense if it meant that Christ's followers were to all become joined in some immeasurable spiritual blob.

Another passage sometimes used by "born-agains" in defense of their "trinity" theory is also recorded in the gospel of John,

> Philip saith unto him, Lord, shew us the Father, and it
> sufficeth us.
> Jesus saith unto him, Have I been so long time with you,
> and yet hast thou not known me, Philip? He that hath seen
> me hath seen the Father; and how sayest thou then, Shew
> us the Father? (John 14:8-9)

Jesus was not saying that He *was* the Father, but that His appearance was *the express image* of the Father. The Son looks like His Father. Christ came to reveal the Father. In His *person* and His works He spoke and did His Father's will. Jesus said:

> And the Father himself, which hath sent me, hath borne
> witness of me. Ye have neither heard his voice at any time,
> *nor seen his shape.* (John 5:37)

So according to Jesus, God the Father has both a voice and a physical shape, but His disciples, who frequently had seen Jesus, had never seen the Father's shape—they had never seen the Father. According to Paul, Jesus was the express image of the Person of God:

> Who being the brightness of his glory, and the *express*
> *image of his person....*(Hebrews 1:3)

Jesus said many things, and did many things (like praying to the Father), which clearly prove the "three-in-one" or the "trinity" theory an unbiblical doctrine. For instance, Christ revealed that He has a tangible resurrected body:

> Behold my hands and my feet, that it is I myself: handle
> me, and see; for *a spirit hath not flesh and bones, as ye*
> *see me have.* (Luke 24:39)

And Christ spoke of His father as being a completely separate individual, located in a different place:

> *I go unto the Father*; for *my Father is greater than I.*
> (John 14:28)

And Jesus told Mary,

> Touch me not; for I am not yet ascended to my Father;
> but go to my brethren, and say unto them, *I ascend unto*
> *my Father, and your Father*; and to my God, and your God.
> (John 20:17)

In an effort to explain their "trinity" theory to Mormons, the "born-agains" offer arguments such as, "Well, I can be a mother, a daughter, and a sister at the same time, can't I?" I usually reply by asking them if they can be a mother, a daughter, and a sister *to their own selves*, which they obviously can't be.

One ex-Mormon for Jesus told me, "Mormons don't understand the biblical truth of the Trinity because they are totally ignorant of the Bible. The Bible says that Jesus is God; they believe such blasphemous and ridiculous notions like God was once a man born on some planet, died, and has a body now!"

When I have dialogues with those who have been deceived by anti-Mormon adversaries, it usually goes like this:

Born-again:	"You Mormons are ignorant of the Bible, which says that there is only one God, a Trinity of three persons, all Spirit. You blaspheme God and the Bible by saying He was once a man like us. How could you believe such unbiblical and ridiculous doctrines?"
Author:	"Do you believe that Jesus is God?"
Born-again:	"I most certainly do!"
Author:	"Is God one substance or three different beings?" (Many born-agains either don't know what the creeds of their churches teach, or hold opinions at variance with those creeds, but the Nicene Creed says they are one substance.)
Born-again:	"God is one substance!"
Author:	"Does Jesus have a body of flesh and bone?"
Born-again:	"Yes." (They often say "no" until they're shown Luke 24:39.)
Author:	"Was Jesus born of a woman? Was He once a man like us? Did He die?"
Born-again:	"Yes."
Author:	"Then according to you, Jesus, the Holy Spirit, and the Father, are one single Being manifest in three persons. This one Being was born of a woman, lived as men do although sinless, suffered and died on the cross, and now is resurrected. Now since you believe that God came down, was born of a woman, died, and has a body of flesh and bone, why do you call me a Satanist and a blasphemer because I believe God has a body, when Jesus, His Son, declared everything He did was only in imitation of what He had seen the Father do?"

Usually the conversation isn't that ideal. "Born-agains" usually use their "flip flop" technique to switch to another subject, or greatly modify their concept of God, as one concerned Christian did who worked for the anti-Mormon movement:

Author:	"Are Eloheim and Jehovah the same Being?"
Concerned:	"The Bible says so!"
Author:	"Does Eloheim, or God, have a body of flesh and bone?"
Concerned:	"Of course not, He is a Spirit!"
Author:	"Is Jesus Jehovah?"
Concerned:	"Yes."
Author:	"Does Jehovah have a body?"
Concerned:	"Well, ah, I suppose He does."

Author: "We've agreed that Jehovah, or Jesus, has a body. But
             you say the Father is only a Spirit. So are Eloheim and
             Jehovah the same Being?"
Concerned: "No!"

Christian Scholars Acknowledge that
the "Trinity" Theory Is Not Biblical

While the average "born-again" Christian sincerely believes that the Bible
teaches the doctrine of the trinity, Christian scholars know better. This is
evident from quotations such as these drawn from various Christian
publications:

> The God whom we experience as triune is, in fact, triune.
> But *we cannot read back into the New Testament, much
> less the Old Testament, the more sophisticated trinitarian
> theology and doctrine* which slowly and often unevenly
> developed over the course of some fifteen centuries.[20]

Also,

> Thus *the New Testament itself is far from any doctrine
> of the Trinity or of a triune God* who is three co-equal
> Persons of One Nature.[21]

And,

> The New Testament *does not contain the developed
> doctrine of the Trinity.*[22]

And also,

> All this underlines the point that *primitive Christianity
> did not have an explicit doctrine of the Trinity* such as was
> subsequently elaborated in the creeds of the early
> Church.[23]

Jesus declared how very important it was to have a correct knowledge
about God in a prayer which he offered to his Father:

> This is *life eternal, that they might know thee* the only
> true God, and Jesus Christ, whom thou hast sent. (John
> 17:3)

The Latter-day Saints declare that God can be known through His Son
Jesus Christ, who came to earth to *reveal* the Father. All other religions

on the globe believe and teach that God is unknowable and incomprehensible.

In order to deny man of the Father's will for him, eternal life, all the Adversary needs to do, and has done around the world, is to deceive man into believing that God is unknowable. Jesus said that it is eternal life to *know* both God and Jesus, who hath revealed or declared Him.

Ancient Christian Writers Rejected and Condemned the "Trinity" Theory

The "trinity" theory, which the Lord warned the people against in the Old Testament (as it came from Babylon), was indeed a false doctrine that was spreading about in the ancient Church. The early Christian leaders and writers condemned the "trinity" theory as *anti-Christ and a doctrine of the devil*. Wrote *Hippolytus*, a disciple of Irenaeus:

> If, again, he alleges his own word when he (Noetus) attends to the fact, and understands that he did not say, "I and the Father am one, but *are one.*" For the word re (*esmen*)) is not said of one person, but *it refers to two persons and one power*. He has himself made this clear, when he spoke to the Father concerning the disciples, "The glory which Thou gavest me I have given them; that they may be made perfect in one; that the world may know that Thou hast sent me." What have the Noetians to say to these things? Are all one body in respect to substance, or is it that we *become one in the power and disposition of unity of mind*?...A man, therefore, even though he will it not, is compelled to acknowledge God the Father Almighty, and Christ Jesus the Son of God, who, being God, became man, to whom also the Father made all things subject, himself excepted, and the Holy Spirit; and that *these therefore, are three.*[24]

This statement by Hippolytus was from his work called *De Antichristo* (The Anti-Christ). Noetus was a false teacher, or anti-Christ, in the ancient Church, who tried to introduce the pagan belief in the trinity into Christianity.[25]

Origen, the great ancient Christian scholar, apologist, and martyr, wrote:

> Those who entertain *false notions about Christ* under pretense of doing him honour are not to be thought of as "for" him: such are *they who confuse the conception of*

Father and Son who suppose that the Father and Son are one in individual being and only admit distinctions of function in the identical subject.[26]

Origen also wrote,

The Son is inferior in relation to the Father, since he touches only things endowed with reason, for he is subordinate to the Father. The Holy Spirit is still lower in degree, pertaining only to the saints. So then the power of *the Father is superior to the Son and the Holy Spirit, while the Son's power is greater than the Holy Spirit*; and again the power of the Holy Spirit excels all other holy things.[27]

Origen also wrote this statement:

And they are *two separate persons*, but *one in unity and concord of mind and in identity of will*; so that he who has seen the Son, "radiance of the glory" and "expression of the being" of God, has seen God in him who is the image of God.[28]

Tertullian, another great ancient Christian scholar and defender of the faith, wrote a book called *Against Praxeas*, another false teacher who tried to introduce the pagan "trinity" theory into the ancient Church. Writes Tertullian:

In various ways has *the devil rivalled and resisted the truth. Sometimes his aim has been to destroy the truth by defending it.* He maintains that there is one only Lord, the Almighty Creator of the world, in order that out of this doctrine of the unity he may *fabricate a heresy.* He says that the Father Himself came down into the Virgin, was Himself born of her, Himself suffered, indeed, was Himself Jesus Christ.[29]

Tertullian also wrote,

He himself, they say, *made Himself a Son to Himself.* Now a Father makes a Son, and a Son makes a Father; and they who thus become so related to themselves, that *the Father can make Himself a Son to Himself,* and *the Son render Himself a Father to Himself....*Now all this must be the device of the devil.*[30]

And also,

> They more readily suppose that the Father acted in the Son's name, than that the Son acted in the Father's; although the Lord says Himself, "I am come in my Father's name;" and even to the Father He declares, "I have manifested Thy name unto these men;" whilst the Scripture likewise says, "Blessed is He that cometh in the name of the Lord," that is to say, the Son in the Father's name.[31]

And again,

> Now, observe, my assertion is that *the Father is one*, and *the Son one*, and *the Spirit one*, and that *They are distinct from Each Other.*[32]

Here, then, is the real perversion of doctrines: the three-in-one concept which crept into the early church after the time of Christ. Those who teach that the "trinity" theory is fact, and Biblical, are based neither in fact nor scripture. They are preaching a heresy which marked the seriousness of the great apostasy which occurred in the first centuries after the time of Christ.

Prophets Have Reintroduced Knowledge of the True God in Every Gospel Dispensation

God has promised the faithful that He would make them His heirs and joint-heirs with Jesus Christ—kings and priests privileged to share their Heavenly Father's power. God has sent His Only-begotten Son in the flesh and first-begotten in the spirit to make atonement for their sins, to reveal the Father to them that they might have eternal life, and to show them the way.

Lucifer, because he wanted to ascend to heaven some other way, was cast out for rebellion, thus becoming Satan, the Adversary. He has been opposing the work of God from the beginning, and in his rage and his jealousy has sent false Gods, false Christs, and false teachers and prophets to deceive mankind. Under his guidance, the false religion of Babylon has repeatedly crept in and perverted the religion of Zion.

In the dispensation of Adam, when the true prophets were killed in favor of such doctrines, and Enoch and his city were taken from the earth, a time of spiritual darkness began.

God opened another dispensation with Noah, and the world rejected the living prophets and built a tower to ascend to heaven. Darkness resumed again.

Then Abraham was called and his dispensation continued until the people of God were seduced by the Babylonian religion of Egypt. They killed and rejected the prophets, and the Egyptians made them their slaves. Another time of spiritual darkness began.

The prophet Moses opened up the next dispensation of living prophets, the ministry of angels, and new scripture. He was opposed by the religious leaders of the day, but triumphed over them. Yet the religion of Babylon crept into Zion again. The people worshipped a strange triune God that the Lord Jehovah condemned. Israel listened to the corrupt pastors and killed or rejected the living prophets, initiating yet another time of spiritual darkness.

Then God sent another great prophet by the name of John who was opposed by the religious leaders of his day. In that dispensation, the Lord of all, the very Jehovah who talked and walked with Adam, who counseled Noah, who called Abraham His friend, who appeared to Moses, came down and was born of a virgin. He lived a sinless life and atoned for the sins of the world by His suffering and death on the cross. He preached to the spirits in prison, arose from the tomb and appeared to many, ascended to heaven, and is now on the right hand of the Father.

John came to prepare the way for the Lord, and to announce a new dispensation with living prophets, apostles, gifts of the Spirit, the ministering of angels, and new scriptures. For this he was opposed by the other churches who labeled the Nazarenes a cult.

After Jesus ascended into heaven, His apostles and prophets travelled far and wide spreading the good news of the Gospel, but they were opposed by many. Even after the Church was well established, the people of God began to reject the true and living prophets. They turned to false teachers who called themselves pastors over the flock, but were in fact teachers who introduced the false triune god of Babylon into Zion. Another time of spiritual darkness occurred.

Then, centuries later, God sent another great prophet by the name of Joseph, who also was opposed by the religious leaders of his day. Joseph was the instrument in the hands of the Lord to restore the truth to the earth, as did the great prophets before him. A new dispensation began, with living prophets and apostles, gifts of the Spirit, the ministry of angels, and new scripture. For this he was opposed by the other churches, and the Mormons were labeled a cult. So what else is new?

This is a time to choose between the *true* God Maker who is God, and the false God Maker who is Satan—he who deceived the religious leaders in Jesus's day into condemning Him for being a *God Maker*! The choice is yours.

4

Early Christian Temple Rites: Ancient and Modern Parallels

A Great Prophet Is Sent by God to Man in Each Dispensation

At the beginning of each new gospel dispensation, a great or high prophet has been sent by God to the earth to bear His message to man. When Adam and Eve were thrust out of God's presence, they and their descendants were not left without guidance. God chose that first man, Adam, to be his prophet and spokesman during the first dispensation or gospel age. Through continuous revelation, God revealed His instructions to His children, and Adam, as a prophet, told the people what the Lord had declared. This has always been the plan of God:

> Surely the Lord GOD will do nothing, but he revealeth
> his secret unto his servants the prophets. (Amos 3:7)

God commanded Adam to offer the firstlings of his flock as sacrifice, this being a similitude of the atonement of Jesus Christ. Other prophets came after Adam in that dispensation: Seth, Enos, Canaan, Mahalaleel, Jared, and Enoch.

But many people turned away from God and His spokemen. By the days of Enoch, so many people had rejected the living prophets and had become so wicked that God removed Enoch and his righteous followers from the earth, leaving behind only the wicked.

That was the culmination of the first apostasy, or falling away from the truth. It was an era in which the world so utterly rejected the living prophets that the heavens were sealed for a time, and man was left alone in spiritual darkness. Because of that spiritual darkness the world became even more wicked; so much so that God decided to cleanse the earth by water and to send a deluge which would destroy the nations.

But to preserve human life upon the earth, God opened a second dispensation. He chose Noah, a meek and righteous man, to be His prophet. Noah's ark was built while the world laughed and scorned. Yet the rains came, and the oceans passed over the continents. Only Noah, the high prophet, and his family were preserved to replenish the new world that was to come. After Noah, the families of his three sons greatly increased and became the three races of man.

Other prophets were sent in the dispensation of Noah, but again, the people began to reject the living prophets. They wanted to ascend to heaven their own way. The nations built a great tower to ascend to Heaven, but the Lord destroyed their foolish effort and confounded their understanding. Because the world once again rejected the living prophets, God gathered the righteous to the city of Salem (the city of peace), and the prophet who was their king was Melchizedek (king of righteousness).

The world was in yet another time of spiritual darkness when God chose to open the third dispensation by calling another high prophet; his name was Abram. Abram lived in Ur of the Chaldees, but God commanded him by revelation to leave his native land for a Promised Land, and changed his name from Abram (Exalted Father) to Abraham (Father of Nations). God promised Abraham that because he was faithful in all things He would send the covenant people to earth as his descendants, and even the great Messiah would be among his seed, thus blessing the entire earth.

Other prophets were sent in that dispensation, including Isaac, Jacob, and Joseph. Because of Joseph, the people of God (now called the Israelites after the new name God gave to Jacob) became secure and numerous in the land of Egypt. Yet, after his day the scriptures say nothing for four hundred years. As before, the people began to reject the prophets God sent them, and were seduced by the false gods and false teachers of the religion of Egypt. The people of God found themselves slaves in Egypt, and another time of spiritual darkness had begun.

God opened the fourth dispensation, and he chose Moses, a Hebrew who was an adopted son of the house of Pharoah, to be His high prophet. Moses, no doubt, was opposed by many of the religious teachers among the

Hebrews, but God worked great miracles through him and the people were set free. During Moses's ministry, God instituted his great preparatory law, the Law of Moses, with its rites of sacrifice and ritual. They were types, shadows, signs and tokens of the light, life and sacrifice of the Only Begotten Son who was to come in the meridian of time.

Other prophets, including Joshua, Samuel, Nathan, Isaiah, Jeremiah, Lehi, Daniel, Ezekiel, Nehemiah, Elijah, and Malachi, all admonished the people to keep the law which God gave to Moses. They saw and knew that God would send a Messiah, a Savior and Redeemer, in the future to save the people from their sins and to establish a universal Kingdom of God. Yet the people, influenced by the religion of Babylon around them, began to reject and kill the living prophets, and there eventually came yet another time of spiritual darkness.

God chose to open a fifth dispensation, and He chose a man named John to be His high prophet. Even before John was born, an angel appeared to his father, Zacharias, in the Temple announcing that he and his wife would have a son who was to be a prophet of the Highest. In that dispensation, too, the Messiah would come, for John was to be the one crying in the wilderness, "Prepare ye the way of the Lord, make his paths straight." (Luke 3:4)

Jesus the Messiah Fulfilled Bible Prophecies

This was the dispensation in which the Lord Himself was born of a virgin, and became the Messiah and Savior. Jesus Christ the Messiah was sent for many reasons, one being that in His birth, life, and death He fulfilled prophecy. It was foretold that the Messiah would be a Jew:

> Behold, the days come, saith the LORD, that I will raise unto David a righteous Branch, and a king shall reign and prosper, and shall execute judgment and justice in the earth.
>
> In his days Judah shall be saved: and this is his name whereby he shall be called, THE LORD OUR RIGHTEOUSNESS. (Jeremiah 23:5-6)

Jesus Christ was a descendant of David, in fulfillment of the prophecy. (Matthew 1:1)

It was foretold that the Messiah would be born in Bethlehem:

> But thou, Bethlehem Ephratah, though thou be little among the thousands of Judah, yet out of thee shall he come

> forth unto me that is to be ruler in Israel; whose goings
> forth have been from of old, from everlasting. (Micah 5:2)

Jesus was born in Bethlehem as the prophet had foreseen. (Luke 2:4-11)
It was prophesied that the mother of the Messiah would be a virgin:

> Therefore the Lord himself shall give you a sign; Behold,
> a virgin shall conceive, and bear a son, and shall call his
> name Immanuel. (Isaiah 7:14)

The mother of Jesus was a virgin, in literal fulfillment of the prophecy.
(Luke 1:26-32)
It was foretold that a star would appear in the heavens announcing the
birth of the Messiah:

> I shall see him, but not now: I shall behold him, but
> not nigh: there shall come a Star out of Jacob, and a Sceptre
> shall raise out of Israel. (Numbers 24:17)

A star in the East announced the birth of Jesus, and led the wise men to
Bethlehem. (Matthew 2:1-2)
It was foretold that a great Prophet would prepare the way for the Messiah
by preaching in the wilderness:

> The voice of him that crieth in the wilderness, Prepare
> ye the way of the LORD, make straight in the desert a
> highway for our God. (Isaiah 40:3)

John the Baptist, whose birth was heralded by angelic visitations, announced
Jesus in the wilderness (Matthew 3:3).
The manner in which the Messiah would be slain was foretold:

> My strength is dried up like a potsherd; and my tongue
> cleaveth to my jaws; and thou hast brought me into the
> dust of death.
> For dogs have compassed me: the assembly of the wicked
> have inclosed me: *they pierced my hands and my feet.*
> I may tell all my bones: they look and stare upon me.
> They part my garments among them, and cast lots upon
> my vesture. (Psalm 22:15-18)

Jesus was crucified, in literal fulfillment of the prophecy (John 19:23-24). It was foretold that the Messiah would rise from the dead:

> Thy dead men shall live, *together with my dead body shall they arise*. Awake and sing, ye that dwell in dust: for thy dew is as the dew of herbs, and *the earth shall cast out the dead*. (Isaiah 26:19)

Jesus Christ was resurrected from death, as the ancient prophet had foreseen (Matthew 18:1-10). These and many more prophecies were fulfilled by Jesus of Nazareth who was the Messiah and Savior.

Ancient Prophets Had Secret Rites, Rituals, and Records

The prophets knew much about the Savior who was to come, and about the message of salvation He would bring for mankind. According to Paul, for instance, they knew the Gospel (Acts 4:12; 1st Corinthians 10:1-4; Hebrews 4:2; Galatians 3:8), but only revealed bits and pieces of it in the Old Testament scriptures.

But there is evidence that they had considerably more knowledge than they passed on in the Old Testament. According to modern scholars, there had been, among believers in the true religion of God a *secret (or apocalyptic) tradition* which asserted that the divine secrets were made known to people who then recorded them in secret or "hidden" books for the instruction of the righteous of God's elect.[1]

The secrets were usually made known to the prophet or seer in a dream or vision in which he was caught up to Heaven. Frequently it took the form of a bodily translation which allowed the prophet to go into Heaven, either in the spirit or in the body, where the seer was introduced to the eternal secrets of the divine purpose, or even into the very presence of God Himself. Sometimes, too, an angelic interpreter was introduced who guided the seer in his heavenly journeyings and explained to him the meaning of things in heaven and earth. The vision would consist of a review of the Creation and Fall of man, plus revelations of things yet future. These revelatory experiences took place not only in Old Testament times, but in the New Testament era also.

The apocalyptic writers (many of them the ancient Christians) wrote that these divine secrets were written down on the "heavenly tablets" by the ancient seers. They wrote that these books related the purposes of God for the whole world from creation to the end-time. They had been hidden away for many generations and handed down in a long line of secret traditions, finally preserved until "the last days."[2] The prophets knew the heavenly secrets, and the mystery of God about the Messiah became a reality in Jesus Christ.

Modern Christian Scholars Have Documented
Aspects of Ancient Christian Temple Ritual

The ancient Christians had secret rites which they did not divulge to the uninitiated, and they practiced these rites in their Christian temples. Before Jesus made His appearance as the Christ, the Saints of God gathered around His prophet, John. The other churches of the day, especially the ministers, rejected John the Baptist because they thought that revelation through prophets had ceased. They called John and his disciples "Nazoreans," a nickname which means *"keepers of the secret teachings."*[3] According to Christian scholar Dr. E. S. Drower:

> Each *raza*, "each mystery," *is a drama,*...but they are still couched in the language of parable and symbol, so obscure in expression that none but a "true Nasorean" can interpret its meaning.[4]

Scholars know that the mystery drama included a representation of the creation of Adam, and a *"ritual handclasp."*[5] According to Christian scholar and historian Dr. Johann L. Mosheim:

> In the ritualism of the early Jewish Mysteries the *pageantry of creation was enacted, the various actors impersonating the Creative agencies.*[6]

Jesus himself made it clear that his most faithful followers were to receive special knowledge of the rites of his kingdom, but that knowledge would not be shared with the uninitiated:

> And the disciples came, and said unto him, Why speakest thou unto them in parables?
> He answered and said unto them, Because *it is given unto you to know the mysteries of the kingdom of heaven*, but to them it is not given. (Matthew 13:10-11)

The Savior had already admonished His disciples to keep holy things secret and to not share them with those who were unworthy:

> *Give not that which is holy unto the dogs*, neither cast ye your pearls before swine, lest they trample them under their feet, and turn again and rend you. (Matthew 7:6)

New Testament Contains References
to the "Mysteries of God"

According to the apostle Paul, along with the public Gospel there were certain secrets called the Mysteries of God, which dated back to the beginning of the world:

> Now to him that is of power to stablish you according to my gospel, and the preaching of Jesus Christ, according to the *revelation of the mystery*, which was *kept secret since the world began*. (Romans 16:25)

He also repeated his teaching that the mystery of God was established before the world began in his first epistle to the Corinthians:

> But we speak *the wisdom of God in a mystery, even the hidden wisdom*, which *God ordained before the world* unto our glory. (1 Corinthians 2:7)

Paul acknowledged that Church leaders had access to the gospel mysteries, and that they were stewards of them:

> Let a man so account of us, as of the ministers of Christ, and *stewards of the mysteries of God*. (1 Corinthians 4:1)

And another epistle of Paul, written to the Saints at Colosse, contains these words:

> For I would that ye knew what great conflict I have for you, and for them at Laodicea, and for as many as have not seen my face in the flesh;
> That their hearts might be comforted, being knit together in love, and unto all riches of the full assurance of understanding, to the acknowledgement of *the mystery of God*, and of the Father, and of Christ.
> In whom are *hid all the treasures of wisdom and knowledge*. (Colossians 2:1-3)

And Paul alluded to these special mysteries in his first epistle to Timothy:

> Likewise must the deacons be grave, not doubletongued, not given to much wine, not greedy of filthy lucre;
> Holding the *mystery of the faith* in a pure conscience. (1 Timothy 3:8-9)

These references give clear indication that the early Church had special teachings which were made available to the selected faithful, but which were not shared with those who were unworthy to receive them.

Numerous Allusions to Temple Rites in the Book of Revelation

The Mysteries of God, a term for their ancient temple rites, are alluded to in several places in the Book of Revelation. John wrote, for instance, of men becoming kings and priests:

> And hath made us *kings and priests* unto God and his Father; to him be glory and dominion for ever and ever. (Revelation 1:6)

He also wrote of men receiving a new name:

> He that hath an ear, let him hear what the Spirit saith unto the churches; To him that overcometh will I give to eat of the *hidden manna*, and will give him a white stone, and in the stone *a new name* written, which no man knoweth saving he that receiveth it. (Revelation 2:17)

And also:

> Him that overcometh will I make a pillar in the *temple of my God*, and he shall no more go out: and I will *write upon him the name of my God*, and the name of the city of my God, which is new Jerusalem, which cometh down out of heaven from my God, and I will write upon him *my new name*. (Revelation 3:12)

John wrote of special clothing which he called garments:

> Thou hast a few names even in Sardis which have *not defiled their garments*; and they shall walk with me *in white*: for they are worthy.
> He that overcometh, the same shall be clothed in *white raiment*; and I will not blot out *his name* out of the book of life, but I will confess his name before my Father, and before his angels. (Revelation 3:4-5)

John wrote of men being privileged to share the throne of Christ:

> To him that overcometh will I grant *to sit with me in
> my throne*, even as I also overcame, and am set down with
> my Father in his throne. (Revelation 3:21)

And John wrote of sealings, which constitute an important part of the temple ritual:

> And I saw another angel ascending from the east, having
> the *seal of the living God*: and he cried with a loud voice
> to the four angels, to whom it was given to hurt the earth
> and the sea,
> Saying, Hurt not the earth, neither the sea, nor the trees,
> till we have *sealed the servants* of our God in their
> foreheads. (Revelation 7:2-3)

John wrote of heavenly temples:

> Therefore are they before the throne of God, and *serve
> him day and night in his temple*: and he that sitteth on the
> throne shall dwell among them. (Revelation 7:15)

And, like Paul, John used the term "mystery of God":

> But in the days of the voice of the seventh angel, when
> he shall begin to sound, the *mystery of God* should be
> finished, as he hath declared to his servants the prophets.
> (Revelation 10:7)

Modern Christian Scholars Bear Witness of Ancient Christian Secret Rites

The fact that the ancient Christians had secret rites is known to Christian scholars and historians. The famous Christian scholar and historian Dr. Johann J. Mosheim testifies:

> That the more learned of the Christians, subsequently
> to the second century, cultivated, in secret, an obtuse
> *discipline of a different nature from that which they taught
> publicly*, is *well known to everyone*. Concerning the
> argument, however, or matter of this secret or mysterious
> discipline, its origin, and the causes which discontinued
> it has caused many disputes among scholars.[7]

Mosheim also wrote,

> Why James, and John, and Peter, should have been, in
> particular, fixed upon as the apostles whom Christ selected
> as the most worthy of *having this recondite wisdom
> communicated to them by word of mouth*, is very easy to
> be perceived. For these were the three disciples whom our
> blessed Saviour took apart with him up into the mountain
> when he was about to be transfigured, Matthew xvii,1.
> Luke, ix.28. To represent them, therefore, as having in a
> particular manner been favored with an *insight into all
> mysteries*, appeared to be but consistent and proper.[8]

Mosheim acknowledged that the ancient Christians reserved the initiation
into their "mysteries" for those who were established members of the
Church:

> The multitude professing Christianity were therefore
> divided by them into the *"profane,"* or those who were
> *not yet admitted to the mysteries*, and the *"initiated,"* or
> faithful and perfect....and as *none were permitted to be
> present at these "mysteries,"* as they were termed, *save
> those whose admission into the fellowship of the church
> was perfect and complete*, so likewise was it expected that,
> as a matter of duty, the *most sacred silence should be
> observed in regard to everything connected with the
> celebration of them*, and nothing whatever relating thereto
> to be committed to the ears of the profane.[9]

According to the ancient anti-Christians, the Nazarenes had special means
established for identifying each other as Christians. It is recorded that "They
recognized each other by *secret marks and signs*."[10]

According to one ancient writer, *Caecilius*, the Christians also had
"distinguishing marks on the body," meaning, no doubt, their
underclothing.[11]

What were those marked underclothing? According to the ancient
Christian scholar and martyr *Origen*, a true Saint had to have and wear
special garments in order to properly offer sacrifices of praise, prayers,
pity, purity, and righteousness:

To offer these aright you have need of clean garments, or vestments kept
apart from the common clothing of the rest of mankind.[12]

These sacred mysteries were conducted in ancient Christian temples, and according to Dr. Mosheim, many temples were destroyed or defiled because of anti-Christian persecution:

> This long and cruel persecution commenced in the month of February or April, A.D. 303,...and it was introduced by the destruction of the spacious *Christian temple at Nicomedia*, and the burning of the *books found in it.*[13]

Ancient Anti-Nazarenes Attacked the Church Because of Its Temple Rites

The anti-Nazarenes, of course, tried, and often succeeded in deceiving the public into believing that the Nazarenes, or Christians, kept some of their rites secret because those rites were occultic and immoral. One ancient "cult fighter" warned:

> And now—for the evil grows apace—the corruption of morals gains ground from day to day, and throughout the entire world *those abominable shrines of the evil confederacy increase in number.* This conspiracy must be radically rooted out and execrated.[14]

In the view of the ancient *gainsayers,* Jesus had been heavily involved in magic and occultism.[15] They also claimed that the Nazarenes had secret rites which were kept secret under, they claimed, a penalty of death.[16] They claimed that the "secret and nocturnal" rites were borrowed from the pagan mysteries.[17] Yet according to a modern Christian scholar:

> There is no relation between the *Discipline of the Secret in early Christianity* and the customs of the pagan mysteries. The similarities are of a purely external nature.[18]

Ancient and modern parallels are immediately apparent. Modern *gainsayers* have repeated the false assertions made by the ancient cult fighters. They have again advanced the falsehoods that latter-day temple rites are immoral, occultic, and drawn from pagan origins, all of which are untrue and without factual basis.

Historians Acknowledge Early Christian Rites Were Reserved for Most Worthy Members

According to Christian historian Edwin Hatch, the ancient Christians "had *mysteries which they disclosed to the initiated* only after long preparation, and with an *oath not to divulge them....*"[19] The Mysteries of God given in the temples were sacred, and not to be given to everyone. They were reserved only for those who were prepared to make the covenants therein.

The fact that the ancient Christians had secret rites reserved only for those who were fully prepared is confirmed by other ancient Christian writers. For instance, *Hippolytus* wrote that

> We have delivered to you briefly these things concerning baptism and the oblation because you have already been instructed concerning the resurrection of the flesh and the rest according to the Scriptures. But if there is any other matter which ought to be told, *let the bishop impart it secretly to those who are communicated. He shall not tell this to any but the faithful* and only after they have first been communicated. *This is the white stone of which John said that there is a new name written upon it* which no man knows except him who receives.[20]

Basil of Caesarea wrote that

> *Secret doctrines* and public teachings have been preserved in the Church, and some of them we have from written teaching and *others we have received handed down to us in a mystery* from the tradition of the apostles.[21]

And also,

> In just the same way, the apostles and fathers who were ordering the institutions in connection with the churches in the beginning used to *preserve that which was sacred in the mysteries by a secret and undivulged method.* For that which is published for common and chance hearing is not properly a mystery. This is the reason for the *tradition of unwritten things*, to prevent the knowledge of *secret doctrines* becoming neglected and through familiarity becoming contemptible in the eyes of the majority. *Secret doctrine is one thing*; public teaching another. *The former is preserved in silence*; the latter is published.[22]

Cyril of Jerusalem recorded his instructions that:

> If after the class a catechumen asks you what the instructors have said, tell outsiders nothing. For *it is a divine secret that we deliver to you, even the hope of the life to come.* Keep the secret for the Rewarder. If someone says, "What harm is done if I know about it too?" don't listen to him. So the sick man asks for wine, but, given to him at the wrong time, it only produces brain-fever, and two evils ensue: the effect on the sick man is disastrous, and the doctor is maligned. So the catechumen, *if he is told the Mysteries by one of the faithful: not understanding what he has been told, the catechumen raves, attacking the doctrine and ridiculing the statement*, while the believer stands condemned as a traitor.[23]

Athanasius instructed that:

> *One must not recite the mysteries to the uninitiated*, lest outsiders who do not understand make fun of them while they perplex and scandalize investigators.[24]

Tertullian recorded that:

> We believe that the apostles were ignorant of nothing, but they did not transmit everything they knew, and were *not willing to reveal everything to everybody.* They did not preach everywhere nor promiscuously....but taught one thing about the nature of Christ in public and *another in secret.*[25]

Paul, in the New Testament, spoke of secrets revealed to him by vision which he was unwilling to divulge:

> I knew a man in Christ above fourteen years ago, (whether in the body, I cannot tell; or whether out of the body, I cannot tell: God knoweth;) such an one caught up to the third heaven.
>
> And I knew such a man, (whether in the body, or out of the body, I cannot tell: God knoweth;)
>
> How that he was caught up into paradise, *and heard unspeakable words, which it is not lawful for a man to utter.* (2 Corinthians 12:2-4).

Christ Revealed Temple Rites
Following His Resurrection

According to the Bible, Jesus was resurrected from the dead, and appeared to and taught the disciples for forty days before ascending into heaven:

> The former treatise have I made, O Theophilus, of all that Jesus began both to do and teach,
> Until the day in which he was taken up, after that he through the Holy Ghost had given commandments unto the apostles whom he had chosen:
> To whom also he shewed himself alive after his passion by many infallible proofs, being seen of them *forty days*, and *speaking of the things pertaining to the kingdom of God*. (Acts 1:1-3)

Of what things did Jesus speak? For the most part, the Bible is silent on this question. According to the ancient Christians, however, it was during His forty-day ministry that Jesus taught His disciples the Mysteries of God, giving them first to Peter, James, and John. The ancient Christian historian *Eusebius* wrote in his "Ecclesiastical History":

> The *Lord imparted the gift of knowledge to James the Just, to John and Peter, after his resurrection*; these delivered it to the rest of the apostles, and they to the seventy, of whom Barnabas was one.[26]

The Latter-day Saints declare that the Church is a restoration of the ancient Christian faith. They have, as the ancient Saints did, apostles and prophets, gifts of the Spirit, new scripture, and those same Mysteries of God.

Modern Gainsayers Ignorant of Evidences
of Ancient Christian Temple Worship

Yet, lacking knowledge of all the evidence of the secret teachings circulated in the early Christian church, such as that which is cited above, anti-Mormons adversaries, the *gainsayers*, erroneously declare:

> Secrecy is contrary to Christianity. Jesus did not found a secret society. When falsely accused of many things before the Sanhedrin, and when the High Priest demanded to know His doctrine, Christ specifically stated: "I spoke openly to the world; I always taught in the synagogue and in the temple where the Jews always resort, and in secret have I said nothing."[27]

What do these adversaries hope to prove by quoting John 18:20? Jesus did not give the Mysteries of God to his disciples until *after* he made that statement—until *after* His death and resurrection. The *gainsayers* are using just another straw man technique. There is a great amount of evidence of the existence of early Christian temple rituals, as has been shown.

These modern *gainsayers* also show their ignorance of historical sources by erroneously asserting that:

> There is no record, however, either in history or tradition to indicate that a "Christian temple" ever existed anywhere, much less that Christians ever practiced the pagan rituals now performed in Mormon Temples.[28]

And they have also said,

> There is not one example in the Bible (or the Book of Mormon, for that matter) of any ritual, ceremony, or act of worship that was practiced in secret—much less an example of an oath forfeiting one's life for revealing something sacred.[29]

The evidence previously cited in this chapter gives clear indication that these *gainsayer* allegations are unfounded. They either are indications of a serious lack of knowledge of the scriptures and historical sources, or an intentional disregarding of a substantial body of evidence, or both. Suffice it to say that in the matter of ancient temple rites, as in numerous other doctrinal and historical matters cited in this book and elsewhere, the *gainsayers* are in error.

Ancient and Modern Attempts to Publicize and Profane the Temple Ritual

Many of the ancient Saints suffered death rather than reveal the Mysteries of God. They suffered death at the hands of anti-Nazarenes, cult-fighters and Romans who demanded that the Nazarenes they persecuted and imprisoned reveal to them what went on in their temples. But the faithful remained silent and suffered death at the hands of their enemies rather than reveal the sacred mysteries.[30]

The ancient anti-Nazarenes sought to reveal to the public the secret rites of the Nazarenes, but their only source of information was apostates who had once been Christian. What those ex-Christians revealed was totally inaccurate and unreliable. Likewise, anti-Mormon adversaries today think they are hindering the Church by publicizing and profaning some of the temple ritual. According to one Latter-day Christian apologist, writing about "The God Makers":

> The producers of the film have admitted their use of *deception* to obtain stock footage of temple interiors from the LDS church information services, and to arrange interviews with church officials who appear in the film. These despicable tactics speak for themselves.[31]

One ex-Mormon apostasized from the Church, but used his unexpired temple recommend to enter the Temple to "worship" there. He entered with a hidden recorder to record the Endowment. Later the transcript went on sale. Was that an honest act? The Endowment had already been published by other anti-LDS persons, so why did this man feel he had to willingly deceive people in the name of Christ? He entered the Temple under false pretenses. Is that not like a wolf in sheep's clothing?

Although their so-called re-enactment of LDS Temple worship in the film "The God Makers" is much better than what had been said in the past (if they told the truth previously, then why did they have to be more accurate now?), it is still a far cry from an honest portrayal, and far from the truth.

More than one adversary has tauntingly said to me, "Well, if we haven't presented what goes on in the Temple accurately, then please correct us in detail and we'll change what we did!" Anti-Mormon adversaries know full well that the Saints will not speak about the Mysteries of God outside the Temple, and will not share sacred insights with non-members.

The ancient Christians were confronted with the same dilemma as the latter-day Christians are now. Wrote the ancient Christian scholar and writer *Lactantius*:

> We do not make a practice of defending and discussing this thing publicly, because, with the help of God, *we quietly keep His secret to ourselves in silence*...for it is proper to withhold and conceal the mystery with all possible care—especially so for us who bear the name of believers.[32]

LDS adversaries have, on occasion, attempted to force various Latter-day Saint members to reveal the Mysteries of God. One ex-Mormon for Jesus, who had never been a Latter-day Saint, tried to do that to me. He mocked, ridiculed, and greatly distorted the Church's temple worship right in front of me, and then, smiling, asked, "Now is what I've shown you true or not? The only way you can convince me that it's not is if you tell me what really goes on in there!''

I replied, "You and I both know that you have twisted and distorted my sacred sacraments. I will ask you a question—if Christ told you that He was indeed the Messiah, but if he commanded you to tell no one of that fact, would you obey Him or would you tell?" My accuser laughed and said, "You Mormons are so ignorant of the Bible and Jesus because He has never, and would never, ask anyone to do that!" I turned to the Scriptures to refute another railing accusation—this time to the book of Matthew:

> He saith unto them, But whom say ye that I am?
>
> And Simon Peter answered and said, Thou art the Christ, the Son of the living God.
>
> And Jesus answered and said unto him, Blessed art thou, Simon Bar-jona: for flesh and blood hath not revealed it unto thee, but my Father which is in heaven.
>
> And I say also unto thee, That thou art Peter, and upon this rock I will build my church; and the gates of hell shall not prevail against it.
>
> And I will give unto thee the keys of the kingdom of heaven: and whatsoever thou shalt bind on earth shall be bound in heaven: and whatsoever thou shalt loose on earth shall be loosed in heaven.
>
> *Then charged he his disciples that they should tell no man that he was Jesus the Christ.* (Matthew 16:15-20)

After reading the scripture my accuser's jaw fell open. He was suddenly silent, and turned from me. I asked again, "Would you tell people that Jesus was the Christ after the Savior Himself charged you not to?" Angered by the embarrassment, my adversary turned around sharply and yelled, "Of course not!" I, of course, countered that I would not tell him details of the temple service because the Savior has charged the Saints not to do so.

Sacred Ordinances Are Covenants for the Life to Come

The Mysteries of God include covenants for the life to come, just as baptism and the Lord's Supper do. At baptism the Saints are immersed in water in the name of the Father, the Son, and the Holy Ghost, symbolically dying and rising with the Savior. As Paul wrote:

> Therefore we are buried with him by baptism into death: that like as Christ was raised up from the dead by the

> glory of the Father, even so we also should walk in newness
> of life. (Romans 6:4)

The Lord's Supper (called the sacrament or communion) is another covenant that Jesus instituted before His death and resurrection. It is a feast of remembrance in which the Saints covenant with God to remember that Jesus shed His blood and died for them, and that they must keep His commandments in order to have His Spirit which He had promised to them.

Those ordinances have been the lesser mysteries. Jesus instituted the greater or higher mysteries during His post-resurrection forty-day ministry, sacraments so sacred that Latter-day Saints partake of them only in temples dedicated to the Lord.

The ancient anti-Christians thought to stop the work of God by distorting and displaying the sacred Mysteries of God before the public, but they only succeeded in showing the people that they used deceit in the name of God. The Mysteries of God among both the former-day and Later-day Saints are concealed in symbol so that only those saints who have the Spirit of God can grasp their meaning. Hence, the only thing that has been exposed is that the *gainsayers* make use of deception. The writing is truly on the wall.

More Evidences of Ancient Temple Worship
Recorded by Modern Scholars

The fact is that the ancient Christians had secret rites. Christian scholar and historian Dr. Morton Smith wrote:

> The central problem, I had gradually come to see, was the element of secrecy in primitive Christian tradition....The synoptic Gospels are full of it. John swarms with contradictions that look like deliberate riddles; *both John and Luke hint at secret teaching to be given by the resurrected Jesus or by the spirit, after Jesus' death.*[33]

The world-famous Biblical scholar, professor Joachim Jeremias, wrote,

> The whole environment of primitive Christianity knows the *element of the esoteric.*"[34]

Professor Jeremias also wrote of "cryptic sayings" recorded by the apostle Paul and of how those special insights had been withheld from the general Church membership:

> When one turns to the *early Christianity*, he repeatedly comes across *cryptic sayings* and a *concern to keep the*

most sacred things from being profaned. Paul, who calls himself and his fellow workers *"stewards of the mysteries of God"* (1 Corinthians 4:1), speaks in general terms in 1 Corinthians 2.6-3.2 of the divine "wisdom" which can only be imparted to the "mature" (2.6), i.e. "those who possess the spirit" (2.13); *it is a secret and hidden wisdom of God* (2.7). Paul had been able to offer the Corinthians only milk (elementary teachings, 3.2), not yet the solid food of "wisdom" for the "mature" (3.2; 2.6). The concern of this "wisdom" is with "the depths of God" (2.10). That *Paul had kept this from the Corinthians*, although they had been Christians for years, shows that *he would never have spoken of these final secrets before non-Christians.*[35]

If the ancient Christians had secret rites, why is it that the modern churches of mainline Christendom don't have them now? According to one Christian historian:

The number of the faithful having greatly increased— the Christians from being persecuted having become persecutors, and that of the most grasping and barbarous kind—the Church in the seventh century instituted the minor orders, among whom were the doorkeepers, who took the place of the deacons. In 692 *everyone was ordered thenceforth to be admitted to the public worship of the Christians*, their *esoteric (secret) teaching of the first ages* was entirely suppressed, and what had been pure cosmology and astronomy was turned into a pantheon of gods and saints. *Nothing remained of the mysteries* but the custom of secretly reciting the canon of the Mass.[36]

Jesus and the apostles had predicted a falling away from the truth, and in this apostasy of the Church many things were lost. Notable among the lost teachings were the sacred rites of the Christian temples.

Anti-Mormon adversaries, or sincere Christians deceived by them, sometime ask Latter-day Saints why their Mysteries, or Endowment as it is called, isn't found in the Bible. As has already been seen, there are numerous allusions to it in the Bible, but in small bits and pieces. But this would not be logical for Jesus to institute a secret tradition just to have it published in the New Testament. According to Christian scholar and historian Dr. Angus:

> An awful *obligation to perpetual secrecy* as to what was said and transacted behind closed doors in the initiation proper was imposed—an obligation so *scrupulously observed* through the centuries that *not one account of the secrets of the holy of holies of the Mysteries has been published* to gratify the curiosity of historians.[37]

An Ancient Description of the Christian Temple Service

To my knowledge at present, there is no surviving written account of the ancient Christian Mysteries of God, though many ancient Christian writers have commented on them, some in considerable detail. *Cyril of Jerusalem*, an ancient Christian scholar and writer, writes in his "lecture on the Mysteries—The Rites of the Inner Chamber:"

> I put before you yesterday's *ordinances of initiation* in their proper order, so that you may learn which tokens must be given by you in the inner temple[38]....Immediately, then, upon entering, you *removed your tunics*. This was a figure of the "stripping off of the old man with his deeds." Having stripped, you were naked, in this also imitating Christ, who was naked on the cross, by His nakedness "throwing off the cosmic powers and authorities like a garment and publicly upon the cross leading them in his triumphal procession." For as the forces of the enemy made their lair in our member, you may no longer wear the old garment. I do not, of course, refer to this visible garment, but to "the old man which, deluded by its lusts, is sinking towards death."...Truly you bore the image of the first-formed Adam, who was naked in the garden and "was not ashamed." Then, when stripped, you were *anointed with exorcised olive oil* from the topmost hairs of your head to the soles of your feet, and became partakers of the good olive tree, Jesus Christ....You are *anointed first upon the forehead* to rid you of the shame which the first human transgressor bore about with him everywhere; so you may "reflect as in a glass the splendor of the Lord." Then *upon the ears*, to receive ears quick to hear the divine mysteries, the ears of which Isaiah said: "The Lord gave me also an ear to hear," and the Lord Jesus in the Gospels: "He who hath ears to hear let him hear." Then *upon the nostrils*, that, scenting the divine oil, you may say: "We are the

incense offered by Christ to God, in the case of those who are on the way to salvation.'' Then *on the breast,* that "putting on the breastplate of justice you may be able to withstand the wiles of the Devil."[39]...*After that we commemorate the heavens, the earth and the sea; the sun and moon, the stars, the whole rational and irrational creation, both visible and invisible....*[40] The Paradise of God from which our First Parent was expelled through transgression...is now opened to you...[41] Now you see the deacon providing wash things for the priest and the Elders *standing in a circle around the alter.*[42]...Next, when the spiritual sacrifice, the bloodless worship, has been completed, over that sacrifice of propitiation *we beseech God* for the public peace of the Churches, for the good estate of the world, for the Emperors, for the armed forces and our allies, for those in sickness, for the distressed: for all, in a word, who need help, *we all pray and offer this sacrifice.*[43]...*You have just seen the prayer circle.*[44]...Then the Assistant cries out: *Exchange signs with each other* and let us embrace![45]

Of the final rite of these particular mysteries a Christian scholar writes:

The explanation probably is that what is being expounded is that part of the service which the congregation were allowed to hear and see, as distinct from the *prayers recited by the celebrant in a low voice and perhaps behind a curtain (veil, screen).*[46]

We have seen beforehand that it was the Lord Himself who first instituted the apocalyptic, or secret, tradition. He gave this hidden wisdom to Adam, and after each apostasy, or time of spiritual darkness, it was restored again in a new dispensation.

Essenes Attempted to Preserve Temple Ceremony

Within each time of spiritual darkness, however, the Mysteries have not been totally lost. For instance, during Israel's apostasy in the meridian of time there was a society called the Essenes which tried to carry on the apocalyptic tradition.

According to one historian, the Essenes were the Freemasons of Israel.[47] The Essenes, like the disciples of John (Nasoreans) and later the disciples of the Lord (Nazarenes) had secret rites:

> In the Qumran writings there are *many references to the mysteries or secrets* (raz) which have been revealed. Some are recorded on heavenly tablets (Cave 4 fragments). The basic *raz* concerns the wonders of God: His grace, mercy, wisdom and truth. These attributes are expressed through the mysteries of the divine plan of history.[48]

The *Essenes* themselves wrote that, "The counsels of the Spirit concerning *the Mysteries are to be kept secret* (1QS 4.6)."[49]

Philo of Alexandria, speaking of Moses, said, "Our lawgiver encouraged the multitude of his disciples to live in community: these are called Essenes."[50] According to the great Jewish general and historian, Josephus, the Essene who was initiated into the mysteries took an oath to *"tell nothing (of their secrets) to others even if he shall suffer violence unto death."*[51]

Why John the Baptist Was an Essene

The great prophet of Jesus, John the Baptist, was himself at one time an Essene. Various Christian scholars and historians have commented on this fact. Dr. Powell Davies wrote, "That John was, in the broader sense of the term, an Essene can scarcely be doubted."[52] Prof. Edmund Sutcliffe observed that "John's spirit and ideals were thus very different from those that were entertained at Qumran. Still it is urged that he must have spent his early years among the monks there."[53] And Bishop Pike commented that "John the Baptist, without any doubt, stemmed from the Qumran tradition."[54] There are many more Christian scholars that testify that John was an Essene like Howlett,[55] W.H. Brownlee, Hastings, etc.[56]

The probable reason why John became an Essene is that when the people of God rejected the living prophets, and the sun of revelation went down again into a time of spiritual darkness, a group of righteous men formed the Order and brotherhood called the Essenes. They were to be guardians of the sacred mysteries during the time of apostasy.

Erroneous Gainsayers' Conclusion:
John and Jesus Borrowed Essene Teachings

John became an Essene because their initial mission had been fulfilled. The enemies of the ancient Saints, of course, seeing the similarities (but not noting the vast differences) with the rites of the Essenes and the rites of the Nazarenes concluded that both John and Jesus had borrowed heavily from the Essene secret rites to form their own mysteries, and that these mysteries were ultimately pagan in origin. This accusation can even be heard today. Wrote Dr. Martin Larson:

We believe, then, that Jesus had been a member of the Essene Order; that, frustrated by waiting, he left it, convinced that he himself was the coming Messiah; that he preached it's basic doctrines in the byways and villages of Judea; that he drew his inspiration and ideology principally from this source; that he consciously modelled his own career on that of the martyred Teacher of Righteousness and upon passages which he discovered in *The Testaments of the Twelve Patriarchs* and in *Enoch*; that he forced his enemies to crucify him by making statements which he knew would bring capital punishment; that he made the most careful preparations to accomplish his own execution in a climactic and spectacular drama; and that he understood clearly that only by this method could he accomplish his world-encompassing objectives.[57]

Some Christian scholars still claim that John and Jesus borrowed from the Essenes. Writes Professor Andre Dupont-Sommer:

The documents from Qumran make it plain that the primitive Christian Church was rooted in the Jewish sect of the New Covenant, the Essene sect, to a degree none would have suspected, and that it borrowed from it a large part of its organization, rites, doctrines, "patterns of thought" and its mystical and ethical ideas.[58]

So the ancient *gainsayers*, and even some modern Christian scholars, have concluded that John and Jesus were both Essenes who received a great deal of their inspiration from the Essenes, including the Christian Mysteries of God. Now is that true? No! The rites of the Essenes and the Christians were similar because the Essenes were the custodians of a corrupted form of the Mysteries and ancient Gospel from the previous dispensation. The Mysteries of God portrayed in detail the birth, life, death and other details of the coming Messiah and the divine purposes of God in symbol.

Attempts to Preserve Temple Ritual
During the Great Apostasy

Jesus was the Christ, we know, because He fulfilled the prophecies of the Scriptures and the Mysteries to the letter! After Christ's death there again came a time when the people began to reject the prophets of God and to slay them. And shortly after Christ's prophets (the Apostles) were killed and rejected, the sun of revelation went down once again, and a time of spiritual darkness covered the earth. The Bible refers to this as the "falling away." Others know this period as the Dark Ages.

Yet, in this era of apostasy, a few righteous men, all of them Saints of the Most High God, formed an Order or Brotherhood called the Templars. This Order, much changed from what it originally was, is called Freemasonry today. It was the object of the Templars, like that of the Essenes, to be the guardians of the Mysteries of God during the time of apostasy.

Erroneous Gainsayers' Conclusion:
Joseph Smith Borrowed Masonic Teachings

Joseph Smith, like John Ben Zachariah (John the Baptist), was a Prophet that cried in the wilderness about the Second Advent of the Christ, as John had declared the first advent. Joseph became a member of the Masonic Order, as John became a member of the Essenic order, to declare unto the withered tree of wisdom, withered and worn from age and lack of revelation's light, that God had restored to the earth again the Kingdom of God.

The anti-Mormons are declaring today that Mormonism is just a borrowing of the Masonic Order, just as the ancient anti-Nazarenes declared that Nazarenism was just a borrowing of the Essenic Order. The parallel is readily apparent. According to LDS adversaries:

> There can be no doubt that Joseph Smith received a great deal of inspiration from Masonry.[59]

The truth is that the ancient Christians had secret rites instituted by Jesus Himself, and these things can only be found today in The Church of Jesus Christ of Latter-day Saints. There is nothing of significance that anti-Mormon accusers have said against the Church that had not been said against Jesus, His Prophet John, and the ancient Saints long before by ancient *gainsayers*.

"Epilepsy" Allegation Copied from
Ancient to Modern Times

This has only been a brief examination, but the truth is that every accusation can be answered to not only refute it, but to bring an added testimony that Jesus is the Christ, and Joseph is His latter-day prophet! One anti-Nazarene writer wrote about the visions of the apostle Paul:

> He even relates how, on this or some other occasion, he was *caught up into the third heaven, whether in the body*

or out of the body he knew not. Thus *caught up into
paradise*, he *had heard unspeakable words, which is not
lawful for a man to utter*...undoubtedly the epilepsy which
often attends such temperaments.[60]

One anti-Mormon writer copied the ancient "epilepsy" allegation and
transferred it to the modern prophet. He wrote about the visions of the
Prophet Joseph:

> Certainly Joe's visions were accompanied by seizures
> which, from his own accounts, appear to have been
> epileptic.[61]

The parallels can go on and on. Detectives look for a fingerprint at the
scene of a crime. I think I have shown you such a "fingerprint"
demonstrating here that it is the work of Satan to oppose the work of God
by trying to deceive men into believing that the truth is a lie and his lie
the truth. His influence is clearly seen on the anti-Christ movement against
the Saints in both former and latter-days!

In the course of seven thousand years, God will finish His eternal purposes
for man on this earth. He has sent a high Prophet over each dispensation,
each restoring the Gospel in its purity and setting up the Kingdom of God
for his particular dispensation. Jesus Christ is Lord over all dispensations,
and greater than all the prophets combined. He has set aside the seventh
dispensation for Himself—the great Millennium.

The Ancient Christian Doctrine of "The Two Eliases"

The ancient Christians had a doctrine which was extremely important
to them. The doctrine was called "The Two Eliases." It was foretold in
the Scriptures and in the Mysteries that two great heralds of the Messiah
would appear—one before the first and another before the second advent
of Christ. It is written in the Old Testament:

> Behold, I will send my messenger, and he shall prepare
> the way before me: and the Lord, whom ye seek, shall
> suddenly come to his temple, even the messenger of the
> covenant, whom ye delight in: behold, he shall come, saith
> the LORD of hosts. (Malachi 3:1)

And also,

> Behold, I will send you Elijah the prophet before the
> coming of the great and dreadful day of the LORD:

> And he shall turn the heart of the fathers to the children,
> and the heart of the children to their fathers, lest I come
> and smite the earth with a curse. (Malachi 4:5-6)

The churches of Israel thought that Elijah would minister in person, but the Saints knew that Elijah would only confer his power and spirit upon the two prophets. Thus, each of the prophets to come before both the Lord's first and second advents was referred to as *Elias,* and that term was used by the ancient Christians to identify one who had come "in the spirit and power of Elijah." Several ancient Christian writers clearly set forth the doctrine of Elias. *Hippolytus* wrote,

> For as two advents of our Lord and Saviour are indicated
> in the scriptures, the one being His first advent in the flesh,
> which took place without honor....But His second advent
> is announced as glorious, when he shall come from heaven
> with the host of angels, and the glory of His Father....Thus
> also *two forerunners were indicated. The first was John,
> the son of Zacharias, who appeared in all things a
> forerunner....*The Saviour is to be manifested again at the
> end of the world as Judge. It is a matter of course that his
> *forerunners must appear first,* as he says, by Malachi and
> the angel. "I will send you Elias the Tishbite before the
> day of the Lord, the great and notable day, comes: and
> he shall turn the hearts of the fathers to the children, and
> the disobedient to the wisdom of the just, lest I come and
> smite the earth utterly."[62]

John Chrysostom wrote that

> As John was the *forerunner of the first coming, so will
> Elias be the forerunner of the second coming....*Christ
> called John Elias on account of his performing the same
> office.[63]

Theophylact expressed his view that

> By saying that *Elias cometh,* He shows that he was not
> yet come; *he will come* as a *forerunner of the second
> advent,* and will restore the faith of Christ...this is he of
> whom the prophet Malachi spoke as the coming of Elias;
> for the forerunner and Elias perform the same service.[64]

Modern Scholars Confirm
the "Two Eliases" Doctrine

"Born-again" Christian scholars also confirm the coming of a prophet called *Elias*. Dr. Dwight J. Pentecost wrote that

> Inasmuch as John could not have fulfilled the prophecies because Israel rejected the offered kingdom, it does not seem possible to assert that the prophecy of Malachi 4:5-6 has been fulfilled. The fact that John could have fulfilled it, even though he was not personally Elijah, seems to indicate that Elijah need not come personally to fulfill the prophecies. *During the period preceding the second advent, and prior to the outpouring of the judgments upon the earth, there will be a ministry by one in the spirit and power of Elijah, which will fulfill this prophecy.*[65]

Reverend L. T. Nichols, observed,

> Every heart, every church member, yea, every minister ought to rejoice, receive and *herald forth the wonderous news of the COMING OF ELIJAH to bring about this state of universal peace and prosperity* carried to the legitimate end by Christ appearing so quickly to judge His people, and *restore again the Kingdom of Israel....*We do not expect every minister to either hold up our hands, or herald forth these wonderful predictions of Holy Writ, for we are told distinctly that when the time comes for us to *"Arise and shine for thy light is come"* and the glory of the Lord is to arise upon us, that "DARKNESS SHALL COVER THE EARTH, AND GROSS DARKNESS THE PEOPLE." It cannot be denied but that *all the world, church members, ministers and all are in darkness in reference to the coming of Elijah, the prophet,* as set forth in the oracles of truth....*This will continue until Elijah appears upon the stage*, for it is prophesied of this people who are in darkness, "STAY YOURSELVES AND WONDER, CRY YE OUT AND CRY," or, as it is in the original and marginal, take your pleasure and riot. "They are drunken, but not with wine; they stagger, but not with strong drink. The Lord hath poured out upon you the spirit of sleep— deep sleep—and hath closed your eyes. The prophets and your rulers, the seers, hath he covered, and the vision of

all is become unto you as the words of a book that is sealed."[66]

Dr. Joseph A. Seiss has written,

> There was a twofold ministry embraced in the ancient promise to send Elijah, just as there was a twofold advent in the predictions concerning the Messiah. In neither case did the Old testament clearly distinguish between these two, but viewed them both as if they were but one. And as the two Messiah-comings are widely separated in time, though belonging to one and the same work; so *there are two Elijah-comings, equally separated in time, and equally comprehended in the predictions.*[67]

He also wrote,

> On the mount of Christ's glorious Transfiguration Elijah appeared. The disciples saw him and knew him. And, as they were coming down from the mount, they asked the Master about this very point, alleging the doctrine of the scribes that "Elias must first come." And he answered and said unto them: *"Elias* TRULY SHALL FIRST COME, AND RESTORE ALL THINGS." (Matt. 17:11) This passage is decisive. "The great Interpreter of prophecy gives right to that interpretation of the prophetic word which the scribes maintained," says Trench. It cannot refer to John the Baptist, for John was then dead, while every part of it specifically related to *the future.* "Elias truly shall come, and *shall* restore all things." Besides, the restoration or "restitution of all things," in the which it is affirmed that the coming of Elias is to take part, is specifically referred by the Apostle Peter to the time of Christ's second coming. (Acts 3:19) In all its terms and relations, therefore, we are compelled to accept this solemn declaration of the Saviour as looking to the future, and meant to set forth what yet awaited fulfillment. John the Baptist is here out of the question, unless indeed he is to come again. Dr. Stier has rightly said: "Whoever, in this answer of Christ, would explain away the manifest and striking confirmation of the fact that a coming of Elias was yet to take place, must do great violence to the words, and will never be able to restrain the future of their form and import so as to be applicable to John the Baptist."

But, it may be asked, Did not Christ say in the same connection, that Elias had come already, leaving it to be understood that He spoke of John the Baptist? The answer is, Yes; but in a way entirely distinct from the declaration we have just been considering. Elsewhere also he says of John: "If ye will receive (*it, him,* or someone else) this is Elias, which was to come." (Matt. 11:14) This proves that there is a sense in which John the Baptist was Elias, but certainly not such a sense as that in which the Jews were expecting Elias, nor yet such a sense as that in which He declared, after John was dead: *"Elias truly shall come and restore all things."*[68]

The doctrine of the two Eliases was simple. The prophet Elijah would appear to and confer his power and spirit on two individuals who would become prophet-heralds of the Lord Jesus Christ—one for His first advent, and the other for His second.

Joseph Smith a Modern Elias

The latter-day Apostle Parley P. Pratt wrote:

And that great Prophet, Apostle and martyr, *JOSEPH SMITH, was the Elias, the restorer, the presiding messenger*, holding the keys of the "dispensation of the fullness of times." Yes, that extraordinary man, whose innocent blood is yet dripping, as it were, from the hands of assassins and their accessories in the United States, was the chosen vessel honored of God, and ordained by angels, to ordain other Apostles and Elders, to restore the Church and Kingdom of God, the gift of the Holy Ghost, and to be a messenger in the spirit and power of Elijah, to prepare the way of the Lord. "For, behold, He will suddenly come to His temple!" Like John, who fulfilled a similar mission preparatory to the first advent of the Son of God, he baptized with water unto repentance, for the remission of sins; like him, he was imprisoned; and, like him, his life was taken from the earth; and, finally, like all other true messengers, his message is being demonstrated by its progressive fulfillment, the powers, gifts, and signs following the administrations of his message in all the world, and every minute particular of his predictions fulfilling in the order of events as wheels of time bring them due.[69]

Modern Gainsayers Parallel Teachings and Activities of Ancient Gainsayers

Those adversaries of Jesus and His Prophet John tried, and unfortunately very often succeeded, in deceiving the people into believing that they were the true Messianists, defending the orthodox beliefs against the cultists like the Nazarenes. Those adversaries believed and proclaimed that the true Christ was on their side, and that John was a false prophet and that the Nazarene Christ was a different Christ from the real One who had not yet appeared.

Modern adversaries proclaim that the "true Jesus" is on their side, and that Joseph was a false prophet and the "Mormon Jesus" is a different Jesus from the real One who has yet to appear again.

The *gainsayers* of two thousand years ago, those anti-Nazarenes and cult fighters, supposedly spoke and acted in the name of the Messiah (Christ), yet they were the ones who confronted Him everywhere to trap Him, who brought false witnesses against Him, who betrayed Him, slapped Him, spit upon Him, scourged Him, had nails driven through His hands and feet, and had a crown of thorns placed upon His head. Certainly they were not the defenders of the true Christ and true Messianity.

They ceased not to persecute His Saints, and as God lives, they do not cease now. Yet Jesus arose from the dead and ascended to heaven. His prophets and Saints may temporarily suffer the abuse of the world, but they eventually shall reign with Him in glory and eternal life in His heavenly mansions above! And those who knowingly persecuted the Christ or His messengers and Saints in the name of God shall indeed experience their day-in-court, confronted by the only Just Judge who presides in the heavenly courts above.

Who are the *gainsayers*? Today as in ancient times, they are anti-Christs who do all they can to thwart the true work of God. The apostle John tells us:

> Little children, it is the last time: and as ye have heard that *antichrist shall come, even now are there many antichrists*; whereby we know that it is the last time.
> *They went out from us, but they were not of us*; for if they had been with us, they would no doubt have continued with us; but *they went out, that they might be made manifest that they were not all of us*. (1 John 2:18-19)

No Salvation in Believing an Evil Report

Jesus is the Christ, the son of the living God. Joseph the Prophet is the high Prophet of God over the sixth dispensation, and the prophet-herald of Christ. *If one rejects the herald the King has sent, he likewise rejects the King that sent him.*
Joseph Smith the Prophet said:

> The Savior has the words of eternal life. Nothing else can profit us. *There is no salvation in believing an evil report against our neighbor.*[70]

The Saints of the Most High God declare nothing but what their Savior Jesus has commanded them to declare—that God has parted the heavens again, and sent messengers to warn the inhabitants of the earth to turn from their sins and the vain philosophies of man: to turn to the Kingdom which has been set up in the latter-days as foretold, to await the coming of the King. Jesus is the Christ, and Joseph is His Prophet.

5
Gainsayer Missionary Strategies

While being trained in the Ex-Mormons for Jesus movement, I was taught a variety of ways to "witness" to Mormons, and I observed other techniques and strategies which they utilized. I believe that it is important for Latter-day Saints to be aware of these "witnessing" techniques so they will recognize them when they encounter them. In this chapter I will summarize some of these anti-Mormon missionary techniques and approaches.

Anti-Mormon Witnessing Technique:
The "Devil's Advocate" Charade

One method that was used was called "The Devil's Advocate." One ministry member would play the Mormon (sometimes pretending to be a returned missionary) and the other would play the Christian. What took place was play-acting.

It was usually staged at places where Ex-Mormons for Jesus or a related ministry had a booth (usually at county fairs, swap meets, etc.) It was often performed on the outskirts of LDS gatherings too; at temple open houses, dance festivals, or wherever there was a large gathering of Mormons.

The idea was to have the pretend-Mormon and the Christian start a dialogue that would attract a large crowd. The pretend-Mormon would first get offended, and sometimes abusive, when the Christian would call Mormonism a cult. The Christian, always cool and logical in these controlled situations, would commence to witness to the pretend-Mormon, at the same time promising that if he said anything that wasn't true then he would stop witnessing to Mormons. The pretend-Mormon would come back with ineffective pat answers: "But I know the Church is true because I had a burning in the bosom," or "No, the Bible can't be trusted; that's why we have the Book of Mormon," etc.

Naturally, the Christian would win the debate, and sometimes the pretend-Mormon would be "brought to Christ." Praise the Lord! The audience of the charade was never given the hint that Mr. Mormon and Mr. Christian were putting on a street play. I even discovered that not one of the players I met had ever been a Mormon.

Anti-Mormon Witnessing Technique:
"Jesus and Satan Are Brothers"

One line that always seemed to get someone's attention at the booths was, "Excuse me, sir (or miss), but did you know that the Mormons teach that Jesus and Satan were brothers?" This would usually elicit shock from the person being addressed.

I remember being at a booth in a county fair, and over the booth was a very large sign that read EX-MORMONS FOR JESUS. Behind the booth stood about a half dozen or so individuals who typically used the "brother" phrase I have mentioned to engage passersby in conversation.

I remember speaking with Dan, one of the group members manning the display, about using this method to attract people to the booth. I knew, and they knew as well, that the Latter-day Saints believe and teach that *all mankind* are spirit children of God, so all mankind are brothers and sisters, including both Jesus and Lucifer.

The Bible alludes repeatedly to the doctrine that everyone is a spirit child of God. One reads in Hebrews:

> We have had fathers of our flesh which corrected us, and we gave them reverence: shall we not much rather *be in subjection unto the Father of spirits,* and live? (Hebrews 12:9)

The book of Ecclesiastes, while describing the death process, says,

> Then shall the dust return to the earth as it was: and *the spirit shall return unto God who gave it.* (Ecclesiastes 12:7)

And God told Jeremiah,

> *Before I formed thee in the belly I knew thee*; and before thou camest forth out of the womb *I sanctified thee*, and *I ordained thee a prophet* unto the nations. (Jeremiah 1:5)

In Job, the angels who dwell in the presence of God are referred to as the *sons of God,* and the Bible says that Satan was among them (Job 1:6). Latter-day Saints believe that man and angels are of the same race, and Jesus, our brother, is also. He is given the highest honor as the "firstbegotten" in the spirit (Hebrews 1:4-6) and the Only Begotten Son of God in the flesh. (John 1:14; 3:16) So Latter-day Saints believe that all mankind are brothers, and there's strong scriptural basis for their belief.

But when anti-Mormons say Mormons believe that Jesus and Satan are brothers, they're trying to twist the perception of that belief in the mind of those to whom they're speaking. They're implying that Latter-day Saints either equate Jesus with evil or equate Satan with good, and that is deception.

I asked Dan why they didn't tell the people the whole story. He replied, "We will, if they ask us." But of course, most people don't know to ask.

Anti-Mormon Witnessing Technique: The "Pat Answer" on Why They Left Mormonism

I found that when stories were told by "Ex-Mormon" adversaries about their experiences as Latter-day Saints, their stories were remarkably similar. Without fail, every time I asked an ex-Mormon why he or she left the LDS Church, I always got the same pat answer. They would claim that after joining the Latter-day Saints they began to read their Bibles for the first time and discovered Mormonism is diametrically opposed to the Bible. Then, at that point, they would assert that they found the "real" Jesus. Well, the reason why that is such a common response is because that "pat" answer is part of the witnessing technique.

I met a young woman by the name of Loretta who was an Ex-Mormon for Jesus. Loretta told me that she had found the "real" Jesus, repeating the pat answer I've just described. She shared lots of other "information" with me too. She told me, for instance, that in the temple ceremony "they really wash you!" She told me she began to doubt Mormonism when in the temple they gave her a "complete and thorough bath just like someone washing you in a tub!" Only after I had been to the temple myself did I find out how she had lied to me.

The more I talked with her, the more revealing the conversation became, which is inevitable. Loretta began to list her grievances. "I was the only one who did my visiting teaching," she exclaimed. "I read all the scriptures, and all the *Journal of Discourses* (there are 26 volumes of 300-plus pages each). And they had the nerve to call me into court...!" She was getting emotional, and I did not pursue the conversation. I had learned everything I needed to know.

I met other ex-Mormons with similar results, and I soon discovered that the great majority of Ex-Mormons for Jesus had never been Mormons in the first place, but they all had a pat answer for how they left the Church!

Anti-Mormon Witnessing Technique: Anti-Mormon "Testimonies" in LDS Testimony Meetings

My efforts to finish up my research took me from the state of Washington to Utah to California and back again several times. I was back in Washington when I heard about an EMFJ (Ex-Mormon for Jesus) meeting close by. I decided to attend. There I heard about incidents where Ex-Mormons for Jesus (who probably had never been Mormons) were attending Testimony Meetings at local LDS Church meetinghouses, going up to the microphone, and giving their "testimonies" that Joseph Smith was a false prophet and that the Mormon Church was false as well.

This sickened my very soul! How could anyone who professed to believe in Christ deceivingly approach and enter any church with such audacious and deceptive conduct as that? Naturally, this conduct was "justified" in their rationalizations. But I couldn't justify this conduct in my heart, to myself, or to my Lord.

Anti-Mormon Witnessing Technique: "Flip-flop"

After I had returned to the Church, I convinced myself that others among my "anti" acquaintances should know what I had discovered. I spoke with several Ex-Mormons for Jesus (one had actually been a Latter-day Saint until he was 12), and I explained to them how I felt and how I couldn't justify the deception involved in their movement to myself. I began to point out to them the deceptive nature of some of their witnessing techniques and to refute their claims.

They stopped me, saying they weren't interested in what I had to say. I shared with them my testimony of the Savior, that He was my Redeemer and Lord—that when we accept Him as our Lord and follow Him, we walk from darkness into light, and that He is our only Savior, who suffered and died to pay the penalty for sin. I reminded them how the Book of Mormon was centered completely around Christ as Lord and Savior:

> We talk of Christ, we rejoice in Christ, we preach of Christ,
> we prophesy of Christ, and we write according to our
> prophecies, that our children may know to what source
> they may look for a remission of their sins. (2 Nephi 25:26)

They then turned to raising their anti-LDS propaganda claims as if I had
said nothing. I began to show them where the answers were to refute those
claims. However, every time I would begin to refute one claim, when they
saw that they couldn't deceive or defeat me by that particular argument,
they would flip to another claim. When I began to answer the other claim,
they would turn to yet another one, constantly changing the subject.

This is known as "flip-flop." Frequent subject changes to prevent an
orderly rebuttal of their false accusations is a common witnessing technique
employed by these anti-Mormon *gainsayers*.

Anti-Mormon Witnessing Technique: Exaggeration and Falsehoods "So Brainwashed People Will See the Light"

I kept them on one subject and challenged them, asking them how it
could possibly be justified for them to lie and misrepresent in the name
of Christ? They replied that they believed the Mormon Church was so
Satanic, and its people so deceived, that sometimes the truth needed to
be "exaggerated" so that people who are brainwashed could see the light.
Constant exaggeration and the deliberate presenting of falsehoods are basic
elements in their witnessing techniques.

Anti-Mormon Witnessing Technique: Accusing Those Who Dispute Their Words of Being "Possessed by Satan"

They began an argument over the interpretation of scripture. All of us
began to raise our voices, and I was upset. They looked at me and said,
"See, we know that Satan is possessing you right now because you're being
argumentative—is that the spirit you call Christian?" This was a common
approach used against those who would disagree with them.

I felt disillusionment because I'd been deceived by the very people who
told me long before that it was the Mormons who had deceived me. I felt
sickened because of their deception, and disturbed over the
misrepresentations that these people presented in a most precious name:
the name of Christ.

Just like their ancient counterparts, the Pharisees and Sadducees before
them, these anti-Mormons knew how to use the tools of mockery and reviling
in order to anger the Saints, and to cause the Saints to say or do something
which they could hold against them.

Anti-Mormon Witnessing Technique:
Provoking Confrontation Incidents

One Ex-Mormon for Jesus (who had never been a Latter-day Saint) told me how they had several members of their ministry dress up in LDS temple robes and parade before people at a county fair. (Something comparable to this act of desecration, if done against a "born-again" Christian, would be like using a cross for a marshmallow roast.)

One member of the ministry would situate himself with a video camera in an unnoticeable spot, hoping for a Mormon to come along and take a swing at one of the people dressed in the temple robes. As it turned out, no one took a swing at anyone, and the only assault which occurred was that the individuals dressed in the temple robes assaulted the sacred beliefs of other human beings. I understand this technique is still being used.

Anti-Mormon Witnessing Technique: Luring
Missionaries Into Unexpected Confrontations

While I served my mission in California, I frequently was confronted with people involved in or influenced by the anti-LDS movement. A technique that became popular in one area in which I served involved situations in which missionaries were invited to go to a certain home where a family or individual was reported to be interested in hearing the missionary discussions. This usually came as a result of the missionaries tracting door-to-door, but I remember that on several occasions calls to the mission office and referrals were used.

The missionaries were led to believe that the people were sincerely interested in hearing their gospel discussion, but after they had arrived, the individual or family was joined by one or more members of the local ministry to the Mormons. It had all been planned beforehand, and naturally, the missionaries were caught off guard. Anti-Mormon adversaries delight in trying to show themselves knowledgeable and the Mormon ignorant—which means the anti-Mormon has his "anti"-literature at his side, but the Mormon has just the Scriptures and a testimony, with no time for advance preparation.

Anti-Mormon Witnessing Technique: Reliance on
Anti-Mormon Literature Rather Than the Scriptures

I've often observed that anti-Mormon accusers rarely use the Bible in their attempts to refute Latter-day Saint doctrines. Instead, they use their "anti"-literature. If Mormonism, as they call it, is so unbiblical, why not just use the Bible to refute it? In any case, this common witnessing technique is just one more act of deception.

Anti-Mormon Witnessing Technique: Creating Distrust and Antagonism by Showing "The God Makers"

The film "The God Makers," with all its distortions and innuendos, was shown and reshown throughout my mission area, and throughout the duration of my mission. Some people became interested and curious about the Church because of it and began to take the missionary lessons, but their numbers were relatively few. Mostly, the showing of the film left an aura of fear, suspicion and antagonism against the Mormons among those people who had seen it, usually "born-again" members of a local congregation.

Showing the film raises strong animosities among some who view it. For instance, a few days after one "God makers" showing in an area where I labored, a group of young toughs who belonged to a local "born-again" church stopped two missionaries, assaulted and threatened them, and told them they didn't want cultists in their neighborhood. Other similar incidents occurred.

Anti-Mormon Witnessing Technique: Falsely Asserting They Have Read Mormon Rebuttals of Anti-Mormon Claims

Books exposing the fraud and deceit of "The God Makers" and other anti-LDS books and tapes are available now, and have been available for some time.

I have asked various Ex-Mormons for Jesus if they had read any of those books exposing the anti-LDS deceit. "Oh yes," said one boastfully, "I've read all that completely, and it's a bunch of lies!" I questioned him on the material, and he finally admitted to me that he hadn't read it or even seen it, but concluded, "I don't even have enough time to read all of my Christian literature, so why should I read that anti-Christian stuff?"

One woman said she had read the book by Robert and Rosemary Brown called *They Lie in Wait to Deceive*, Vol. 1., which is a penetrating expose of anti-LDS writer and lecturer Dee Jay Nelson. Then she said she was even more convinced since she read the book that the Mormon Church was a fraud.

"What was the book, I mean volume one, about?" I asked her. She said, "Well, it was about the Tanners, Dr. Martin, and Saints Alive. You know what? They call our people the anti-Mormons." I immediately knew she hadn't even seen the book because it was about Dee Jay Nelson. "Is Dee

Jay Nelson in the book?" I asked. She responded "Oh, ah, I think they mentioned him too!"

I told her I knew she hadn't read the book and asked her why she felt she had to lie to me. She became angered and exclaimed, "Why should I read books by Mormons—all it is is lies—just like anything you could tell me would be a lie!"

I have often wondered why LDS adversaries hypocritically expect Latter-day Saints to see a film and read books which falsely portray their sacred beliefs as Satanic, but they don't want their people reading Latter-day Saint books or to see the LDS side of the story?

Just as many of the "Ex-Mormon" *gainsayers* have a "pat answer" concerning why they left the LDS Church (though most of them have never been Latter-day Saints), I find that many of them also will profess to have read Mormon rebuttals of their claims, though they have not read them.

Anti-Mormon Witnessing Technique:
Non-stop Badgering of LDS Investigators

One young Baptist girl had been taking the discussions from the missionaries and was preparing for baptism when she went to a youth camp sponsored by her "born-again" church. When they found out she intended to become a Mormon, they kept her up all night and into the morning (they took shifts), witnessing to her and repeating many anti-Mormon falsehoods. Her pastor made her promise not to have the missionaries over again.

We finally got a chance to talk with her, and she told us that they had brought her to tears and almost to an emotional breakdown before she finally placated them by agreeing to drop contacts with us and with the Church. We talked with her and gave her a book called *They Lie In Wait To Deceive.* This is a book by Robert and Rosemary Brown, of Mesa, Arizona, who are writing a series of books exposing the frauds and deceptions of the anti-LDS movement.

The next day her pastor visited her, and she told him that she was going to hold fast to her original intent: she was going to become a Latter-day Saint. Seeing nothing would persuade her otherwise, he cursed her to hell and left. She was shunned by her Baptist friends, but she knew the gospel was true and was baptized accordingly into the Church.

Anti-Mormon Witnessing Technique:
Social Pressures Against Latter-day Saints

Another woman I met, a recent convert who worked at an evangelical Christian day-care center, was told by her employers she had to see the movie "The God Makers" with them or lose her job; she saw the film.

Many of the Latter-day Saints in the Southern California area had their children enrolled in private Christian schools because they disliked the public school system. After the showing of the film, some of the parents had their children removed, or were talking about it, because their children were coming home crying because the other children were calling them names or refusing to play with them—all because they were Mormons.

In one area of my mission, flyers announcing the showing of "The God Makers" were plastered all over the entrance doors and windows of the LDS meetinghouse. Someone had to literally cut through the flyers just to get inside. There are events all over the country that are similar to these and worse.

One returned missionary told me of an incident that happened to him while he served his mission in the South. A youth pastor at a "born-again" church began to investigate Mormonism with an eye to begin a class on it at his church. His intent was to refute Mormonism, but he made a "mistake" by going to the missionaries before he started reading the anti-LDS literature. After his initial combativeness and defensiveness was over, the pastor agreed to read the Book of Mormon and to pray about the doctrines and principles the missionaries had shared with him. He did, received a testimony, and requested baptism.

When other members of his church found out what he was doing they told the senior pastor. They sent this fellow many anti-LDS books and tracts, but the youth pastor still remained determined to become a Latter-day Saint.

Finally, in an act of desperation, they literally kidnapped him from his home by force and drove him to their church. There they tried to persuade him not to become a Latter-day Saint. When that failed they began to try to "drive the devil out of him" by using the name of Jesus.

When the man bore his testimony to them, a testimony about his love for Jesus and that Joseph Smith truly was the Lord's prophet, he was met with cursings. Upset, the young man said, "I'm leaving, and according to the law you can't stop me!" They didn't, and the youth pastor was baptized.

The senior pastor, however, did not let it rest, but found out where the missionaries lived and, late at night, met them at the door and said, "I know that you brainwashed him! I don't know how you did it, but if you try it again with any of my sheep I will personally kill both of you!" The missionaries responded to him with courteous silence.

The Confrontation Question: "Is Your Purpose to Catch Us in a Snare?"

All the endings weren't so happy, however. The missionaries would lose some investigators directly or indirectly because of "The God Makers" film. I remember a girl whose parents were leading members of a huge "born-again" church in the area, and that particular church was very active in anti-LDS rallies—they even had a "Christian Ministry to Mormons" headed by several members of the Ex-Mormons for Jesus organization. The girl wanted the missionary discussions and wished to be baptized right away, but the missionaries tried to slow things a little to be sure she was properly prepared.

The missionaries called me (I was in a different area of the same mission) when she invited them to her parent's home and told them there would be some people from her church to question them. This sounded like another set-up to the Elders, and they wanted to get my input because they knew what my background on this subject was. I suggested to them that they not attend, because if it was a set-up the last thing those people from her church would be interested in was honest answers to questions about the Gospel. They told me that they had promised her they would come, and that they couldn't back away from their word.

I then suggested to them that if it was a set-up, they should ask the anti-Mormon challengers this question: *"Are you asking us these questions because you sincerely are interested and don't know the answers, or are you, like the Pharisees and Sadducees when they would ask Jesus questions, just trying to catch us in a snare?"*

I told the elders if those people answered honestly that they truly were seeking information about the Latter-day Saint faith, then any argumentation would be avoided. But if they admitted that "We are trying to catch you in a snare!" then the missionaries were not bound, as the Savior Himself wasn't, to answer their questions. I suggested to the elders that in that case, they should briefly share their testimonies and then leave.

Bearing Testimony as a Witness Against Gainsayers

Anti-Mormon adversaries often say that when Latter-day Saints share their testimonies in these confrontation situations it is just an effort on their part to avoid the truth. But the truth is that when the Saints boldly declare their testimonies in the face of *gainsayers'* criticisms they are obeying the admonition of the Savior. He told His followers:

> They shall lay their hands on you, and persecute you, delivering you up to the synagogues, and into prisons, being brought before kings and rulers for my name's sake.
> *And it shall turn to you for a testimony.*
> Settle it therefore in your hearts, not to meditate before what ye shall answer:

For *I will give you a mouth and wisdom*, which all your adversaries shall not be able to *gainsay* nor resist. (Luke 21:12-15)

The elders called me later after their meeting with the girl, her parents, and the people from her church. They had asked those people the question, and to their surprise they answered, "We are trying to catch you in a snare!"

Anti-Mormon Witnessing Technique: Planted Mormon Investigators Who Apostatize Immediately After Baptism

For some reason the elders didn't leave; perhaps because the young girl asked them to stay. The elders were subjected to the usual tactics, and when they tried to explain a doctrine or refute a point they were continually interrupted or the subject was quickly changed (flip-flop). The man who did most of the talking was in charge of the "Christian Mission to the Mormons" at the large local church.

When it came time for the elders to leave, the man pointed to the young girl and to the elders and said, "Don't forget what I'm telling you tonight, boys. This young girl that you have blinded with your Satanic powers may join your cult next Sunday, but I tell you in the name of Jesus that she won't stay a Mormon very long!"

Her baptism was scheduled for the next Sunday. The elders confided in me that there seemed something that just wasn't right about it; the Spirit wasn't there. But she insisted that she believed in all the teachings and wanted to be baptized that Sunday. The elders realized that the eternal consequences rested upon the girl's shoulders, so they acquiesced to her wish. The preparations had already been made, and she was baptized. A few days later she called the missionaries and requested that her name be taken off of the Church records. They were upset, but not totally surprised.

I had a chance to talk with her over the phone. She knew too much anti-Mormon propaganda to have been introduced to it only days before—it clearly had been another set-up to provide her with the "credentials" of LDS Church membership, brief though it was. The following week the young woman joined in the Christian Mission to Mormons as a full-fledged ex-Mormon!

They seek Mormon apostates to add "legitimacy" to their organization, recognizing their vulnerability because so low a percentage are literal ex-Mormons. But think of the eternal condemnation this foolish girl brought upon herself by being baptized by one holding the holy priesthood and then rejecting the efficacy of that sacred ordinance!

Anti-Mormon Witnessing Technique: Asserting that the LDS Church Can't Refute Their Charges

According to "The God Makers,"

> Mormons attending various showings of the film in order to publicly refute it during the open discussion time that always follows have invariably charged that it is full of lies. When asked to be specific, they have just as invariably failed to substantiate their accusations. One would think that if the Mormon Church, which has been carefully examining the film for months, had been able to find any inaccuracies it would have published an official refutation instead of remaining silent.[1]

I have not found, in my own personal experience, that the above statement holds true at all. I have seen Latter-day Saints refute anti-Mormon charges on many occasions. But what the *gainsayers* mean by "substantiate their accusations" is that they want Latter-day Saints to prove to them that the Church is true. Yet when the Pharisees and Sadducees saw the miracles of the Savior, those proofs still did not convert them.

Many times on my mission people would say, "What they're saying must be true because your own Church has remained silent about it!" According to that logic Jesus must have been a magician, conspirator, and everything else His enemies accused Him with because He was silent before them.

Anti-Mormon Witnessing Technique: Prohibiting Questions and Rebuttals from Informed Latter-day Saints

I was at a showing of the "The God Makers" film one particular time and I sat front row and center so that I could ask questions. When the question and answer period commenced I was called upon to ask a question and I arose. When I stood, the speaker suddenly recognized me and knew that I wasn't an easy mark; in other words, that I was very familiar with their tactics and claims. He immediately called upon another before I could finish my sentence, and a man came over to me and told me, while grabbing my elbow forcefully, that I wasn't allowed to speak.

Anti-Mormon Witnessing Technique: Diverting the Saints from Building the Kingdom to Debating Their Accusations

In the days of King Artaxerxes of Persia, there was a noble servant of the king named Nehemiah, a Jew. Nehemiah desired of his king that he might travel back to Jerusalem, then lying in ruins, and rebuild it. The king granted the request of his faithful servant, and gave provisions to Nehemiah to help him accomplish the work. However, the enemies of the Jews still lurked in the land of Palestine: Sanballat, Tobiah, and Geshem the Arabian. The enemies of the Jews feared that the Jews would rebuild the walls of Jerusalem and become a mighty people again, so they conspired one with another on just what to do. Nehemiah and his men were doing a great work in building up the walls of Jerusalem, and their enemies knew that they needed to divert the efforts of the Jews to slow this rapid progress:

> Now it came to pass, when Sanballat, and Tobiah, and Geshem the Arabian, and the rest of our enemies, heard that I had builded the wall, and that there was no breach left therein; (though at the time I had not set up the doors upon the gates;)
> That Sanballat and Geshem sent unto me, saying, Come, let us meet together in some one of the villages in the plain of Ono. But they thought to do me mischief.
> And I sent messengers unto them, saying, I am doing a great work, so that I cannot come down: why should the work cease, whilst I leave it, and come down to you?
> Yet they sent unto me four times after this sort; and I answered them after the same manner.
> Then sent Sanballat his servant unto me in like manner the fifth time with an open letter in his hand;
> Wherein was written, It is reported among the heathen, and Gashmu saith it, that thou and the Jews think to rebel: for which cause thou buildest the wall, that thou mayest be their king, according to these words.
> And thou hast also appointed prophets to preach of thee at Jerusalem, saying, There is a king in Judah: and now shall it be reported to the king according to these words. Come now therefore, and let us take counsel together.
> Then I sent unto him, saying, *There are no such things done as thou sayest, but thou feignest them out of thine own heart.* (Nehemiah 6:1-8)

Why should Nehemiah go down and answer the questions of his adversaries when both he and his adversaries knew they were lying? Why should he leave building up the wall, and do exactly what his enemies wanted?

The same situation exists today. The anti-LDS claims have been answered long ago. Both the Latter-day Saints and the *gainsayers* know that. The gainsayers are trying to divert the Saints' attention from building the kingdom to debating on accusations that both groups know have long since been refuted. The Church has already answered its adversaries. Its present answer is called missionary work! The Mormons have more than thirty thousand representative who are ready and waiting to offer anyone who cares to listen a thorough explanation of the gospel of Jesus Christ.

According to the great ancient Christian scholar and apologist, Origen:

> When false witnesses testified against our Lord and Saviour Jesus Christ, He remained silent; and when unfounded charges were brought against Him, He returned no answer, believing that His whole life and conduct among the jews were a better refutation than any answer to the false testimony, or any formal defense against the accusations.[2]

Anti-Mormon Witnessing Technique: "Jesus Christ or Joseph Smith?"

The Church of Jesus Christ of Latter-day Saints proclaims to the world the wonderful message that Jesus is the Christ. Yet the churches of today, who deny the literal resurrection of Christ by teaching that he is only a spirit, without flesh and bones, attempt to portray the Christ worshipped by the Latter-day Saints as a "different" Jesus than the one in the Bible. And since the literal, truly resurrected Christ taught by Joseph Smith differs from the bodiless spirit of their creeds, they try to use this doctrinal difference as a witnessing technique against the Mormons.

They blindly assume the correctness of their creeds when they pose the question, "Whom are you going to follow—Jesus Christ or Joseph Smith?" Many times the *gainsayers* of today use this query in an attempt to convince people not to let the missionaries into their homes.

To a Latter-day Saint, that question is like asking someone, "Who are you going to follow: Jesus Christ or John the Baptist?" The Saints declare that just as God sent his prophet John the Baptist to prepare the way for Christ's first advent, He has sent another prophet, Joseph Smith, to gather the elect and sound the warning voice in preparation for the second advent of Christ! Both were forerunners, preparing the way for the restoration of the Gospel in different dispensations.

In the days of the former prophet there were many different churches, all claiming to believe and teach the scriptures, and all claiming to be followers of the Lord and the expected Messiah. Yet when the Christ came He was rejected and killed, as well as the prophet who prepared His way.

In the days of the latter prophet, there also were many different churches, all claiming to believe and teach the Bible, and all claiming to be the followers of God and the expected Christ. Yet when the prophet Joseph came to prepare His way he was killed; along with hundreds of Saints, and this was done in the name of God.

The parallel to the Lord's prophecy concerning His New Testament saints is inescapable:

> These things have I spoken unto you, that ye should not
> be offended.
> They shall put you out of the synagogues: yea, the time
> cometh, that *whosoever killeth you will think that he doeth
> God service.* (John 16:1-2)

The question men should be asking themselves today is, *"Am I following the Christ taught by His prophet John and the Saints, or am I following the Christ of the philosophies, precepts, and churches of men?"*

Latter-day Saints proclaim that Joseph Smith the prophet is the modern parallel of John the Baptist, and that he was called to prepare the world for Christ's second coming. They regard Joseph Smith as no more and no less than that. If they should reject the message and conclude that they must deny even the possibility of the ministering of angels, apostles and prophets, then they would be doing exactly what those did who opposed Jesus and His prophet John two thousand years ago!

6
"The God Makers" Film: An Example of Extreme Anti-Mormon Propaganda

Because of the extensive advertising and marketing effort which has brought it broad exposure, "The God Makers" has had more extensive impact upon the public than typical anti-Mormon propaganda pieces.

The film is described by its authors as "A shocking expose of what the Mormon Church really believes." In reality, the people who are most shocked are Latter-day Saints who see the film and find Mormonism misrepresented to such an extreme that they don't recognize it.

Strong Criticism of "The God Makers" Issued by The National Conference of Christians and Jews

The National Conference of Christians and Jews did a study of the film, compared it to what the Latter-day Saints really believe, and came to this conclusion:

> The film does not—in our opinion—fairly portray the Mormon Church, Mormon history, or Mormon belief. *It makes extensive use of half-truth, faulty generalization, erroneous interpretations, and sensationalism.* It is not reflective of the genuine spirit of the Mormon faith.[1]

Unfortunately, the film, and the book by the same title which contains much of the same misinformation, has influenced the perception of The

119

Church of Jesus Christ of Latter-day Saints held by many non-Mormon Christians across the nation.

The God Makers' Author: J. Edmund Decker—Former "Member of the Select Senior Melchizedek Priesthood"

I have read the book, "The God Makers" and have seen the film and its short sequel numerous times, and I have spoken and written to anti-Mormon adversaries on numerous occasions about it.

J. Edward Decker is the instigating force behind the book and the film, and he has written of himself:

> As an ex-Mormon who spent nearly 20 years in the Mormon Church and was a member of the select senior Melchizedek Priesthood, I spent much time as a missionary for the LDS church.[2]

That does sound impressive! Here we have a former member of the select senior Melchizedek priesthood telling his Christian brothers to beware of the Latter-day Saints.

What does he mean by "select senior" priesthood? Hundreds of thousands of Latter-day Saint men hold this same priesthood. The nineteen- and twenty-year-old missionaries that go door-to-door with their message of Christ have this very same "senior select" priesthood. And course, every member is to be a missionary, according to the Saints.

His claim to being a "member of the select senior Melchizedek Priesthood," of course, is an attempt to establish augmented authority and credentials for himself. To uninformed non-Mormon readers, this self-serving portrayal makes it appear as if he held positions among the highest councils of the Church, which he did not.

Turning Criticisms Made of Born-Again Christians Against the Mormons: Parallels Between "Holy Terror" and "The God Makers"

There is a book to which "The God Makers" bears an uncanny resemblance. It is a book named "Holy Terror: The Fundamentalist War on America's Freedoms in Religion, Politics, and Our Private Lives." This book is an expose of the "born-again" Christian movement.

I believe that the authors of "The God Makers" copied many of the charges set forth in "Holy Terror," rewriting them to be criticisms of The Church of Jesus Christ of Latter-day Saints. There are far too many parallels between the two books for the similarities to be happenstance.

Like the book "The God Makers," "Holy Terror" has two authors; in this case they are men with impressive credentials. Flo Conway worked for the *Saturday Evening Post* and completed a doctorate in communications. The co-author, Jim Siegelman, graduated from Harvard with honors.

Their articles have appeared in the *New York Times*, which described their book as "well researched and very frightening."[3] The *New York Post* wrote, "It is a book of investigative reporting at it's best."[4] The book promised to expose *"the truth about"* "born-again" Christianity.[5]

What are some of the numerous parallels between the two works—parallels which make it appear that many of "The God Makers'" allegations are copied from "Holy Terror"? The film and the book "The God Makers" assert that "The Brethren," meaning Mormon leaders, teach Mormons to practice and believe doctrines that are detrimental to normal family life— doctrines which break up families, cause divorce, suicide, etc. The book and film also assert that Mormon leaders are building a huge financial "Invisible Empire" for the sole purpose of gaining enough power to take over the United States Government. The book and the film contain testimonies from ex-Mormons which supposedly lend credence to what the film and book put forth.[6]

"Holy Terror" also describes how "The Big Fathers," or "born-again" leaders, teach fundamentalists to practice and believe doctrines that are detrimental and break up families, cause divorce, suicide, etc. It also asserts that "born-again" Christian leaders are building a huge financial "Invisible Empire" for the sole purpose of gaining enough power to take over the United States Government. The book contains testimonies from ex-born-again Christians which supposedly offer credence to what the book puts forth.[7] The authors of "Holy Terror" have written:

> It is the broad program of intimidation, manipulation and control in the name of religion that we call *Holy Terror*....Before our appearance on "The Tonight Show" with Johnny Carson, we received repeated anonymous phone calls in our hotel rooms in Hollywood warning: "If you say anything about born-again Christianity, you'll be sorry."....Suddenly, disaffected born-agains started coming

out of the woodwork, and we began to see a side of this sprawling movement that no one is talking about. Over the years, we've spoken with many born-agains who were sincere in their beliefs and warmhearted in their desire to make their religion a living part of their daily lives. But we've also met people whose faith has filled them with contempt for their fellow man; people who had been browbeaten and confused to the point of surrender by unyielding preachers and proselyters. We've seen marriages broken up and families split apart over absurd tests of true conversion, whole communities turned against one another in heated battles over trivialities of fundamentalist dogma. Worst of all, we've seen real tragedy: people tormented, driven to emotional breakdown and, in some cases, to suicide, while fellow crusaders stood by, unfeeling and uncaring....Long term effects included emotional problems such as depression, suicidal tendencies and feelings of guilt, fear and humiliation, and mental disorders such as disorientation, amnesia, nightmares, hallucinations and delusions. The anguished comments we received in personal replies only added to our concern over the effects of fundamentalist ritual practices on individuals and families in America....These were our first contacts with the fragile lambs we came to call ex-Christians. As they told their stories, we learned about the silent suffering of what may be a considerable number of America's born-agains.[8]

If you want to compare some of the many parallels between "The God Makers" and "Holy Terror," here are enough comparison references to get you started in your quest. You can read how "The Big Fathers" are trying to take over the U. S. on page 66 of "Holy Terror," and how "The Brethren" are planning the same thing on page 241 of "The God Makers."

You can read about the "born-again" missionary and C.I.A. connection on pages 318-320 of "Holy Terror," and about the Mormon missionary and C.I.A. connection on pages 238-239 of "The God Makers."

You can read about how "The Big Fathers" oppose the First Amendment on pages 163-65 of "Holy Terror," and how "The Brethren" oppose the First Amendment on pages 7-8 of "The God Makers."

You can read how "born-again" Christianity is likened to Hitler's "Big Lie" on page 265 of "Holy Terror," and you can read how the LDS Church is likened to Hitler's "Big Lie" on page 208 of "The God Makers."

The similarities go on and on, but I think the point has been made: many of the anti-Mormon allegations made in "The God Makers" appear to be adapted rewrites of criticisms leveled against "born-again" Christians in "Holy Terror."

"Born-again" Christians attempt to dismiss "Holy Terror," with its testimony from ex-born-agains and all as an attempt by humanistic authors to manipulatively discredit fundamentalist Christianity. However, many of them at the same time readily accept the same allegations as unquestionably true when they're rewritten and leveled against the Latter-day Saints.

Synopsis of "The God Makers"

Most Latter-day Saints have not seen, and never will see, the film "The God Makers." Yet many of them may encounter non-Mormon friends and neighbors who will have seen it, and who will want to discuss it with them.

Latter-day Saints who have seen the film have typically indicated their personal responses as feelings of "revulsion," "personal distress because of the film's continual distortion of LDS doctrines and practices," "disgust because it makes light of sacred things," "concern because it is filled with yellow journalism techniques," etc.

Though the film's contents and stylization presumably would be perceived as repugnant by most knowledgeable LDS viewers, they still need to be aware of its message and potential impact on uninformed viewers. Because of that need, the film and its sequel are summarized here. No effort is made, in this context, to refute the many distortions and inaccuracies the film contains. The following summary merely describes the film's contents. Key words are given in italics, paragraph by paragraph, to summarize the themes of many of the film's assertions and portrayals.

Documented Evidence Claim. The first scene begins with an aerial shot of the Hawaiian Temple. The narrator declares, "It looks beautiful from the outside, but when you peal off the mask and talk to the victims, you uncover another part of the story," and "the documented evidence you are about to see may seem unbelieveable, but its all true!"

Brainwashing. The next scene has a man declaring that the Church stole his family from him, and that he tried to commit suicide because of it. Another man declares that the Church turned his children against him, and that its brainwashing techniques "are incredibly effective!"

Implied Law Suit. The next scene shows Ed Decker and his cohort in the film, Richard Baer, at an airport. The narrator tells us that they are among many "victims" that are trying to file a class-action suit against the church through an unnamed Los Angeles law firm.

Church Wealth. The next scene shows Decker and Baer sitting across a table from two attorneys. Decker tells the attorneys that the Church has "billions," that he has "records of many, many homes that have been shattered by these people," and that he "considers it to be one of the most deceptive and most dangerous groups in the entire world!"

Occult and Satanism. Decker declares that he has "documentation that ties it in to the occult and Satanism...." One attorney declares that he knows Mormons, and that they seem to be very moral and family oriented.

Incredible Deception. Decker quickly responds, "That's part of the incredible deception, and that's what we have to dig into. We need to expose it; we need to open it up to the truth!" The music swells and the title "The God Makers" appears across the screen.

The unseen and unnamed narrator now shows scenes from Temple Square in Salt Lake City, which he calls the "Mecca of Mormonism."

Carefully Groomed Image. The scene then shows a Pioneer Day parade, and the narrator declares that to the outside world the Church presents itself in "a carefully groomed Osmond family image."

Characters Introduced. The next scene introduces Dr. Harold Goodman, a former Brigham Young University professor and former mission president. It shows Goodman discussing the Family Home Evening program and shows a family singing a Primary song.

Brian Grant is introduced as the Church director of public relations in the British Isles. Grant briefly discusses missionary work in the Church and how the Church is family oriented.

The next scene introduces Jim and Judy Robertson—Ex-Mormons who head an anti-LDS "ministry" in Arizona. Judy tells how they were introduced to Mormonism, and Jim declares that before that time he always thought Mormons were people dressed in black that had sixteen wives, but he knows now that this isn't true. Judy declares that the Mormons "seemed to be Christian." Another ex-Mormon, a young woman, is shown, and she tells how the Mormons "took me in" by dances and other peer pressures.

Temples Only for Elite Few. Goodman is shown again telling about the youth programs in the Church. The narrator now declares that in Mormon Temples no Church services are held; only "secret ceremonies which are reserved for an elite few." Goodman is now featured speaking on Temple marriage and eternal families.

Became a God with Goddess Wives. Grant is shown in the next scene speaking about temple work, and telling that one needs a temple recommend to enter an LDS temple. Goodman talks about the recommend, and the film makers edit Goodman. The narrator declares that to go to the temple, Mormons must abstain from "tea or coffee" and must "pay" a substantial portion of their income to the Mormon Church, and must be giving free labor to various Church-run organizations. The worthy Mormon can become a god himself in the life hereafter, ruling over his own planet, with "a number of goddess wives." Goodman is quickly reedited back in saying, "So you can see why the temple is so important to the Latter-day Saint!"

Temple for Select Few Mormons. The next scene shows the open house for the Seattle Temple, and the narrator declares that after the open house the Temple will close its doors forever except to "a small select group of Mormons" and that "for many of these Mormons that came from thousands of miles away and stood for hours in the rain, this may be the only time that they are ever allowed to enter a Mormon Temple"

Mormons Dodge Questions. The next scenes show an unseen woman asking Mormons (?) at the open house simple questions on the nature of God, etc, and the Mormons (?) try to dodge her questions.

Billions of Humanoid Gods. The next scene is back at the attorney's office, and Dick Baer declares to the attorneys that the Mormon gods and goddesses were once mere humans, according to Joseph Smith, and that "there are supposed to be billions of these highly evolved humanoids somewhere out in space overseeing their own planet."

Eternal Progression. Floyd C. Mc Elveen, an anti-LDS author and minister, is now shown. Mc Elveen declares, "They believe that God eternally progressed, that once he was a man, and that he became God; from that comes their doctrine that all can progress to be gods."

Information with a Taste of Truth. The film returns to the attorney's office again, with an attorney declaring that tales of gods and goddesses "just won't fly in the jury room" and that a jury needs "information that has a taste of truth to it, and what you're telling us I really don't think they're going to swallow, do you?" Decker responds, "I did for nineteen years," and says that the Mormon concept of godhood is tied around Temple Marriage.

Gods Required to Populate Planets. The next scene introduces Jolene Coe, one of the most featured ex-Mormons in the film. Jolene describes how she was taught that she couldn't go to heaven unless she had a worthy Mormon man to take her to the temple. The narrator now declares that according to "Mormon theology, husbands and wives who have successfully achieved godhood will be required to populate their own planet by procreating as many spirit-children as possible."

Eternally Pregnant. Jolene continues by saying, "Ever since I was a little girl I was taught that my primary purpose was to become a goddess in heaven so that I could multiply an earth, and I wanted that. I wanted to be eternally pregnant, and look down on an earth and say 'that's mine, I populated that whole earth and all those little babies I had.'"

Celestial Sex an Embarrassment. The next scene is in the attorney's office again, with one of them saying that he finds it hard to believe that the Mormon attorneys and Judges he knows could believe that they "could become infinite gods, peopling new worlds, and engaging in celestial sex with their goddess wives." Baer responds, "Why don't you ask them?" The attorney replies, with subdued laughter, "Ah, well, I would be, eh, embarrassed, to be honest with you," and "I'd rather not know about it!" Decker quips, "That's why it's such a secret. That's why even the Mormons don't talk about it—they're embarrassed by it too!"

Extraterrestrial Humanoids. Decker then comments, "Look, Mormonism is based upon the belief that extraterrestrial humanoids from a star in a distant place called Kolob visited this earth, came down to this earth and visited a young boy, a fourteen-year-old boy by the name of Joseph Smith."

Difference Between Mormonism and Christianity. Decker then tells the attorneys that he has had an animation done "to show the difference between Mormonism and Christianity." The scene now pans from Decker to a screen in the attorney's office, and the cartoon begins. Accompanying the eery music is the voice of a new narrator who tells the viewers that Mormons believe in trillions of humaniod gods ruling their own planets scattered across the cosmos. The cartoon shows scenes of worlds and stars travelling to and fro.

Eloheim in Diapers. The narrator declares that Mormons believe that long ago Eloheim was born to an unnamed goddess, and that he was then born to human parents, and went through death and resurrection, while adhering to the Mormon gospel. The scenes include Eloheim in a crib with diapers, and growing to manhood.

Old God, Young Wives. The next scene shows a gray-haired and bearded Eloheim upon a planet with what seems to be innumerable beautiful young women wearing practically see-through clothing. The narrator declares, "Mormons believe that Eloheim is their Heavenly Father, and that He lives with His many goddess wives on a planet near a mysterious star called Kolob." The narrator continues, "Here the god of Mormonism and his wives, through endless celestial sex, produce billions of spirit children."

Heavenly Council Meeting. The screen shows traveling worlds, and innumerable young women taking care of babies in cribs. The travelling worlds are accompanied by sound effects. The cartoon continues with the narrator telling how "the Head of the Mormon gods" called a "heavenly council meeting."

Beer-hall Council. The narrator continues, "Both of Eloheim's eldest sons were there: Lucifer, and his brother Jesus." The cartoon depicts what looks strikingly like a beer hall; this being the site for the heavenly council meeting. At this meeting are a lot of Viking-looking types sitting around a table with jugs at hand. Suddenly, Lucifer scoots his chair back, stands, and advocates a plan. The narrator says, "Lucifer stood and made his bid" and "he wanted the glory for himself." The narrator goes on to say that "the Mormon Jesus suggested giving man his freedom of choice as on other planets," and "the vote that followed approved the proposal of the Mormon Jesus who would become Savior of the planet earth."

Lucifer with Horns. The narrator then declares that "Lucifer became the Devil," and the cartoon shows Lucifer suddenly sprout a wicked smile and a pair of horns (audience laughter). The cartoon then shows a group of blond-haired, blue-eyed demons suddenly sprout horns and wicked smiles just like Lucifer, and they all fly off together from Kolob to earth.

Neutrals Become Negros. The narrator continues, "Those who remained neutral in the battle were cursed to be born with a black skin; this is the Mormon explanation for the Negro race." The cartoon depicts blond-haired blue-eyed neutrals suddenly turning black with kinky hair and other Negroid features (audience laughter). The narrator then exclaims that those who fought valiantly for the Mormon Jesus would be born to Mormon families on earth.

Eloheim was Adam. The narrator continues, "Early Mormon prophets taught that Eloheim, and one of his goddess wives, came to earth as Adam and Eve, to start the human race." The scene shows Eloheim and a young woman coming down and transforming themselves into Adam and Eve.

Eloheim Had Sex with Mary. The cartoon then depicts Eloheim/Adam suddenly materializing (with accompanying sound effects) out of nowhere. He starts to walk around through a village that is supposed to be Bethlehem. The narrator of the cartoon continues, "Thousands of years later Eloheim, in human form once again, returned to earth from the star base Kolob; this time to have sex with the Virgin Mary—in order to provide Jesus with a physical body." The cartoon shows Eloheim knocking on a door, and a young woman (Mary) opens it. Eye meets eye, and the film-makers let the viewer's imagination fill in the rest.

Jesus Was Married. The cartoon then shows Jesus playing with His children, and captions of three young women. The narrator says, "Mormon Apostle Orson Pratt taught that after Jesus Christ grew to manhood, he took at least three wives; Mary, Martha, and Mary Magdalene." He says that Jesus Christ had children by them, and says that "Joseph Smith claimed" direct descent from Jesus.

Jesus Preached to the Indians. The narrator then tells the viewers that Mormons believe that after Jesus's resurrection, He came to the New World to "preach to the Indians." In the cartoon, a few American natives are shown with their teepees in the background. Suddenly, Jesus materializes out of thin air and starts walking around.

Cartoon-style Nephite-Lamanite Battle. In the next few scenes, about a dozen "Nephites" are shown having a little battle with about the same number of "Lamanites;" the sound effects during the battle remind one of a Saturday morning cartoon. The narrator says that by 421 A. D. "the dark-skinned Indian Israelites, known as Lamanites, had destroyed all of the white-skinned Nephites in a number of great battles."

Joseph Smith Known for Tall Tales. The cartoon now shows Moroni, the last of the Nephite prophets, burying the gold plates, and then Joseph Smith uncovering them. The narrator declares, "Fourteen hundred years later, a young treasure seeker named Joseph Smith, who was known for his t-a-l-l tales, claimed to have uncovered these same gold plates near his home in upstate New York," and that "he is now honored by Mormons as a prophet, because he claimed to have visions from the spirit world in which he was commanded to organize the Mormon Church because all Christian creeds were an abomination!"
The next few scenes depict Joseph Smith preaching.

Joseph Smith Central Figure in Final Judgment. The next scene in the cartoon is the judgment scene, and in that scene a timid little fellow is shown looking up in awe at the great judgment bench. In the cartoon Joseph Smith sits in the center seat at the great judgment bench (the prominent position) with God (Eloheim) and the Lord (the Mormon Jesus) at his flanks. The narrator informs the viewers, "The Mormons teach that everyone must stand in the final judgment before Joseph Smith, the Mormon Jesus, and Eloheim."

Joseph Smith Did More Than Jesus Christ. The last scenes of the cartoon depict Joseph Smith putting on his robes and ascending to Kolob. The narrator of the cartoon concludes, "The Mormons thank God for Joseph Smith, who claimed that he had done more than any other man, including Jesus Christ," and "The Mormons believe that he died a martyr—shed his blood so that we too may become gods." The narrator uses very sarcastic tones in the last part of the sentence.

Space Gods from Kolob. The eery music stops, and the screen at the attorney's office goes blank. One of the attorneys, now smiling, exclaims, "Space gods from Kolob! Sounds like Von Dieneken or Battlestar Galactica!" Baer agrees with the attorney, and then tells a story about his wife divorcing him because he couldn't believe that he could become a god.

Church Encourages Divorce of Non-members. One attorney now conveniently asks if it is a Church policy to encourage people to divorce non-members or inactive spouses. Decker quickly tells a story about his children being "pulled" from him, and how he knows of similar stories that "could break your heart."

Divorced Because of the Church. The narrator then introduces Greg and Jolene Coe as "Divorced because of the Mormon church, and are now remarried." Jolene tells a story of trying to convert her "Christian" husband to "Mormonism," but when that failed "I was advised to divorce him."

Freedom to Break Up Families. The scene then goes back to the attorney's office, with one attorney saying, "Gentlemen, this isn't helping your case!" and "These people have the religious freedom to believe anything they want to...." Baer interrupts, "But why should they have the freedom to break up families and destroy lives?"

Mormon Woman's Depression. The next scenes show Decker explaining about the Mormon woman. He says that there is an entire division of psychiatric care that "deals with the depression in the Mormon woman."

Mormon Psychiatric Patients. The next scene shows Judy Robertson telling a story about how she worked in a hospital, and a nurse from the psychiatric ward asks her why so many patients in her ward are Mormons. No names of the woman or the hospital are given.

High Divorce and Suicide Rates. In the next scene the narrator introduces yet another anti-Mormon writer, saying she is "Sandra Tanner, ex-Mormon, author, researcher, considered to be one of the greatest living authorities on Mormonism." Sandra says, "Utah has a higher-than-average rate of divorce. It has higher than the national rate of suicide. Especially teen suicide is much higher than the national rate."

Perfection Goal Causes Suicide. Sandra goes on to say that the Church's moral and ethical code is so high that Mormon youth feel defeated in their goal of perfection and commit suicide.

The film then introduces the father and brother of Kip Elison; a young Latter-day Saint that committed suicide at age 16.

Temple Ceremony Mocks Christian Pastor. The next scenes have Decker explaining his version of Mormonism: how the Mormons believe that Christians are the "Whore of Babylon" and how the temple ceremony mocks the Christian pastor, portraying him as a "hireling of Satan."

Church Isn't Christian. The next scenes show a young woman who declares that once she was lured into the church she discovered it wasn't

Christian. Goodman then is shown stating that anyone who believes in Jesus Christ is a Christian.

Missionaries Instructed to Use Christian Terminology. Various scenes of missionaries at doors or on bikes are shown. The narrator informs the audience, "Mormons are instructed to use Christian terminology when talking to potential converts."

Mormon "Pat" Answers. The scene now goes back to the Seattle Temple open house, with the unseen woman asking Mormons (?) if they believe Mormonism is Christian. The Mormons (?) respond with very pat answers that seem hollow and staged.

Goodman is shown again declaring that Latter-day Saints believe that they have the fulness of the gospel.

Contradictory Versions of First Vision. The scene now shows various publications dealing with Joseph Smith's first vision. The narrator asserts that "Joseph Smith's first vision is the cornerstone of the Mormon Church, and yet there are nine versions, each of which contradict the other."

Church Leaders Hide Mormon History. Sandra Tanner is presented again, telling the viewers that Church leaders are hiding from Mormons the true history of their religion. She gives an example by saying, "In the unpublished accounts we find that Joseph Smith first said that it was just Jesus who appeared to him. The second time he wrote the story down, a few years later, he said many angels appeared to him, and then some years later he said two beings appeared."

Joseph Changed First Vision Accounts. Sandra accuses Joseph of "changing the date, and changing how old he is. He changes the motivation—why he went into the woods to pray. He changes who was there, and he changes what the message was of what they gave him."

Newly Canonized Revelations Omit Words. Decker claims that a recently canonized revelation had 200 words omitted because these words would prove the revelation to be false. Decker does not tell us which revelation this is, nor where it can be found.

Moon and Sun Inhabited. In the attorney's office again Baer exclaims, "You know that Joseph Smith said that the moon was inhabited with people dressed like Quakers, and living to be about a thousand years of age, and

Brigham Young seconded it when he said that the moon was not only inhabited, but the Sun was inhabited!"

Best Anti-Mormon Writing is Church Publications. The next scene is Sandra Tanner again, telling the viewers that the best anti-Mormon writing can be found in the publications for and by the Mormon Church.

Eternal Life Requires Polygamy. Decker is then shown again, in his office, saying that the "true doctrine teaches that there is no eternal life without a polygamous relationship."

John D. Lee. The narrator now introduces Thelma "Granny" Geer, "author, lecturer, outspoken ex-Mormon, great granddaughter of convicted Mormon assassin John D. Lee." Geer tells about her great grandfather John D. Lee, describing him as a Mormon pioneer, bodyguard to Joseph Smith and Brigham Young, and polygamist himself.

Emma Compelled to Accept Other Wives. The following scene shows Decker in his office again telling the viewers that Emma Smith was admonished to be obedient to the principle of other wives "or receive the penalty thereof."

Joseph Lied to Practice Polygamy. Sandra appears again and discusses a "diary" that she claims proves that Joseph Smith was "sneaking around Emma's back to practice polygamy," and that he lied to her to continue it. Sandra does not tell whose diary it is.

25,000 Polygamous Marriages in Utah. Decker is shown again and claims that "in Utah there are approximately 25,000 polygamous marriages."

Early Church Publications Deliberately Hidden. Sandra appears again, saying that Church leaders "deliberately hide" early Church publications from the Church members.

Seventh-East Press Exposed Cover-ups. The following scene features a very brief excerpt from an interview with Ron Priddis, a former business manager of the Seventh-East Press, a newspaper run mainly by BYU students. The narrator declares that the Press operated "to expose Mormon Church cover-ups." Priddis is quoted as saying that the Press did articles on Church history, and on "some of the dishonesty on the part of some of the administrators in dealing with students."

Church Records Not Open for Inspection. Sandra is shown again saying that if the "Church records" were open for public inspection it would tarnish the beautiful, but false, image the Church puts out.

LDS Leaders Rewrite History. Decker is shown in his office again, and declares "in the Christian faith we find our scholars looking for earlier manuscripts," but in Mormonism this isn't the case. Sandra says, "The leaders have to go back and reword, rewrite, cover-up, change, delete, add, all the way through in all of their books."

No Archaeological Evidence for the Book of Mormon. The next scene introduces Charles Crane, yet another anti-LDS author. The narrator introduces Crane as "Dr. Charles Crane, author, college professor, expert on Mormon archaeology." Crane tells the viewers that he has checked maps and archaeological information, but he still has to wonder. He declares, "Where is the land of Zarahemla? Where is the Valley of Nimrod? Where are the plains of Nephihah?" Crane says that he has been "unable to find the record of even one city as mentioned in the Book of Mormon." Sandra is shown again claiming that there is no evidence for the Book of Mormon.

No Excavated Artifacts Support Book of Mormon. The next scene introduces "Dr. Richard Fales, author, lecturer, archaeologist." Fales tells the viewers that "We have never excavated one single artifact that even remotely relates to this alleged civilization that the Mormons claimed existed in the United States, Central America, and in South America." The narrator then declares that no archaeological evidence can be found to support the civilizations described in the Book of Mormon, but that "archaeology has been able to prove the existence of all great civilizations, including those of Biblical times." The narrator mentions coins being found to confirm Biblical archaeology and shows various Old and New Testament coins.

No Book of Mormon Coins Found. The next scene features Crane again, and he claims that in Alma 11:5-19 "is a listing of the coinage of the period of time that was used by these people," but adds that "needless to say, at this point not one of these coins has ever been found."

Harold Goodman appears again on the screen, giving a very brief description of the Book of Mormon.

Book of Mormon a Fairy Tale. Crane appears again suddenly and declares that he is "led to believe" from his research that the Book of Mormon "is a fairy tale, much like Alice in Wonderland."

Mormon Archaeologists Have Failed to Find Evidence. Fales appears again and says that "decades of searching by Mormon archaeologists have failed to uncover one scrap of evidence regarding the people or the places or the events in the Book of Mormon."

Missionaries Claim Archaeological Proofs. The next scene is Decker at his office describing how "Mormon missionaries throughout the world are converting people to the Mormon Church by explaining to them that archaeology has proven the Book of Mormon to be true."

Book of Abraham Has No Relation to Abraham's Time. Crane now discusses the Book of Abraham. Fales appears again and declares that the Book of Abraham "has now resurfaced. Several famous Egyptologists have now looked at it, translated it, and found that it doesn't have anything to do with the time of Abraham at all." Crane appears again and says that Joseph Smith "did not get right even one word in his whole translation." Priddis is spliced in, quickly saying, "Well, there are certain things which are embarrassing to the Church." Crane now declares that Mormons get "locked-in" and are afraid to look into their religion or question it.

Revelation on Blacks the Result of Social Pressure. The narrator declares that President Spencer W. Kimball had a revelation on blacks and the Priesthood because of "increasing social pressures." Scenes are of President Kimball at conference, etc.

Mormons Marrying Blacks to be Killed. The narrator claims that Mormons had believed that blacks were "low in their habits, inferior in their looks, mischievous, treacherous, and generally deprived of intelligence." The narrator claims that Brigham Young taught that "any Mormon marrying a Negro would be killed on the spot, and that this sacred law must never change." The narrator, as usual, gives no reference.

Prophet a Liason Between Man and God. Jim and Judy Robertson appear again declaring that the Mormon prophet believes he is a "liaison between man and God." Brian Grant is then shown briefly speaking on prophets.

Scripture Not to Be Tested. Decker then appears again, in his office, and says that a Mormon testimony is not based upon evaluation of scripture, but the "burning in the bosom," and says "scripture is not to be tested."

Burning in the Bosom. Jim Robertson appears again and describes his experience as an investigator by saying that the missionaries "encouraged us to read the Book of Mormon, nothing in the Bible!" Decker then says, "When we discuss these things with Mormons someone will say 'I don't care if every prophecy of Joseph Smith is proven wrong! I had a burning in my bosom that I know that the Church is true!'"

Reenactment of Temple Ceremony with Eery Music. The scene now shows a replica of an Ordinance Room of a Temple. The narrator, along with more eery music, declares that what the viewer is seeing is a first-ever authentic reenactment film of the Mormon temple ceremony, which "most Mormons never see," and those who have seen it "have sworn never to reveal these secrets under penalty of death!"

Music, Black Background, Zombie Temple Workers. Chuck Sackett, another anti-LDS author and lecturer, appears as a temple officiator behind the altar. The clothes seem very precise, but the shrieking background music which raises thoughts of dark villiany, together with the pitch-black background, hinders the set from appearing authentic. The temple workers and worshippers in the film resemble zombies.

Oaths Consenting to Being Put to Death. Baer is shown again in the attorney's office telling the attorneys that "All of us who have been to the temple have sworn solemn oaths consenting to having our throats slit, and our heart and our vitals thrown—torn out!"

Sealed in Mason-like Rituals. Sackett appears again very briefly in the mock ordinance room describing another token and sign. The narrator then declares that Mormon men and women are sealed together for eternity "in Mason-like rituals," and "without this ceremony, no one can enter the presence of Joseph Smith and become a god."

Fear and Disgust of Temple Ordinances. The scene is again at the mock ordinance room, with the zombie-like temple-goers repeating three Hebrew words. The next scene depicts washings and anointings. Chuck and Dolly Sackett play the temple workers. The violins begin to shriek feverishly at this point, and the washing and anointing rooms appear to be almost pitch-black. The expression on the faces of the actor and actress playing the part of the temple goers are ones of fright and disgust.

Encounter with Demon Dead. The narrator declares that "Mormons are encouraged to have encounters with the dead, and it's not uncommon for demons impersonating the dead to appear to Mormons stating that they've been converted to the Mormon Church in the spirit world and now want their family history traced." The mock washings and anointings continue on the screen.

Genealogy a Fanatical Program. Dr. Goodman is shown again speaking on genealogical work. The narrator calls genealogical work in the Church "a fanatical program to evangelize the dead." Scenes are shown of the Church Genealogical Center, Granite Mountain, etc. The camera returns to Dr. Goodman speaking on genealogical work and its relation to temples.

Mormon Underwear Magical and Dehumanizing. Jolene Coe is presented once again, and says that when "a Mormon goes through the temple to receive his endowments he's given a pair of this holy Mormon underwear, and he is instructed to wear it at all times." Jim Robertson then is shown declaring that the garment is supposed to be "all magical and all protective," but that the garment is probably "the most unattractive, dehumanizing piece of material that can be worn." Decker, in his office again, declares that no statistics can be found to prove that the garments have saved anybody from anything.

Garment a Superstition. The next scenes are of Robertson and Geer describing how Mormon women refuse to remove the garment, even in childbirth, and the assertion is made that Geer's grandmother had to be washed one side at a time because the garment had to be upon her, or at least upon half of her, at all times. Judy Robertson says that the garment "is like a rabbit's foot—it's a superstition!"

Joseph Smith Involved in the Occult. Decker, in his office, declares that Joseph Smith was "heavily involved in the occult," and that he used a "Seer stone as a crystal ball to divine the location of hidden treasures and to translate the golden plates." Baer, in the attorney's office, tells the attorneys that "in 1826 Joseph Smith was arrested for pretending to find buried treasure with that stone."

Temple Garment Markings. Decker, again in his own office, points to the temple garment markings, calling them talismans and amulets.

Mormons Follow the God Mormo. Decker then reaches for a book and says, "Here in Anton Le Vey's Satanic Bible, under the section called

'Infernal Names,' I want to show you something!" The music gets eery again. Decker says, "Here we have the god, Mormo, who's king of the ghouls, god of the living dead. Those people that follow him are called Mormons!" The older attorney breaths heavily and says, "That's the kind of conclusion we can't jump to, it could be a coincidence!"

"Mormon" Means "Gates of Hell" in Chinese. Decker replies that "Mormons are obsessed with genealogies and temple rites and rituals for the dead, whom they believe can visit the living and who can convert to Mormonism even in the grave!" Baer quickly adds, "In Chinese Mormon means gates of Hell."

Vast Wealth of the Church. The narrator then introduces John L. Smith as "Dr. John L. Smith, author and expert on the vast wealth of the Mormon Church." Smith describes the Church as the second largest financial institution west of the Mississippi. The narrator lists some Church holdings, claiming that "two-thirds of their properties are tax-exempt" and "billions of dollars are extracted from Church members each year through their mandatory tithing program."

Church Owns a Major Portion of Hawaii. Decker is then shown, along with scenes of the Polynesian Cultural Center, In Hawaii. Decker claims that the Church owns a major portion of Hawaii. Another anti-Mormon woman is introduced who discusses the referral program of the Hawaiian Temple Visitors' Center.

Utah Leads Nation in Bankruptcy and Stock Fraud. The narrator then declares, "And for all it's talk of building an ideal society, Utah, which is 75% Mormon, leads the nation in bankruptcy and stock fraud, and ranks among the highest in divorce, suicide, child abuse, teen-age pregnancy, venereal disease, and bigamy."

Many Mormons Don't Believe in the Church. Sandra Tanner appears again, telling the viewers that many people in the Church don't really believe in it at all.

No Love in the Church. The next scenes show various ex-Mormons (?) asserting that they found "no love" in the Church. Sandra appears again, claiming that Mormonism undercuts the Bible and all other churches.

No Association with Apostates. Jolene Coe appears again, claiming that as a Mormon growing up, her sisters and brothers were best of friends, but "since I've come out of this Mormon Church my sisters and I have had no relationship at all. One of the rules in the Mormon Church is that if you want to go to the temple you can't associate with an apostate member."

Ex-Mormons Ostracized by Church Members. The next few scenes are of other ex-Mormons describing how they were ostracized by former friends and family because they left the Church. Doug and Janet Webster, with their family, are introduced on the scene, and Janet alleges that the Church spread a false rumor that she and her husband had been excommunicated for adultery. Sandra Tanner then asserts that, in Utah, if someone tries to leave the Church, their jobs and families are threatened. Sandra says she knows of a Mormon bishop that doesn't believe in Mormonism. Again, no name is given.

Staying Mormon the Easy Road. Jim Robertson tells a story of a man he knew that admitted to him the falsehood of Mormonism, but he couldn't come out of it because he would lose his family and career. Sandra describes Mormonism as "the easy road," saying that this is why a lot of people stay with it.

Not a Christian Church, a Cult. A young woman is presented again, saying that it was only after "they took me in" that she discovered "it wasn't a Christian Church—it was a cult."

Satan Convinced Eve She Could Become a God. Jim Robertson appears on the screen again, declaring, "Instead of going back to one of the Standard Works of the Church I went to the Bible, and...and in the second chapter of Genesis, I studied how Eve was convinced by Satan to eat the fruit— that she could become a god. And in the fourteenth chapter of Isaiah, Lucifer was cast out of heaven because he, too, wanted to be equal to or greater than God." An ex-Mormon is presented again, saying that she began studying the Bible, finding the "real Jesus."

Mormons Have Inner Pride and Problems. The scene cuts again to the Webster family, with Janet declaring, "We lived the Word of Wisdom, we attended our meetings, we paid our tithing, we had Family Home Evening, we did all the things we were supposed to do, and when I became a Christian I suddenly discovered that I was not the good person I thought I was, because God revealed to us our inner pride, er, ah, our inner problems...."

Lonely in the Church. An ex-Mormon woman describes how she was always lonely in the Church. Janet then describes how she became "born-again." The Webster family describes their conversion to "Jesus."

Fraud and Misrepresentation. The next scene is in the attorney's office again. The older attorney says, "Mr. Decker, Mr. Baer, I don't think we can take the case." Baer, looking shocked, cries, "But there's fraud! Deliberate misrepresentation! And the families, the lives that are being destroyed!"

The Church Has Billions. The younger attorney tells Decker and Baer, "You don't have the money to fight the Mormon Church, they have billions!" Seriously, the older attorney declares, "This thing can go on for years, and you haven't the resources to do it." The four men arise, and the younger attorney puts out his hand to Decker saying, "You've taken us to Kolob and back, but I don't think we can get a jury to accompany us."

Cults Protected at the Expense of Families. While the attorneys shake hands with a disappointed Decker and Baer, the narrator gives his final plea to the audience: "Cults are protected under the present legal system, and will continue to proliferate at the expense of human lives and families."

Suicide Linked with Leaving the Church. The next scene portrays Gene Eliason reading his son's suicide note, and finally breaking down into tears. The following scene is that of a Mormon (?) at the Seattle Temple Open House. A woman asks the Mormon (?) woman what she would miss the most if she had to leave the Church. The woman says, "I would rather be dead!"

Final Coffin Scene. The last scene begins pitch-black. Slowly, a door creaks open like that of a coffin. On the other side are two Mormon missionaries. One of the missionaries declares, "Good afternoon, ma'am, we'd like to talk to you about The Church of Jesus Christ of Latter-day Saints." The eery music returns and builds into one final screech of doom.

Synopsis of "Temple of the God Makers"

The film, "Temple of the God Makers" cannot literally be classed as a sequel to "The God Makers." Rather, it is a condensed version of it. Like its predecessor, it is summarized here without comment.

Temple Signs and Tokens Portrayed. The first scene begins with various signs and tokens being portrayed in a mock ordinance room. The sound effect is that of a heart beat.

The film begins essentially the same as the longer version, by introducing Decker, this time in his office.

The cartoon is also repeated.

Garment Worn During Physical Intimacy. Chuck Sackett is introduced again, as before, and describes the garment as having to "be worn 24 hours a day," saying it even is to be worn "for moments of physical intimacy."

Nude Paintings Represent Endowment Ceremony. Decker then describes the Endowment ceremony, but on the screen, old Renaissance paintings are shown of a fully naked Adam and Eve in the Garden of Eden. Decker claims that the fig-leaf apron (Genesis 3:7) represents Lucifer's powers, and is therefore evil.

*Temple Rituals from Scottish Rite Masonry.*Decker declares that the temple goer "becomes immersed in a series of rituals directly lifted from Scottish Rite Masonry." Decker, in his office, goes on to say that all the Temple signs, tokens, etc., come from "Scottish Rite" Masonry, and that Joseph Smith became a Mason in 1842.

Temple Signs and Tokens Portrayed. Chuck Sackett then goes into more temple signs and tokens, while acting them out on the screen.

Danites Cut Throats of Mormon Transgressors. The next scene is that of Thelma "Granny" Geer. She claims that "Mormonism teaches that there are certain sins for which the blood of Jesus Christ cannot atone, but the Mormon's own blood must be shed—my great grandfather was one of those men known as the Destroying Angels, or the Danites, who cut the throats of certain Mormon people who had committed a sin against Mormonism."

Geer then declares that Mormons have had their throats cut for such offenses as adultery, stealing, marriage to a Negro, and "not living up" to the temple oaths. The music begins an eery swell. Geer goes on to assert that Mormon fathers would shoot their own sons "right out of the saddle" because of apostasy, and for "trying to leave the Salt Lake Valley to get away from Mormonism."

Demons Visited Genealogical Worker Regularly. The scene goes back to the mock ordinance room, and the narrator repeats his oration on genealogical work. Dolly Sackett, who the narrator claims was a Genealogical Specialist for the Church, claims that her dead relatives, whom she now knows were demons, visited her regularly.

Temple Oaths Place Persons Under Satanic Spell. The next scene is again in the mock ordinance room, this time at the veil. Chuck Sackett declares that the temple oaths place the person, plus future generations, under a Satanic spell.

Early Mormon Architecture Used Satanic Symbols. The next scene shows Decker in his office, declaring that "a further indictment to the non-Christian nature of Mormonism is the fact that not a single cross appears in or on any Mormon temple; however, the pentagram, hexagram, and goat's head, which are the highest of Satanic symbols, were used extensively throughout early Mormon architecture!" Decker then shows a book with a picture of the Goat of Mendes.

Altar Statue Depicts Cain's Offering. Decker then describes the Altar Statue at the Salt Lake Temple Visitor's Center. The statue is that of Adam and Eve worshipping at the Altar. Upon the altar are fruits and grains, and beside the altar is a lamb. Decker exclaims "This is the offering of Cain, which God rejected in Genesis 4!"

Missionaries Use Christian Terminology. The narrator then repeats statements about missionary work from "The God Makers," asserting that Mormon missionaries "are instructed to use Christian terminology when referring to Mormon doctrine." Then the scene with the missionaries and the creeking door is repeated.

Weapons Characterize Food Storage Program. The following scene shows guns, machine guns, grenades, and ammunition, with the narrator saying, "Mormons are urged to store two-years' worth of food and supplies to help see them through the ensuing period of turmoil."

LDS Leaders Will Try Government Takeover. The narrator then asserts that "leaders of the Mormon Church" will try to take over the U. S. Government. Then, according to the narrator, all property and possessions would "be signed over to the Mormon priesthood, and the Church would then redistribute the wealth to those who are in good standing with Mormon officials; a form of theocratic Communism."

Mormons Hold Key Government Positions. The narrator goes on to say that "in preparation for this, the Church has already secured a large number of high level governmental offices," and that "Mormons now hold key positions in the White House, the Cabinet, Congress, the State Department, the Pentagon, the FBI, the CIA, as well as in State and local government and law Enforcement." The next scene is that of a traffic cop writing a ticket.

Mormonism Not Needed Because of Christ's Atonement. Thelma Geer is now shown again, telling how much she regrets giving 31 years to Mormonism. Geer states that she wants Mormons to know that Jesus died for all men's sins, so Joseph Smith, temple marriage, temple garments, blood atonement, etc., are not needed.

The final scene is of Granny Geer calmly picking flowers in front of an old barn.

7

Responses to Other Anti-Mormon Distortions and Misrepresentations

Like the anti-Nazarenes of Christ's day, modern anti-Mormons have adopted two very obvious tactics:

1. they accuse the Saints of believing doctrines which the Saints do not believe, and

2. they radically distort their portrayals of doctrines which the Saints do believe so those doctrines are perceived as offensive or unacceptable by non-Mormons.

This chapter will comment on examples of these types of misrepresentations and distortions commonly advanced by modern anti-Mormon *gainsayers*.

False Anti-Mormon Concept: Mormons Believe the Bible is "Basically in Error"

According to many anti-Mormon adversaries, the Latter-day Saints believe that the Bible is "basically in error."[1] This anti-Mormon allegation is a falsehood which they perpetuate though they know it is untrue. The LDS acceptance of the Bible as revealed scripture is clearly set forth in one of the Church's thirteen basic statements of belief, the eighth Article of Faith,

"We believe the Bible to be the word of God...." Joseph Smith the Prophet was once asked if the Saints believed in the Bible. He replied,

> If we do, *we are the only people under heaven that does*, for there are none of the religious sects of the day that do.

He was then asked how the Saints differ from other sects. He replied that they differ

> In that *we believe the Bible*, and *all the other sects profess to believe their interpretations of the Bible, and their creeds.*[2]

Joseph Smith frequently called the Bible "the record of truth" and the "sacred volume," but added:

> *I believe the Bible as it read when it came from the pen of the original writers.*[3]

And also,

> Our latitude and longitude can be determined in the *original Hebrew with far greater accuracy* than in the English version.[4]

Concerning the Latter-day Saints' regard for the Bible, Brigham Young has said:

> *We are believers in the Bible*, and to our *unshaken faith in its precepts, doctrine, and prophecy*, may be attributed the strangeness of our course, and the unwarranted conduct of many towards this people.[5]

He also said, "We have a holy reverence for a belief in the Bible,"[6] and unequivocally asserted that "The Bible is true."[7]

Brigham Young also commented,

> But I want to know if we agree with the teachings of the bible, in our belief and practice. *The Latter-day Saints believe in doing just what the Lord said in that book.*[8]

And also,

> We as Latter-day Saints have confessed before Heaven, before the heavenly hosts, and before the inhabitants of the earth, that *we really believe the scriptures as they are given to us, according to the best understanding and knowledge*

that we have of the translation, and the spirit of the Old and New Testament.[9]

He also said,

> *You say, I have thrown away the New Testament. I say I have not. You say, I have sacrificed it for the Book of Mormon. I say, I have not.* I have acknowledged the Bible from the time I could be taught by my parents to revere it. They taught me that it was the sacred word of God. And *as far as it could be translated correctly from the Hebrew and Greek languages, it is given to us as pure as it possibly could be given. The Bible is mine, and I am not prepared to have you rob me of it without my consent.* The doctrine in it is mine, which I firmly believe. I believe that Father begot the Son, and gave him to be a propitiation for the sins of the world. I believe he died for the redemption of man, and rose again the third day.[10]

The Saints believe totally that the Bible is the word of God. But what did Joseph Smith and Brigham Young mean when they said "as far as it is translated correctly?" They proclaimed their belief that the Bible was without error of any sort in the original manuscripts but that certain errors have crept in after—the errors of translators and copyists. Of course, anti-Mormon adversaries distort this reservation, depicting it as evidence that Mormons don't use or trust the Bible. In truth, the Saints fully trust the Bible, and what few errors have crept into it are not regarded as significant. The late Joseph Fielding Smith wrote:

> We are all aware that there are errors in the Bible due to faulty translations and ignorance on the part of translators, but *the hand of the Lord has been over this volume of scripture* nevertheless, and *it is remarkable that it has come down to us in the excellent condition in which we find it.*[11]

Modern scholarship has shown that the Latter-day Saints have taken an appropriate position in their assertion that the Bible is correct except for the minor errors of translators and copyists. In the late 19th century it was discovered that ancient manuscripts of the Bible varied in places and different readings. It was conceded that there were indeed errors in the various copies which have been found to date. Some Christian scholars formed the mistaken opinion that the errors were most likely in the originals too, and drew the unwarranted conclusion that the Bible contains much myth and cannot be trusted. This belief is held by many of the "liberal" Christians of today. Since the world doesn't have the original manuscripts, the "liberals" have no evidence that the original writings contained errors.

Other Christian scholars, with "evangelical" or "fundamentalist" backgrounds, took the more correct view that even though the copies may contain errors, the originals which were directly inspired by God do not contain errors.

The International Council on Biblical Inerrancy (a "born-again" Christian scholarly group which believes opposite of the "liberal" Christians) has said:

> Inerrancy means that when all the facts are known, the Scriptures, in their original autographs and properly interpreted, will be shown to be wholly true in everything they teach, whether that teaching has to do with doctrine, history, science, geography, geology, or other disciplines or knowledge.[12]

It also said,

> Finally, there are people who say, "Since translations of the Bible differ, and since both cannot be right, inerrancy is a mistaken notion." The misunderstanding here is to suppose that inerrancy applies to the copies of the original documents or to translations of these documents. Actually, it applies only to the original manuscripts, called autographs.[13]

These statements reflect the views commonly held by most Latter-day Saints. The assertion of anti-Mormon adversaries that Mormons regard the Bible as "basically in error" is an intentional and unwarranted misrepresentation and distortion of Latter-day Saint doctrine and belief.

False Anti-Mormon Concept: God the Father Had Sex with Mary So She Was Not a Virgin

Another belief anti-Mormon activists falsely attribute to the Latter-day Saints, but which is not LDS doctrine, is that God came from Kolob to have sex with Mary to produce Jesus.[14] This accusation is a parallel of the same anti-Christ claim made in the days of Jesus. Wrote an anti-Nazarene in the days of the ancient apostles:

> Then was the mother of Jesus beautiful? And because she was beautiful did God have sexual intercourse with her, although by nature He cannot love a corruptible body? It

is not likely that God would have fallen in love with her since she was neither wealthy nor of royal birth, for nobody knew her, not even her neighbors. When she was hated by the carpenter and turned out, neither divine power nor the gift of persuasion saved her. Therefore, these things have nothing to do with the kingdom of God.[15]

In the days of Joseph Smith and Brigham Young, and even up to the present day, so-called "liberal" Christians have denied the virgin birth of Jesus, regarding it as myth, while "fundamentalist" Christians defend the true and Biblical doctrine of the virgin birth of Christ.

Anti-Mormon adversaries quote statements by Brigham Young and other LDS leaders which state the Church's belief that Jesus is the literal Son of God. Those statements were made in response to the "liberal" Christians and deists who have proclaimed for hundreds of years that Jesus was the son of Joseph and Mary, and that His being a son of God is only in a figurative, unliteral way.

The Saints have always taught the doctrine of the virgin birth, and held that Mary was a virgin till after Jesus was born. Anti-Mormon adversaries, however, claim that their use of the word "literal" means that they believe God had sexual intercourse with Mary and that the Saints don't believe that Mary was a virgin at all.

The *gainsayers* quote the late apostle, Elder Bruce R. McConkie, in his book "Mormon Doctrine" where he wrote that Jesus was begotten and conceived in the natural way as sons are by their mortal fathers. What Elder McConkie was putting forth was a denial of the ancient agnostic heresy that Jesus was not begotten and conceived in the womb, but rather that he suddenly appeared as a man without going through the process of mortal birth. What the late apostle also denied was the modern heresy that Jesus was the Son of God only in a figurative sense and in the flesh was the son of Joseph and Mary.

Elder McConkie, under the section "Virgin Birth" in his book "Mormon Doctrine," boldly declares that the "liberal" Christian teaching denying the virgin birth is utterly false and apostate. He goes on to say that Jesus was the only man ever to be born of a virgin. Somehow the *gainsayers* have managed to never read this statement, though they have obviously given Elder McConkie's book intense scrutiny. I have never seen acknowledgment of it in any of their books or writings. Could it be that they are willfully suppressing it?

Statements by LDS leaders have continually asserted the virginity of the mother of Jesus. Brigham Young said:

When the *Virgin Mary* conceived the child Jesus, the Father had begotten him in his own likeness.[16]

He also said,

The question has been often asked, who it was that begot the Son of the *Virgin Mary*.[17]

Another latter-day apostle, Orson Pratt, also wrote that Mary was a virgin:

Even our great Redeemer, whose death and sufferings we are this afternoon celebrating, was born up in yonder world before he was *born of the virgin Mary*.[18]

The late apostle Bruce R. McConkie wrote:

Our Lord is the only mortal person ever born to a *virgin*, because he is the only person who ever had an immortal Father. Mary, his mother, "was carried away in the Spirit" (1 Nephi 11:13-21), was "overshadowed" by the Holy Ghost, and the conception which took place "by the power of the Holy Ghost" resulted in the bringing forth of the literal personal Son of God the Father. (Alma 7:10; 2 Nephi 17:14; Isaiah 7:14; Matthew 1:18-25; Luke 1:26-38). Christ is not the Son of the Holy Ghost, but of the Father. (*Doctrines of Salvation,* vol. 1, pp. 18-20) *Modernistic teachings denying the virgin birth are utterly and completely false.*[19]

And he also wrote,

She conceived and *brought forth her Firstborn Son while yet a virgin* because the Father of that child was an immortal personage.[20]

False Anti-Mormon Concept: God the Father Not the Father of the Spirits of All Mankind

Other LDS doctrines also are twisted out of shape by anti-Mormon antagonists. One sacred belief that has been misunderstood and misrepresented is the LDS belief that God is the Father of the spirits of all flesh. The Bible affirms this teaching (Numbers 16:22; Jeremiah 1:5; Ecclesiastes 12:7; Hebrews 12:9, etc.) and so does ancient Christianity.

For instance, ancient Christian scholar and apologist *Lactantius* wrote:

And thus, when all things were disposed in a marvelous arrangement, He decided to prepare an eternal kingdom for Himself and *to procreate innumerable souls to whom to give immortality.*[21]

And *Origen* wrote:

> ...it is to expiate this sin that Jesus Christ came to the world. *His soul, created from the beginning with the other spirits*, alone remaining absolutely faithful to God....[22]

These spirits, begotten by God before the world began, are the spirits of all mankind. And Jesus is the brother of mortal man, because God is the Father of all the spirits who come to this earth. This is why the risen Christ told Mary, "Go to my brethren, and say unto them, *I ascend unto my Father, and your Father; and to my God, and your God*" (John 20:17).

False Anti-Mormon Concept:
Lucifer Not One of the Sons of God

Anti-Mormon *gainsayers* have long ridiculed the Latter-day Saints for their acceptance of the Biblical teaching that God the Father is the father of the spirits of all mankind, including both Jesus and Lucifer, thus making the Savior and Satan brothers. Yet their ridicule is directly counter to the conclusions of many Christian scholars. Ignoring the findings of competent scholarship, even of respected Christian scholars, is one of the identifying characteristics of the deceptive intent of the anti-Mormon movement.

Many Christian scholars recognize that Lucifer is a son of God. For instance, a prominent "fundamentalist" Christian scholar, Arno C. Gaebelein, acknowledged that Lucifer was a son of God when he wrote:

> The sons of God, revealed as morning stars, include Gabriel and Michael. As stated in our opening chapter, *Lucifer, the Son of the Morning, should also be included*, though he became the enemy of God by his fall.[23]

Gaebelein also wrote,

> We have stated before that, before his fall, the *devil was probably originally an archangel, one of the Morningstars*, as we learned from the Book of Job, which sang together God's praises in the hour of creation.[24]

Jesus is called the first begotten in the spirit (Hebrews 1:6), and all mankind are His brothers and sisters. Latter-day Saints do not attribute to Satan any special relationship—as a brother to Jesus he is only one of the billions of spirit children of God the Father. Anti-Mormon adversaries don't tell the people the whole truth about the matter, intentionally withholding this insight when using this subject as one of their principal witnessing techniques.

Yet the Latter-day Saints, the Bible, and ancient Christianity agree that our Heavenly Father is truly the Father of the spirits of all mankind, and that Jesus is the First begotten in the spirit and the Only Begotten in the flesh.

The so-called "orthodox" belief was a fabrication of 4th-century false teachers. They adopted the belief that the Son is somehow "eternally begotten" by the Father.

The adversaries of Jesus and His Prophet John, in the meredian of time, scoffed at the idea that God would have a Son. To them, the very idea was not only blasphemous, but ridiculous and unscriptural. To convince the Jews that God could and did have a Son, the Gospel writers and Paul used terminology and language also utilized by the great Jewish scribe Philo, of Alexandria, to prove their point. The apostle John wrote that Jesus was the Word of God:

> *In the beginning was the Word, and the Word was with God, and the Word was God.*
> The same was in the beginning with God.
> *All things were made by him*; and without him was not anything made that was made....
> And *the Word was made flesh*, and dwelt among us, (and we beheld his glory, the glory as of *the only begotten of the Father*,) full of grace and truth. (John 1:1-3, 14)

The apostle Paul referred to Christ as "The image of the invisible God, the *firstborn of every creature*" (Colossians 1:15).

Most of the scribes believed that the Word of God was just a figurative expression for God's creative power, but the great scribe Philo of Alexandria recognized that the "*Logos*" (Word) was "the first-begotten Son of God" by whom the world was created, and "the light" by which man could attain the knowledge of God. Philo believed that the Logos, or Word of God, would take human form.[25]

According to a Christian scholar writing about Philo's view of the Logos:

> Philo calls him the firstborn of God, the highest in age of the angels, the image of God. He even designates him as God (Theos), without the article which qualifies the perfect Being (ho Theos).[26]

To Philo the Word of God (Logos) is mediator between God and man. Philo wrote:

> For if we have not yet become fit to be thought sons of
> God yet we may be sons of His invisible image, the most
> holy Word.[27]

The ancient Christians, writing in defense of their doctrine that Jesus Christ is the Son of God, also used the language of Philo to make their point. Even today the term *Logos* is used for Jesus, and born-again Christians use the Greek word quite often. There are "born-again" magazines, several bookstores, and various ministries that use the name.

Although some of Philo's doctrines were viewed as heretical by the other scribes, it is clear that what he wrote on this subject was true because the Word of God did indeed appear among men as a mediator and he appeared in the image of God.

False Anti-Mormon Concept: Rejection of the "Heavenly Mother" Concept

Along with believing God could have a Son, *Philo* also believed that God has a companion. Philo called the "Mother" by the scriptural title of "Wisdom." According to a Jewish scholar who is an expert on the writings of Philo:

> Philo states unequivocally that God is the husband of
> Wisdom.[28]

Philo believed and wrote that God was the Father, and Wisdom the Mother of innumerable spirits, among whom was the first-begotten Logos. According to an ancient work called "The Wisdom of Solomon," which was accepted by the ancient Christians as inspired, God is the husband of Wisdom, and "She proclaims her noble birth in that it is given to her to live with God, and the Sovereign Lord of all loved her..."[29]

Like Philo, the ancient Christians shared a belief in a Heavenly Mother. *Origen* writes about Jesus:

> He left the Father and the heavenly Jerusalem, *the
> Mother*, and came to this earthly place, delivering up His
> soul into the hands of His enemies.[30]

The ancient Christian writer *Tertullian* wrote:

> In Him, at any rate, and *with Him, did Wisdom construct
> the universe*, He not being ignorant of what *She was
> making*.[31]

The mystery hidden in God about His Word (*Logos*) has been revealed in Christ Jesus, and the Saints and Christians in general talk about that revealed mystery all the time. The hidden mystery about Wisdom (*Sophia*) has not yet been fully revealed. That is why much less is said about Her.

All that is presently known, as Philo and the ancient Christians knew, is that a Heavenly Mother exists. If anti-Mormon *gainsayers* dismiss Wisdom, they shall dismiss the Word as well because early sources refer to both of them.

Anti-Mormon adversaries conveniently overlook the writings of early Christian leaders who assert the existence of a Heavenly Mother, preferring instead to deceptively portray the Heavenly Mother concept as an unwarranted figment of modern Mormon imagination.

False Anti-Mormon Concept: Rejection of Evidence of the Plurality of Gods

Latter-day Saints worship God the Father, but they also acknowledge that there are many who inherit the Father's power and glory and ultimately attain the powers of godhood. The Prophet Joseph Smith said:

> Paul says, "There is one glory of the sun, and another glory of the moon, and another glory of the stars; for one star differeth from another star in glory. So also is the resurrection of the dead." They who obtain the glorious resurrection from the dead, are exalted far above principalities, powers, thrones, dominions and angels, and are expressly declared to be *heirs of God and joint heirs with Jesus Christ, all having eternal power.* These Scriptures are a mixture of very strange doctrines to the Christian world, who are blindly led by the blind. I will refer to another scripture. "Now," says God, when He visited Moses in the bush (Moses was a stammering sort of boy like me) God said, "Thou shalt be a God unto Aaron, and he shall be thy spokesman." I believe those Gods that God reveals as Gods to be the sons of God, and all cry, "Abba, Father!" *Sons of God who exalt themselves to be Gods, even before the foundation of the world, are the only Gods I have reverence for.*[32]

God has many sons who bear His exalted title because of their faithfulness. To them and their descendants the Father is God of gods, or the Most High God, as the Bible repeatedly testifies:

And Melchizedek king of Salem brought forth bread and wine: and he was a priest of the *most high God*.

And he blessed him, and said, Blessed be Abram of the *most high God*, possessor of heaven and earth:

And blessed be the *most high God*, which hath delivered thine enemies into thy hand. (Genesis 14:18-20)

And Abram said to the king of Sodom, I have lift up mine hand unto the LORD, the *most high God*, the possessor of heaven and earth. (Genesis 14:22)

He hath said, which heard the words of God, and knew the knowledge of the *most High*. (Numbers 24:16)

But there are also numerous references in the Bible to a plurality of Gods. Note that these references are not speaking of heathen deities, nor of pagan gods. These are speaking of divine personages who dwell on high. Though they are not Gods of this earth, their existence is clearly and reputably acknowledged in the Bible, and they are alluded to with respect by inspired Biblical authors.

Who is like unto thee, O LORD, *among the gods*? (Exodus 15:11)

Now I know that the LORD is *greater than all gods*. (Exodus 18:11)

For the LORD your God is *God of gods*, and *Lord of lords, a great God*. (Deuteronomy 10:17)

For thou, LORD, art high above all the earth: thou art *exalted above all gods*. (Psalm 97:9)

For I know that the LORD is great, and that our Lord is *above all gods*. (Psalm 135:5)

O give thanks unto *the God of gods*: for his mercy endureth for ever. (Psalm 136:2)

I will praise thee with my whole heart: *before the gods will I sing praise to thee*. (Psalm 138:1)

...the *God of gods*. (Daniel 11:36)

Jesus answered them, Is it not written in your law, I said, *ye are gods*? (John 10:34)

For though there be that are called gods, whether in heaven or in earth, (as *there be gods many, and lords many*,)

But to us there is but one God, the Father, of whom are all things, and we in him; and one Lord Jesus Christ, by whom are all things, and we by him. (1 Corinthians 8:5)

These verses, and many more verses in the Bible, clearly indicate that the Biblical prophets and writers knew and taught that there are many who have become Gods. And these verses are not speaking of false gods—pagan deities. They're speaking of Gods in the heavens—beings accepted and respected by God the Father and the Lord Jesus Christ.

Thus it is clear that both the Bible and the ancient Christian writers taught that there is a plurality of gods. The Latter-day Saints proclaim that God has, through this dispensation, simply restored the ancient Christian faith; for which many sincere Christians have been looking and praying for centuries.

And again, this fundamental Biblical doctrine has been rejected by anti-Mormon agitators, who attempt to misrepresent Latter-day Saint doctrine on the subject, portraying it as unscriptural.

False Anti-Mormon Concept: Rejection of Evidence that Jesus Was Married

Another concept which anti-Mormon adversaries distort and for which they intentionally ignore conclusions drawn by competent Christian scholars, is the large body of evidence which seemingly indicates that Jesus was married while here in mortality. They assert the teaching that Christ was married to be Latter-day Saint doctrine, while in fact no official LDS doctrine exists concerning the marital status of Jesus Christ during his mortal ministry. There is no firm scriptural basis nor official pronouncement issued by the First Presidency on the subject, so Latter-day Saints have no official doctrinal stance on the matter.

There is, however, some strong historical evidence on the subject, and many Christian scholars have taken the stance that Jesus was married. Only a small portion of that evidence can be cited in this context.

Some Latter-day Saints have adopted the personal belief that Jesus was married, based on the evidence and opinions of those researchers. For instance, according to Jedediah M. Grant, a latter-day apostle,

> The grand reason why the gentiles and philosophers of his school persecuted Jesus Christ was because he had so many wives; there were Elizabeth and Mary and a host of others that followed him.[33]

What have various non-LDS scholars had to say on the subject? Christian scholar C. J. De Catanzaro tells his readers that in one ancient Christian text, "Mary Magdalene is referred to as Jesus' spouse."[34]

And according to Christian scholar William E. Phipps, "Some other ancient manuscripts support the assertion...that Mary Magdalene was Jesus' wife."[35] Phipps adds that "This authentic tradition would outweigh the late speculation and dogma in Gentile Christianity that Jesus was unmarried."[36]

According to Phipps and others who have investigated the subject, the early belief about Jesus being married was replaced by a later speculation that He couldn't have been, mainly because of the influx of pagan philosophy into Christianity.[37] Dr. M. Zvi Udley has written:

> *Did Jesus have children? There seems to be evidence that such was the case*; in 1873 M. Clermont Gannaeu discovered near Bethany on the Mount of Offense certain sarchephagi of extremely ancient times.[38]

Dr. Udley goes on to say that on one of the tombstones there was the name "SIMEON, SON OF JESUS" and that the other names on the tombstones bore the names of the persons mentioned in the Gospels near the site of the village of Bethany. This Simeon was at one time the Bishop of Jerusalem, and Dr. Udley concludes:

> In all probability *Simeon was a son of Jesus and Martha*, and was that child who appeared at the crucifixion.[39]

The Latter-day Saints, as a church, have no established doctrine concerning whether or not Jesus was married. But some LDS individuals acknowledge that numerous clues seem to indicate that He may have been, and they recognize that many non-Mormon Biblical scholars also conclude that Jesus had one or more wives while here on earth.

Anti-Mormon adversaries, however, attempt to assert that it is official LDS doctrine that Jesus was married, which is not true. They also refuse to recognize the research of many non-Mormon scholars whose research indicates that the Savior was married and had a family, attempting to make it appear to the world that the possibility of his married status is without evidence and is purely a Mormon belief, one not shared by others.

False Anti-Mormon Concept: Social Statistics Fail to Demonstrate the Fruits of Mormonism

Mormon Saints sometimes cite the Bible passage "by their fruits ye shall know them" (Matthew 7:20), accompanying it with recitations of the results of various comparative studies which seem to depict Mormons in a favorable light. But anti-Mormon critics often try to turn this line of thought against them by attempting to report negative statistical data from various sociological studies. Yet, when one checks their alleged sources of information, one frequently comes up blank. The "evidence" they cite usually is non-existent, or taken out of context and presented in a manner designed to present a warped portrayal of the truth.

Even the slightest amount of research shows that LDS "fruits" really compare quite favorably in many fields of endeavor and in numerous aspects of day-to-day life style. For instance, the U. S. Government did a study of illegitimate birth rates during the years from 1970-76. Of the 39 states included in the study, Utah ranked 39th, the lowest of all, with a birth rate per thousand of only 33.0. "Born-again" Christian states such as Alabama (7th), Tennessee (11th) and Missouri (13th), were very high; as were the "born-again" Christian states of Texas with a rate of 89.4, and Oklahoma with a rate of 89.6.[40]

In 1975, Utah had a divorce rate of 5.1, while "born-again" Christian states such as Oklahoma (7.6) and Texas (7.3) had substantially higher rates.[41] Divorce rates in 1970 were even more revealing. In 1970 the divorce rate for Salt Lake City, Utah was 4.1. Provo, Utah, with a much higher percentage of Latter-day Saints, had a divorce rate of only 2.8, an extremely low rate. In contrast, "born-again" Christian cities such as Springfield, Missouri (6.4), Columbus, Georgia (6.5), Chattanooga, Tennessee (5.6), Oklahoma City, Oklahoma (6.6), Tulsa, Oklahoma (9.4), and Witchita Falls (5.6) had much higher rates of divorce than the cities with predominately LDS populations for the same year. Latter-day Saints who marry in the temple have extremely low divorce rates, especially compared to the divorce rate of other Christians in Utah.

Utah is ranked 47th among the states in venereal disease; "born-again" Christian states were ranked much higher because their venereal disease problem is far more extensive.[42]

The same type of comparison holds true in the matter of mental health. According to Dr. Joe J. Christensen:

> It is interesting to note how the average number of daily resident patients in state mental hospitals throughout the country compares with that of the state of Utah, where members of the Church constitute the majority. One study, prepared by the Joint Information Service of the American Psychiatric Association and the National Association for Mental Health, indicated that the number of average daily resident patients in public mental hospitals per 100,000 civilian population was 61.0 in 1964 and 54.8 in 1966 in Utah, compared with a national average of 262.3 in 1964 and 237.9 in 1966. Utah has consistently been ranked 51st in comparison with all other states and the District of Columbia.[43]

False Anti-Mormon Concept: Mormons Pass Themselves Off as "Just Another" Middle-class Fundamentalist Religion

Another charge made by the *gainsayers* is that:

> The Mormon Church has not only brainwashed its own members, but almost everyone else into viewing the Church as just another middle-class fundamentalist Christian denomination. Yet in actuality Mormons never refer to themselves as Christians but take pride in using the term "Saints," believing themselves to be far superior in enlightenment, truth, and knowledge to those Christians lost deep in apostasy.[44]

Here anti-Mormon adversaries claim that Mormons brainwash everyone into believing that they are just another middle-class fundamentalist denomination. And at the same time they claim that Mormons never refer to themselves as Christians. Mormons are surely being charged with amazing stunts. Never have I seen, read, or heard from anyone within the Church that the Latter-day Saints are trying to brainwash, or convince people in any other way, that they are just an average, run-of-the-mill, "just another" fundamentalist Christian denomination.

To the contrary, Latter-day Saints boldly proclaim, as the former-day Saints did in the time of Jesus and His Prophet John, that God has again opened another gospel dispensation, that the heavens are open once more after a long, dark age of apostasy, and that Jesus has sent a great prophet by the name of Joseph Smith to set up a Kingdom for the coming King, who is Jesus Christ.

The Church, while very willing to work hand-in-hand with other Churches in efforts to solve various social problems, displays no inclination to "blend in" as just another Church. It in no way has abandoned its unwavering proclamation that it is the "The only true and living church upon the face of the whole earth" (D&C 1:30).

False Anti-Mormon Concept: Latter-day Saints Don't Refer to Themselves as "Christians" and Abuse the Term "Saint"

In the same vein, anti-Mormon adversaries say that the Saints never refer to themselves as "Christians." This foolishly false assertion ignores numerous statements on the subject made by Latter-day Saints, such as this forthright announcement by Brigham Young: *"We are Christians professedly,* according to our religion."[45]

But an even more foolish assertion made by anti-Mormon accusers is the claim that Latter-day Saints pride themselves in using the term "Saint," and that they believe themselves to be far superior in enlightenment to those Christians lost in apostasy. Mormons do refer to themselves as the "Saints" or the "Latter-day Saints" much more often than they refer to themselves merely as "Christians," because that is the term the Church members in New Testament times used to refer to themselves.

In the New Testament, the ancient disciples of Jesus Christ only referred to themselves as Christians once (1 Peter 4:16), but they called themselves by the title of Saints many times (Matthew 27:52; Acts 9:13, 32, 41; Romans 1:7; 8:27; 12:13; 15:25; 1 Corinthians 1:2; 6:2; 14:33; 2 Corinthians 1:1; 8:4; 9:12; Ephesians 1:1; 2:19; 3:8; 4:12; 5:3; 6:18; Philippians 1:1; Colossians. 1:2; 1 Thessalonians 3:13; 2 Thessalonians 1:10; Hebrews 6:10; 13:24; Jude 1:3; Revelation 5:8; 8:3; 13:10; 14:12; 15:3; 16:6; 17:6; 18:24; 20:9).

Furthermore, Latter-day Saints are known to themselves as "Christians" and "Saints," and not as Christians and Roman Catholics, nor Christians and Episcopalians, nor Christians and Methodists, or Baptists, Presbyterians, Adventists, Jehovah's Witnesses, Pentecostals, Christadelphians, Christian Scientists, Lutherans, or any other name for a church men have devised without inspired instruction from God on the matter.

Do the Latter-day Saints believe that they are superior to other Christians? No, they believe that God is far superior to all mankind, and that when He speaks again from the heavens they should heed his message. They are commanded by the Lord to share this message with all mankind: that Jesus lives, and that He has set up His latter-day kingdom on the earth in preparation for His glorious return.

Was it prideful for the Saints in the time of Jesus to go by the name their Lord gave them, and to announce to the world that God had separated the dark clouds of apostasy and spoken to His prophet John and sent His Only Beloved Son to be a sacrifice for sin? The ministers of the other churches thought it was very prideful and arrogant for the despised Nazarenes to call themselves Messianists and Saints. So much so that the cult fighters spent much time and effort to revile, say all manner of evil against, and mock Jesus, His prophet John, and the Saints.

False Anti-Mormon Concept: Mormons Teach Salvation by "Works," not by "Grace"

While I served my mission, people influenced by anti-LDS propaganda repeatedly parroted the false understanding of the Mormon doctrine of salvation which is continually disseminated by modern *gainsayers*. They told me that I didn't believe in Jesus and that I believed that a certain number of brownie points would get me into heaven. If and when they would let up a bit from reciting their anti-Mormon propaganda, I would try to share with them my testimony and explain the truth about the matter, occasionally with marvelous results.

In the LDS-written *Bible Dictionary* that missionaries carry with them, under the subject "Atonement" it says:

> Jesus Christ, as the Only Begotten Son of God and the only sinless person to live on this earth, was the only one capable of making an atonement for mankind. By his selection and fore-ordination in the Grand Council before the world was formed, his divine Sonship, his sinless life, the shedding of his blood in the garden of Gethsemane, his death on the cross and subsequent bodily resurrection from the grave, he made a perfect atonement for all mankind. All are covered *unconditionally* as pertaining to the fall of Adam. Hence, all shall rise from the dead with immortal bodies, because of Jesus' atonement. "For as in Adam all die, even so in Christ shall all be made alive" (1 Cor. 15:22), and all little children are innocent at birth. The atonement is *conditional*, however, so far as each person's individual sins are concerned, and touches every one to the degree that he has faith in Jesus Christ, repents of his sins, and obeys the gospel.[46]

In other words, because of Adam's fall, two deaths occurred: a separation of body and spirit called physical death, and a separation between God and man called spiritual death. Because of Adam, all men die, and because of the Atonement of Christ all shall live again, or be resurrected. Thus all are saved from physical death. But being saved from spiritual death is predicated on their personal relationship to Christ. Because of Christ's atonement, men are saved from spiritual death when they accept Him as Lord and keep His commandments.

Here's where the syntax gets sticky. When a "born-again" Christian accepts Christ as Lord it usually means that he's repeated a prayer which the minister or someone has suggested that he repeat. After that, he supposedly is saved. "Born-again" Christians often refer to the very date and hour of that prayer as the moment of their salvation. When a Latter-day Saint accepts Jesus as Lord, it means much more than repeating a short prayer. A Lord is someone who gives commands and he obeys. What good is calling Jesus Lord if men don't obey His commandments?

There is still much argument going on today among "born-again" Christians about the meaning of salvation. One theory is called the "eternal security" of the believer. This theory holds that after one makes that initial mouth confession, inviting Jesus into his heart, he is saved forever, and nothing can change that, no matter what.

Other "born-again" Christians argue that many people fall from grace after they are initially saved; hence, salvation is more of an active, ongoing thing that a once-and-for-all-time experience.

The "eternal security" "born-again" Christians counter the latter belief, asserting that people who were once saved and then fall from grace were never really saved in the first place. The other "born-again" Christians refute the "eternal security" viewpoint by saying that there is no such thing as "eternal security" because if many people already saved aren't really saved after they fall from grace, then how is one to know that he has "eternal security"? Both sides sincerely believe they are right and the other side is wrong, and they offer numerous Bible scriptures to "prove" their case.

Out of this confusion, it was refreshing to see the Biblical truth as presented by the Saints. While on my mission, one woman told me the date and time when she was saved, and asked me, "You Mormons don't even know if you're saved. Do you know when you were saved?" "Yes ma'am!" I said confidently. "I was saved on the 6th of April, 33 A.D.!"

Sometimes we were accused, after anti-Mormon adversaries regretfully conceded that Mormons *do* look to Christ's atoning blood for salvation, that Latter-day Saints believe that Christ paid for their personal sins in the Garden of Gethsemane and not on the cross, as is taught in the Bible. The Saints believe that Christ began to atone for the sins of the world as soon as He began to suffer and shed His blood. He began his suffering for all mankind in the Garden, and His suffering and shedding of blood ended on the cross with His death.

One ex-Mormon for Jesus said to me, "You can't look at Gethsemane for any atoning value—that was just some personal suffering of Jesus!" I replied,

> What suffering of Jesus was not personal? According to the Bible, Jesus suffered so in the Garden that He bled from every pore, and the tortures He endured under the hands of the Romans fulfilled the prophecies which foretold that by His wounds our transgressions were paid for, and that by His stripes we are healed. His atoning sacrifice for us did not begin on the cross, but began before that and was fulfilled on the cross. The Saints look at the cross

not as the beginning but as the climatic end of an infinite
atonement.

In the days of the beginning of the Protestant movement, the leaders of
the Roman Catholic Church had men sell what was called indulgences.
For a certain payment of money to the church, one could be forgiven of
even the most terrible of sins. According to Catholic doctrine, one is saved
by the body and blood of Christ in the sacraments of the Lord's Supper,
or communion; the bread and wine only saving, or becoming effectual,
on account of personal righteousness in the form of doing good deeds like
alms-giving, penance, etc. Many good Catholics *protested* such ideas about
salvation as being wrong and unscriptural, these becoming the Protestant
Christians.

Martin Luther proclaimed that while reading an epistle of Paul he
discovered that it was by *faith*, and not the works of the law, that man is
saved. Of course, by *works* Paul meant the works of the Law of Moses.
Often, especially to missionaries, this statement made by the Apostle Paul
is quoted:

> For by grace are ye saved through faith; and that not of
> yourselves; it is the gift of God:
> Not of works, lest any man should boast. (Ephesians
> 2:8-9)

Sometimes the finger of accusation is pointed at Latter-day Saints as being
boasters, and the assertion is made that Mormons think that they can save
themselves without Christ's help. Usually, the ones doing the pointing are
ignorant of how Latter-day Saints view salvation. The Saints firmly believe
that the grace of God is absolutely necessary for men to be saved. They
do not believe that they can save themselves from spiritual or physical death
by their own good works, because they know no matter how perfect they
try to be, they will always fall short of the glory of God.

In the LDS *Bible Dictionary*, it says under "Grace":

> *It is through the grace of the Lord Jesus, made possible
> by his atoning sacrifice, that mankind will be raised in
> immortality,* every person receiving his body from the grave
> in a condition of everlasting life. It is likewise *through the
> grace of the lord* that individuals, through faith in the
> atonement of Jesus Christ and repentance of their sins,
> receive strength and assistance to do good works that they
> otherwise would not be able to maintain if left to their own
> means. This *grace is an enabling power* that allows men

and women to lay hold on eternal life and exaltation after they have expended their own best efforts....*It is truly the grace of Jesus Christ that makes salvation possible.*[47]

Often, missionaries and other Latter-day Saints try to explain to others that they do believe that salvation is through faith in the atonement of Jesus Christ, but they also use the admonition of James:

> Even so *faith, if it hath not works, is dead*, being alone.
> (James 2:17)

Martin Luther, in his strong reaction against the Catholic doctrine of salvation by good works, at first condemned the epistle of James. He called it an "epistle of straw," suggesting it was fit only for the fire because it seemed to disagree with his theory about salvation. Later in life, however, Luther saw clearly that faith had to be an active thing, or it wasn't faith at all.[48]

The Savior said that His people had to be baptized by water and by the Spirit to enter the Kingdom of God, but most "born-again" Christians today deny this because they claim baptism is a "work." However, I read recently in an evangelical Christian magazine where the author was raising the question of whether or not the Protestant "mouth confession" hadn't replaced baptism as the saving good work of the Christian.

As the churches of Christendom battle between themselves about salvation, the Saints know assuredly that salvation comes by grace through the atoning blood of their Redeemer Jesus Christ, when one has faith in Him. Their scriptures proclaim it. Their prophets and apostles proclaim it, and whosoever says that they deny these things is only trying to deceive.

False Anti-Mormon Concept: Mormons Use Water in the Sacrament Because They Reject the Blood of Christ

What other reasons do the *gainsayers* give in their false assertions that Latter-day Saints are not Christians? They claim, for instance, that

> Because they reject the full value of Christ's blood poured out in death for sin on the cross, Mormons take bread and *water* at their communion services instead of bread and *wine* (or grape juice) as Christ commanded....[49]

The truth is, according to the Saints, the blood of Christ gave the free *unconditional* gift to all men of the resurrection, and the blood of Christ *also* gives the free *conditional* gift of Eternal Life to those that follow Him. To the "born-again" Christian, the blood of Christ only affects those who conditionally follow Him (accept Him as Lord). I ask, which belief has a fuller value?

The Saints, in the early days, did use wine in the partaking of the sacrament, but the enemies of the Saints, because they didn't believe that God had opened a new dispensation, plotted to poison the wine that the Saints were using in their sacrament. The Prophet Joseph inquired to the Lord about the problem and received this response:

> Listen to the voice of Jesus Christ, your Lord, your God, and your Redeemer, whose word is quick and powerful.
>
> For, behold, I say unto you, that *it mattereth not what ye shall eat or what ye shall drink when ye partake of the sacrament, if it so be that ye do it with an eye single to my glory*—remembering unto the Father my body which was laid down for you, and my blood which was shed for the remission of your sins. (D & C 27:1-2)

Every week, among Latter-day Saints all over the world, this very same prayer is offered as part of the sacramental ordinance:

> O God, the Eternal Father, we ask thee in the name of thy Son, Jesus Christ, to bless and sanctify this water to the souls of all those who drink of it, that they may *do it in remembrance of the blood of thy Son, which was shed for them*; that they may witness unto thee, O God, the Eternal Father, *that they do always remember him*, that they may have his Spirit to be with them. Amen.

To assert that Mormons reject the full value of the atoning blood of Jesus Christ is, once again, an intentional falsehood circulated by *gainsayers* seeking to profit from the falsehoods they circulate.

False Anti-Mormon Concept: Mormons Are Not Christians Because They Don't Display the Cross

The last part of the accusation cited above says that Latter-day Saints are not Christians because they display no cross inside or outside their chapels and temples.

I ask them, "Do you not know that the *cross* is used in occult symbols? Does that mean all Christians are occultists because the cross is used by occultists?" Their own logic affects them as much as the Latter-day Saints. According to the *gainsayers*:

> Our ultimate goal is to see *Christian crosses* replacing the naked spires and idols atop every LDS edifice in the

world, signifying that the Mormon Church, from the top
down, has officially repented and turned to the true and
living Savior.[50]

It's interesting how anti-Mormon critics choose to call LDS spires
"naked," as if to suggest they somehow are immoral. How does one clothe
a spire? These critics certainly don't want to clothe them. They want to
replace them.

The spires which accompany most Latter-day Saint buildings signify the
resurrection and ascension into heaven of their Lord and Savior Jesus Christ.
The Saints prefer to focus on the glory of the Lord's resurrection rather
than the agony of His crucifixion.

I shall now quote from a very popular fundamentalist Christian writer
and scholar, the Reverend Alexander Hislop, to show in part just why the
Latter-day Saints don't use the amulet of the cross:

That which is now called the Christian cross *was
originally no Christian emblem at all, but the mystic Tau
of the Chaldeans and Egyptians....Now, this pagan symbol
seems first to have crept into the Christian Church in Egypt,
and generally into Africa.* A statement of Tertullian, about
the middle of the third century, shows how much, by that
time, the Church of Carthage was infected with the old
leaven. *Egypt especially, which was never thoroughly
evangelized, appears to have taken the lead in bringing
in the Pagan symbol.* The first form of that which is called
the *Christian Cross*, found on *Christian* monuments there,
is the unequivocal Pagan Tau, or the Egyptian "*Sign of
Life*." Let the reader pursue the following statement of Sir
G. Wilkinson: "A still more curious fact may be mentioned
respecting this hieroglyphic character (the tau), that *the
early Christians of Egypt adopted it in lieu of the cross,
which was afterward substituted for it*, prefixing it to
inscriptions in the same manner as the cross in *latter times*.
For, though Dr. Young has some scruples in believing the
statement of Sir A. Edmonstone, that it holds that position
in the sepulchers of the great Oasis, I can attest that such
is the case, and that *numerous inscriptions, headed by the
Tau, are preserved to the present day on early Christian
monuments*." The drift of this statement is evidently this,
that in Egypt *the earliest form of that which has since been
called the cross, was no other than the "Crux Ansata,"*

or "Sign of Life," borne by Osiris and all the Egyptian gods; that the *ansa* or "handle" was afterwards dispensed with, and that it became the simple Tau, or ordinary cross, as it appears at this day, and that *the design of its first employment on the sepulchers, therefore, could have no reference to the crucifixion of the Nazarene, but was simply the result of the attachment to old and long cherished Pagan symbols*, which is always strong in those who, with the adoption of the Christian name and profession, are still, to a large extent, Pagan in heart and feeling. *This, and this only, is the origin and the worship of the cross.* This, no doubt, will appear all very strange and very incredible to those who have read Church history...even among Protestants....[51]

Note, now, that I have not quoted from a Mormon scholar, but from a highly read "born-again" Christian scholar who has told us that the cross, as an amulet, is Pagan. Are the Latter-day Saints then un-Christian because they do not use this symbol on top of their buildings, or inside them, nor hang this pagan amulet around their necks?

The ancient Pharisees hypocritically and boastfully displayed their phylacteries (strips of scripture fastened to the forehead or arm; see Matthew 23:5) as a visual sign of their "righteousness." Today at least one anti-LDS minister wears a huge leather cross around his neck, as if he is saying, "Look at me, I follow the Lord!"

In the film, "The God Makers," in one scene it is insinuated that Mormons are occultists and asserts that in early Mormon architecture a goat is displayed.[52] Ed Decker shows the attorneys in the film (who are actually actors) a book showing the Goat of Mendes, a Satanic symbol, as if early Mormons had used that symbol. The symbol is the Goat's head in a five-pointed star. Latter-day Saints have never used that symbol!

On the outside of the Salt Lake Temple there are five-pointed stars, but no goat heads. Just what is the five-pointed star, and why is it on the outside of the Salt Lake Temple? According to the Reverend Friedrich Rest, in his book *Our Christian Symbols*:

The five-pointed star is symbolic of the Epiphany, or the manifest nature of God. In Matt. 2:2, it is recorded that the wise men came from the east and asked, "Where is he who has been born king of the Jews? For we have seen his star in the east, and have come to worship him." The five-pointed star is the star out of Jacob (Num. 24:17),

Jesus Christ, the bright and morning star (Rev. 22:16) who manifested himself to the Gentiles.[53]

Is this symbol un-Christian? You can't get any more Christian than the Star of the East because it represents Jesus Himself. So what has happened to the *gainsayers'* assertions that Latter-day Saints are not Christian because of symbols used in their architecture? Have they told the truth? No! Once again their claims are shown to be based on distortions and falsehoods.

This chapter has been a brief refutation of some of the major accusations that are the very foundation of the film and book "The God Makers" and other similar anti-Mormon works. Have the *gainsayers* been accurate in portraying what Latter-day Saints "really" believe? It is obvious that accuracy has not been their objective. Instead, they have intentionally sought to distort the truth and to malign the Saints.

What Jesus said in response to His accusers seems to apply equally well to those modern *gainsayers*:

Ye are of your father the devil, and the lusts of your father ye will do. He was a murderer from the beginning, and abode not in the truth, because there is no truth in him. When he speaketh a lie, he speaketh of his own: for he is a liar, and the father of it.

And because I tell you the truth, ye believe me not.

Which of you convinceth me of sin? And if I say the truth, why do ye not believe me?

He that is of God heareth God's words: ye therefore hear them not, because ye are not of God. (John 8:44-47)

8
Answering Anti-Mormon Objections: The "Truth Will Prevail" Dialogue

Saints Commanded to Preach to All the World

When the Savior was upon the earth in His mortal ministry, He gave a command to His disciples to preach the Gospel to all the world. His instructions were:

> Go ye therefore, and teach all nations, baptizing them in the name of the Father, and of the Son, and of the Holy Ghost;
> Teaching them to observe all things whatsoever I have commanded you; and, lo, I am with you alway, even unto the end of the world. Amen. (Matthew 28:19-20)

The Saints of the Most High try to obey that command of their Master. That is why the Church sends out thousands of missionaries each year to spread the Gospel around the world. They proclaim that Jesus is the Christ, the Son of the living God, and that Joseph the Seer is His Prophet in these last days. LDS missionaries labor at their own expense because they love the Lord and seek to obey His command to preach.

Gainsayers Attempting to Counter the LDS Missionary Effort

There are some in the world who attempt to counter this great missionary effort and seek to destroy testimonies by spreading false reports about the Church, its teachings and practices. The *gainsayers* now have a national and international program in which they train people to become anti-Mormon "experts" at the local level. In the near future, LDS missionaries will be constantly harassed with anti-Mormons who will locate their investigators through friends, relatives, and co-workers. Missionaries, and LDS members involved in missionary work, will need to be prepared to give answers to the sincere investigators that seek them out.

The "Truth Will Prevail" Dialogue—Suggested Answers to Anti-Mormon Propaganda Ploys

The following dramatization deals with accusation techniques currently used by anti-Mormons, and shows ways to refute them using only the scriptures. In the dialogue, the sincere investigator "Linda" responds well to the teachings of the Latter-day Saint elders, but the anti-Mormon minister, her Uncle Ed, is never convinced, no matter how obvious or scriptural the answer given.

This "dialogue" is *not* intended to train Latter-day Saints to "Bible bash," but is designed to suggest possible answers to anti-Mormon propaganda ploys and to answer anti-Mormon challenges effectively. Subjects are not treated fully, but enough is supplied to suggest ways to handle various objections quickly and effectively.

*   *   *   *   *   *   *   *   *   *   *   *   *

The missionaries are outside the door of Linda's apartment. They are concerned because she didn't come for her baptismal interview.

Elder Smith: "Well, let's try this again, Elder."

Elder Jones: "I sure hope she'll be home this time. I wonder why she didn't show up for her baptismal interview."

Elder Smith: "Let's see if we can find out. I know she felt the Spirit when we taught her." (Elder Jones knocks on the door.)

Elder Jones: "We both know she had a testimony."

Elder Smith: "What do you mean *had?*"

Elder Jones: "Don't you remember? Linda told us that she had an uncle who's an anti-Mormon minister."

Elder Smith: "Great! Do you think he's gotten to her?"

Elder Jones: "It certainly is beginning to look that way."

Elder Smith: "I hope not."

(Linda opens the door very slowly and shows concern when she sees the Elders.)

Linda: "Oh, Elders, I, ah, didn't expect you back so soon."

Elder Smith: "We tried calling a number of times, and we came over yesterday...."

Linda: "Oh, ah, I wasn't home!"

Elder Jones: "We missed you at the interview, but that's fine—we know things come up."

Linda: "That's right—I'm really sorry—well, you see, I've had a relative visiting me for the past week now...."

Elder Smith: "Your uncle?"

Linda: "That's right! How did you know?"

Elder Jones: "Just an educated guess on my companion's part. May we come in?"

Linda: "Well, I...."

Uncle Ed: (A voice is heard from far inside the house.) "Linda, who's that at the door?"

Linda: "Ah, huh, just some friends of mine, Uncle Ed."

Uncle Ed: "They wouldn't be the Mormon missionaries, would they?"

Linda: "Yeah, ah...."

Uncle Ed: "Well, have them come in—I'd like to ask them a couple of questions."

Elder Jones: "Your Uncle Ed seems to be a pretty good guesser too."

Linda: "Ah, yeah—well—why don't you come in?"

Uncle Ed: "Hello. My name is Ed Brown, and you're...?"

Elder Jones: "I'm Elder Jones."

Uncle Ed: "Hello—very happy to meet you."

Elder Jones: "And this is my companion, Elder Smith."

Elder Smith: "How do you do, sir?"

Uncle Ed: "Couldn't be better—I've had good news recently. It's great meeting you two fine young men."

Elder Jones: "Thank you very much."

Uncle Ed: "Please sit down, boys—Linda has some news for you, and you might not want to remain standing for it."

Elder Smith: "Thank you, we will sit down."

Elder Jones: "What news is this, Linda?"

Linda: "Ah, well, you see, I was going to call you when I got the chance...."

Uncle Ed: "Linda, could you get to the point with these young men?"

Linda:	"All right, Uncle Ed. You see, Elders, I consider both of you my friends and all, but I've changed my mind about being baptized into your Church."
Elder Smith:	"Is that true, Linda?"
Linda:	"Yes, I think so."
Uncle Ed:	"Of course it's so, and praise the Lord for it. When I heard from her parents that you boys had her under, eh, were teaching her, I came straight over, and I've been sharing the biblical truths about Jesus and Christianity with her."
Elder Jones:	"Is that what you've been studying with your uncle, Linda?"
Linda:	"Well, not exactly. Uncle Ed has been showing me stuff on Mormonism for about the last...."
Uncle Ed:	(Uncle Ed cuts Linda off.) "That's right. You see, young men, I have no doubt in the world that you two are very sincere in your convictions that Mormonism is of God, and that Joseph Smith communicated with extraterrestrial humanoids, but, you see, Mormonism is diametrically opposed to biblical Christianity."
Elder Smith:	"No, Sir, I bear you testimony that...."
Uncle Ed:	(Angrily) "Now just wait a minute! I know what you're going to do—you're going to give your 'pat-answer' testimony."
Elder Jones:	"Mr. Brown, we're not here to get into an argument...."

Answer Investigator's Sincere Questions, Not Anti-Mormon Criticisms

Uncle Ed:	"No! No! I agree, and please don't get me wrong. I really admire you guys for coming out for two years to preach what you think you believe in, but all I'm asking is: Is Mormonism Christian? You *do* proclaim yourselves to be Christians, don't you?"
Elder Jones:	"Yes, we certainly do!"
Uncle Ed:	"All right then. All I'm asking is that we compare Mormonism with historic Christianity and see if it fits."
Elder Smith:	"Mr. Brown, what we're trying to say is that we have met with people like you before, and such situations typically turn into a Bible bash. We've observed that they're usually not seeking for truth and honest

	answers; they're trying to argue and debate. They bring a spirit of contention with them that drives away the Spirit of the Lord. We've even had people call us names when we pointed out scriptural passages that refuted their accusations. And then they'd flip flop from one subject to another when they'd find a particular line of reasoning wasn't holding up against us. So you see, it's both fruitless and pointless!"
Elder Jones:	"I agree with my companion. All throughout our discussions we teach from the Bible and testify to the things that we've· taught. And then we tell our investigators about the scripture in the epistle of James that reads, 'If any of you lack wisdom, let him ask of God, that giveth to all men liberally, and upbraideth not; and it shall be given him. But let him ask in faith, nothing wavering." (James 1:5-6)
Uncle Ed:	"I know all about that."
Elder Jones:	"Okay, but what we're trying to say is that one must go to God in prayer, and not trust himself nor anyone else but God to answer him, and he must ask sincerely."
Uncle Ed:	"Oh, don't get me wrong—I'm very sincere! If you can prove to me that Mormonism is biblical I'll become a Mormon, and I'll try to convince Linda likewise."
Elder Smith:	"Sir, Linda is the reason why we are here. Linda, may we meet with you and talk to you about the questions your uncle has raised?"
Linda:	"Sure, I...."
Uncle Ed:	"She *is* meeting with you. I'm meeting with you."
Elder Jones:	"Mr. Brown, we meant alone."
Uncle Ed:	"Ha, ha, I'm sorry, boys. If you have anything to say to her you say it to me!"
Linda:	"But Uncle Ed, I think...."
Uncle Ed:	"Linda, did you not agree with me the other evening that you would only see these young men again in my presence?"
Linda:	"I suppose I did, but now...."
Uncle Ed:	"Listen, I promised your parents that I would look after your spiritual welfare while I was here, and this I intend to do—you're a very important young woman to them and to me."

Linda: "All right, Uncle Ed. I'm sorry, Elders."

Uncle Ed: "Well, gentlemen, again, if you could clear up these few questions I have I would be most grateful."

Elder Smith: "No, Mr. Brown, we will not answer your questions."

Uncle Ed: "You see Linda, just like I told you. They can't answer because they don't have the answers."

Elder Jones: "That's not what my companion said, Mr. Brown. He said that we won't answer *your* questions, but we will answer Linda's."

Elder Smith: "That's right. Since she promised not to meet with us without you here then we must have you here, but we shall answer *her* questions."

Base Discussion on the Scriptures, Not Anti-Mormon Literature

Uncle Ed: "That's fine by me, because my questions *are* her questions. The first thing I want to bring up is in this book right here. Now, why is it that Brigham Young...."

Elder Smith: "May I see that book, Mr. Brown?"

Uncle Ed: "Why, ah, of course you may."

Elder Smith: "*The Mormon Delusion.* Mr. Brown, didn't you say to us just moments ago that Mormonism, as you call it, is diametrically opposed to what you call biblical Christianity?"

Uncle Ed: "Yes I did, but here you have to...."

Elder Smith: "Don't you believe that biblical Christianity can be proven directly from the Bible itself?"

Uncle Ed: "I most certainly do, and not only that, I can *prove* that Mormonism is incorrect directly from the Bible."

Elder Smith: "Very well then, Mr. Brown, then we shall use the scriptures, and only the scriptures in our discussion. Or don't you think the scriptures are sufficient?"

Uncle Ed: "Unlike you Mormons, I believe that the Bible is the inspired Word of God!"

Elder Smith: "Very good, Mr. Brown, then let's use the scriptures, and the scriptures alone."

Set Discussion "Ground Rules"

Elder Jones:	"And if we're going to have a rational discussion of these things we should have a few rules."
Uncle Ed:	"For instance?"
Elder Jones:	"I'd suggest that we agree on three rules. First, that each should be given his turn without being interrupted. Second, that we shouldn't argue over the true or false meaning of a scripture, but simply state what each believes about it; and third, that neither side will flip-flop from one subject to another until we've agreed the question we are discussing has been answered."
Uncle Ed:	"That sounds perfectly agreeable to me."
Elder Jones:	"And one more thing, Mr. Brown. Both sides should regard as sacred the things that the other side holds to be sacred. In other words, we should not deride nor belittle nor profane the other's worship."
Uncle Ed:	"I would never think of it. In fact, it is Mormonism that derides, belittles, and defames...."
Elder Jones:	"Do you agree to these terms, Sir? Linda?"
Uncle Ed:	"We agree to them, so let's get on with it."
Elder Smith:	"Okay, Linda, do you remember about prayer? We would like you to offer an opening...."
Uncle Ed:	"Now, wait, if there is any praying to do, then I must give it!"
Elder Smith:	"Perhaps we should just start with your questions, Linda."
Linda:	"I really don't know where to begin."

The Articles of Faith:
A Systematic Discussion Outline

Elder Smith:	"Do you remember our discussion of the Articles of Faith?"
Linda:	"Yes."
Elder Smith:	"Let's begin there. They provide a systematic outline for discussing the basic doctrines of Christianity. We'll read off an Article of Faith, and then you may ask us your questions about it. Is that agreeable with you?"
Linda:	"Yes, that would give some order and continuity to our discussion."

Elder Smith: "Good, let's use them as our discussion outline. Elder Jones, could you read for us the first Article of Faith?"

"Adam Is God" Objection Answered

Elder Jones: "Sure. It reads, 'We believe in God, the Eternal Father, and in His Son, Jesus Christ, and in the Holy Ghost.'"

Linda: "Elders, I can't remember everything my uncle said to me about that, but I remember him telling me that Brigham Young taught that Adam was God."

Uncle Ed: "That's right Linda, you young men doubtless have never heard this before, but your second prophet taught that Adam was God. But the Bible teaches us in Genesis that Adam was created by God out of the dust of the earth. To say he was God is not only ridiculous, but absolutely contrary to the Bible!"

Elder Smith: "I'm glad that you mentioned the book of Genesis, Mr. Brown, because that is where we can find the answer to Brigham Young's statement in which he refers to Adam as God. But, to answer Linda's question, let me first ask you a question. Who is the god of this world?"

Uncle Ed: "Why, ha, that's Jesus, of course, and I don't mean the Mormon Jesus!"

Elder Smith: "The Apostle Paul says, in 2nd Corinthians 4:3-4: 'But if our gospel be hid, it is hid to them that are lost: In whom *the god of this world hath blinded the minds of them which believe not*, lest the light of the glorious gospel of Christ, who is the image of God, should shine unto them.' So, Mr. Brown, according to the apostle Paul, who is the god of this world?"

Uncle Ed: "That scripture implies that it's Satan."

Elder Smith: "Exactly. Linda, your uncle has just said that Satan is the god of this world, but this was not always so. We read in Genesis 1:26 that God created Adam and Eve, and gave them dominion over this earth. It reads, 'And God said, Let us make man in our image, after our likeness: and *let them have dominion* over the fish of the sea, and over the fowl of the air, and over the cattle, and *over all the earth*, and over every creeping thing that creepeth upon the earth.' So, a Lord is one that has dominion, and the Bible teaches that God gave to Adam dominion over all the earth. But he fell because of transgression, partaking of the forbidden fruit, and Satan, that great deceiver, took over and claimed to be the god of this world in Adam's place. But when Jesus comes again, Satan will be bound for a thousand years and ultimately banished. Adam will then regain the dominion God gave him over this earth; ruling under God the Father and His Son Jesus."

Linda: "That explains why this earth is such an evil place, because Satan took dominion over it from Adam by deception."

"Only One God" Objection Answered

Uncle Ed: "You see, you admit that Adam is a God, but the Bible plainly teaches that there is only one God, not two, nor trillions of extraterrestrial spacemen like Mormonism believes. Listen to what it says in Isaiah 44:6. 'Thus saith the LORD the King of Israel, and his redeemer the LORD of hosts; I am the first, and I am the last; and beside me there is no God.' That verse alone puts an end to Mormonism, because Mormonism teaches people to worship many gods."

Linda: "How do you explain that, Elders?"

Elder Jones: "Linda, we do not worship many Gods. We worship God the Father in the name of Jesus Christ through the Holy Ghost. But let's look at what Isaiah was saying in context. Isaiah says in verses 8 and 9 of chapter 44 the following: 'Fear ye not, neither be afraid: have not I told thee from that time, and have declared it? ye are even my witnesses. *Is there a God beside me? yea, there is no God*; I know not any. They that *make a graven image* are all of them vanity; and *their delectable things* shall not profit; and they are their own witnesses; they see not, nor know; that they may be ashamed.' And in the next verse, verse 10, it reads, '*Who hath formed a god, or molten a graven image that is profitable for nothing?*' So, the Israelites were making heathen idols, gods of wood and stone and metal, and placing those false gods along side, or beside, their worship of the Lord. But the Lord says through His prophet Isaiah that He is their only God, and that the gods of the pagans are nothing more than dumb idols, the works of men's hands."

Elder Smith: "Linda, probably the best response we could give to this is the one given by the Apostle Paul in 1st Corinthians 8, verses 5 and 6: 'For *though there be that are called gods,* whether *in heaven* or in earth, (as *there be gods many, and lords many,*) But *to us there is but one God, the Father,* of whom are all things, and we in him; and one Lord Jesus Christ, by whom are all things, and we by him.'"

Uncle Ed: "Yes, but Paul meant to say that all these gods are false gods—they are idols!"

Elder Jones: "Not so, Mr. Brown. I have made a list here of scriptures in the Bible that speak of more than one God—passages that aren't referring to pagan dieties but to bonafied beings of the same order as our Heavenly Father. These passages call God the God of gods and the Most High God, clearly indicating that there are other Gods besides the Father and the Son. For instance, in Genesis 14:19 Melchizedek said, 'Blessed be Abram of the *most High God.*' Genesis 14:22 says, 'And Abram said to the king of Sodom. I have lift up mine hand unto the LORD, the *Most High God*, the....'"

Uncle Ed: "Well, what I want to know is about the over 4,000 changes in the Book of Mormon, and...."

Elder Smith: "Mr. Brown, do you remember about agreeing not to interrupt until we have a chance to answer, and sticking to one subject until it has been dealt with? Go ahead Elder Jones."

Elder Jones: "'...the possessor of heaven and earth.' Moses says in Exodus 15:11, 'Who is *like unto thee,* O LORD, *among the gods?*' And he says in Deuteronomy 10:17, 'For the LORD your God is *God of gods*, and *Lord of lords, a great God.*' David, in Psalm 97:9, says, 'For thou, LORD, art high above all the earth: *thou are exalted above all gods.*' And...."

Uncle Ed: "You boys don't understand a word of the Bible. These scriptures obviously are talking about idols!"

Elder Smith: "Are they, Mr. Brown? Using that logic, then, God would be the Idol of idols and the Most High Idol."

Uncle Ed:	"Eh, ah, what I meant to say is that those passages refer to judges and rulers."
Elder Jones:	"Then why don't the scriptures say judges and rulers, Mr. Brown?"
Uncle Ed:	"Oh, ha ha, I see what you're trying to do. Well, ha, I have something here that will give the death blow to your false prophet, Joseph Smith."
Elder Smith:	"Before we get to that, Mr. Brown, we would like to conclude on this subject by reiterating what Paul said. We believe in the One True God; He is our Heavenly Father. Under Him, and not beside of or along side of Him, there are those that are called "gods" whether in heaven, meaning the angels, or on earth."
Uncle Ed:	"That is blasphemy—you have no proof! You Mormons teach that God is just one of billions of other gods."
Elder Jones:	"What we teach, Mr. Brown, is what the Bible reveals. Namely, that angels and men are called gods."
Uncle Ed:	"Where is that found in the Bible?"
Elder Jones:	"Let's turn to Ephesians 3:14-15. The Apostle Paul writes: 'For this cause I bow my knees unto the Father of our Lord Jesus Christ, Of whom the *whole family in heaven and earth is named.*' What is the name of the Father of Jesus Christ?"
Linda:	"God!"

"God Is a Spirit" Objection Answered

Uncle Ed:	"Linda?.... Now, here is a scripture that you've probably never heard before. It says in the Bible that 'God is a Spirit,' and you can find that in John 4:24. What about that! You see, right here in this verse, Mormonism is destroyed!"
Elder Smith:	"Not so fast, Mr. Brown, let's take a closer look. According to your reading of this scripture we must leave our bodies to worship God, since the verse goes on to say, 'they that worship him must worship him *in spirit* and in truth.'"
Uncle Ed:	"That's right!"
Elder Jones:	"I believe in that version it says 'God is spirit' and not 'God is a Spirit.'"
Uncle Ed:	"Yes it does, so what of it?"

Elder Jones:	"We see that it is to be taken metaphorically, just as in 1st John 4:16 it says that: '*God is love*; and he that dwelleth in love dwelleth in God, and God in him,' or in 1st John 1:5 where it says '*God is light.*' Using your interpretation, Mr. Brown, then we must call God *a* light and *a* love, and we would have to leave our bodies, be *in* the Spirit, to worship Him correctly."
Elder Smith:	"In other words, Mr. Brown, some scriptures are figurative, not literal, and John 4:24 is clearly a figurative reference to God."

"Anthropomorphic Scriptures are Figurative" Objection Answered

Uncle Ed:	"What you've said is true. Some scriptures are figurative, and that's *exactly* why I can't accept your prophet, because you teach that God is a man, and not a Spirit, and that He has hands, fingers, toes, and eyes. I know where you get your scriptures to back this up, how it says in the Bible that the Lord has his eye upon us, and that He smells sweet savours, and about His mouth and hands and the rest, but what you boys don't understand is that *those* scriptures describing God in human form are just figurative, and I can prove this to you. In Psalm 36:7, here in the Bible, it says: 'How excellent is thy loving kindness, O God! therefore the children of men put their trust under the shadow of thy wings.' So there, you see, according to your interpretation of the Bible then, God must have wings!"
Elder Jones:	"Not quite, Mr. Brown. Maybe we can share this other scripture with you. But first, let's ask you a question: Do you believe that Jesus had a body? That He had eyes and fingers, and toes and a nose?"
Uncle Ed:	(Laughing) "What are you trying to get at?"
Elder Smith:	"Please answer our question, Mr. Brown."
Uncle Ed:	"Yes, I do. Of course He did!"
Elder Jones:	"All right, let's read here in Matthew chapter 23, verse 37. Jesus is speaking: 'O Jerusalem, Jerusalem, thou that killest the prophets, and stoneth them which are sent unto thee, how often would I have *gathered thy*

children together, even as a hen gathereth her chickens under her wings, and ye would not!''

Elder Smith: "Here, Mr. Brown, Jesus is referring to himself as a chicken. If this is only figurative language, then must all the other things the Bible says about the person of Jesus—that He walked, talked, saw, and that He spoke with a mouth, and so forth—must all that be figurative language as well?"

Uncle Ed: "Of course not! That would be ridiculous!"

Elder Jones: "Exactly!"

Linda: "Oh, I see what you mean!"

Elder Smith: "Good, Linda! We know in the Book of Genesis that God walked with Adam in the cool of the day, and in Exodus it reads that God spoke with Moses face-to-face. And in the book of Daniel, the Prophet Daniel had a vision of God where He is described as having a face as the appearance of lightning, and his eyes as lamps of fire, and his arms and feet like in color to polished brass, and...."

Uncle Ed: "What I want to know about is why do Mormons wear the apron that symbolizes...."

Elder Jones "Mr. Brown, do you remember your agreement not to try to 'flip-flop' the subject?"

Uncle Ed: "Don't *you* change the subject; now why is it that Mormons...."

Elder Smith: "Good Mr. Brown, that's why we're going to stick to this subject we're discussing—the nature of God. Now, Linda. Do you have any more questions?"

"Man Can Become God" Objection Answered

Linda: "Well, ah, I remember my uncle mentioning to me before that Mormons believe that God the Father has a Father, and that *He* has a Father, and on and on!"

Uncle Ed: "That's right, boys! How can you explain that? Do you honestly believe that you're going to become gods, and that you're going to have many wives, and have celestial sex with them to produce billions of spirit babies to populate your own world? Isn't that the most ridiculous thing you've ever heard in your lives?"

Elder Smith: "Yes, the way you put it!"

Uncle Ed: "Isn't it blasphemous towards God?"

Elder Jones:	"Your demeaning language is certainly blasphemous towards God, but our belief in eternal lives is not!"
Uncle Ed:	"Just tell me one place in the Bible where it talks about becoming a god over your own planet and producing billions of offspring into the eternities?"
Elder Jones:	"Mr. Brown, the Bible is built upon this doctrine!"
Uncle Ed:	(Laughing) "That is the *most* absurd thing I have ever heard! You boys are more ignorant than I thought!"
Linda:	"Elders, can you explain what you said? that the Bible is based upon this?"
Elder Jones:	"Yes we can Linda. Do you have the scripture, companion?"
Elder Smith:	"Right here!"
Elder Jones:	"Please read it."
Elder Smith:	"In Genesis chapter one, verses 26-28 we read, 'And God said, Let us make man in our image, after our likeness; and let *them* have *dominion* over the fish of the sea, and over the fowl of the air, and over the cattle, and *over all the earth*, and over every creeping thing that creepeth upon the earth. So God created man in his image, in the image of God created he him; male and female created he them. And God blessed them, and God said unto them, *Be fruitful, and multiply*, and *replenish* the earth, and subdue it: and have *dominion* over the fish of the sea, and over the fowl of the air, and *over every living thing* that moveth upon the earth.'"
Elder Jones:	"Now Linda, what…."
Uncle Ed:	"Now wait a minute…."
Elder Jones:	"Now Linda, what did God give to Adam and Eve?"
Linda:	"Dominion over all the earth!"
Elder Smith:	"Good Linda. And what did god command Adam and Eve to do?"
Linda:	"To multiply and fill up the earth."
Elder Smith:	"That's right, you're so good! And Mr. Brown, how many descendants of Adam and Eve have been born upon this world?"
Uncle Ed:	"Oh, I see what you're doing, you're trying to manipulate me into an answer *you* want to hear!"
Elder Jones:	"Very well, since it was Linda's question anyway, or it is supposed to be, we'll ask her. Linda, how many

descendants of Adam and Eve have been born upon this world?''

Linda: "Why, ah, billions!"

Elder Jones: "So, according to the book of Genesis, in the Bible, God made Adam, with His wife, a god of this world, to have lordship over it, and they now have had billions of descendants. So what is so unbiblical about this?"

Linda: "Nothing."

Uncle Ed: "Linda! You don't know what....I mean *they* don't know what they're talking about. How can you believe in some sort of extraterrestrial humanoid god who was once born a man to a human mother on some other planet, and that he had to die after living a sinful life? That this little man has a Father who is also a God, and on and on. You two never answered this! The Bible says that 'God is not a man, that he should lie.'"

Elder Smith: "That's in Numbers chapter 23, verse 19, but the verse says 'God is not a man, that he should lie; *neither* the son of man, that he should repent!' Jesus refers to Himself as the Son of Man many times in the New Testament. (See Matthew 11:19; 12:8, 16:13, 18:11, etc.) Don't you believe Jesus was God?"

Uncle Ed: (Angrily) "Yes, I do. *You* don't believe he is God, and that's why I'm trying to drive some sense into your th—I mean, explain what the Bible really has to say!"

Elder Jones: "It's obvious, Elder Smith, that he hasn't heard your point. But let's not bother to repeat it; let's answer Linda's questions as we agreed."

Elder Smith: (As Elder Jones is speaking) "You're right, Elder—you're right!"

"Resurrected But No Body" Objection Answered

Elder Jones: "Do you believe, Mr. Brown, that it is unbiblical to believe that God was born of a woman, and that He lived and died, and now has a resurrected body of flesh and bone in heaven?"

Uncle Ed: "It's not only blasphemous, but ridiculous, absurd, and Satanic!"

Elder Jones: "Is Jesus God?"

Uncle Ed: "That's what I've been trying to tell you!"

Elder Smith: "Does God have a body?"

Uncle Ed:	"No, he is Spirit!"
Elder Jones:	"But sir, is Jesus God?"
Uncle Ed:	"You're saying that I can't hear you. Can't you hear me? Yes—praise the Lord—Jesus is God!"
Elder Jones:	"Okay, Jesus is God! Is he fully God or partially God?"
Uncle Ed:	(Smirking) "You don't listen too well, do you! Jesus is fully God—the fulness of the Godhead is dwelling in Him bodily!"
Elder Jones:	"But you believe that God doesn't have a body, that He is a Spirit, and yet you say you believe Jesus is fully God!"
Elder Smith:	"Do you see any contradictions there?"
Uncle Ed:	(Clearing his throat) "No, I don't! And...."
Linda:	"I do!"
Uncle Ed:	(Angrily) "Now just wait! You two boys are trying to confuse things here. Neither of you understand the biblical doctrine of the Trinity!"

"Christ Ascended Without a Body" Objection Answered

Elder Jones:	"Do you understand the Trinity, Mr. Brown?"
Uncle Ed:	"Well, yes!"
Elder Smith:	"We thought that the Trinity was a mystery too high for human reason to grasp. So are you claiming to be able to understand it?"
Uncle Ed:	"No, I never had said that I did! All I'm saying is that *you're* not interpreting the Bible correctly!"
Elder Smith:	"All we are saying is that if Jesus is fully God, and the fulness of the Godhead dwells in Him bodily, then God must have been born of a woman, been a little baby, grown to manhood, died, was resurrected, and has a glorified body of flesh and bone that resembles a man!"
Uncle Ed:	"You're not listening! The Bible says that God is a spirit. We know that Jesus must have been a spirit or else he couldn't have walked through walls."
Elder Jones:	"Well, let's refer to the New Testament, where it talks about the resurrection of Jesus. In the gospel of Luke...."
Uncle Ed:	"What about the hundreds of changes in the Doctrine and Covenants? what about...."
Linda:	"Uncle Ed, please, the Elders weren't finished!"

Elder Jones:	"Mr. Brown, we've been through this before...."
Uncle Ed:	"Well, I don't care...."
Linda:	(Impatiently) "Uncle Ed, please—I want them to finish!"
Elder Jones:	"Thank you Linda. In Luke 24:39 Jesus answers your question. Here he appears to his disciples after His resurrection and apparently walks through a wall to do so. And it reads, 'Behold my hands and my feet, that it is I myself: handle me, and see; for *a spirit hath not flesh and bones*, as ye see me have.'"
Elder Smith:	"So, Linda, if Jesus is God, then God could not possibly be only a Spirit, because Jesus just told us that he has a body of flesh and bones."
Uncle Ed:	"Then he got rid of his body as he ascended up into heaven!"
Elder Smith:	"Where is that found in the Bible, Mr. Brown?"
Uncle Ed:	(Long pause)
Elder Jones:	"In fact, in the Bible, in the Book of Acts, chapter one, beginning with verse 9 it reads, 'And when he (meaning Jesus) had spoken these things, *while they beheld, he was taken up*; and a cloud received Him out of their sight. And while they looked steadfastly toward heaven as he went up, behold, two men stood by them in white apparel; Which also said, Ye men of Galilee, why stand ye gazing up into heaven? this same Jesus, which is taken up from you into heaven, *shall so come in like manner as ye have seen him go into heaven.*'"
Elder Smith:	"Linda, if Jesus ascended into heaven with a resurrected flesh-and-bone body, and the angels say that He will descend the very same way, then what kind of a body does he have in heaven today?"
Linda:	"A body of flesh and bones."
Elder Jones:	"Does this make sense to you, Linda?"
Linda:	"Yes, it does!"

"Three-in-One Trinity" Objection Answered

Uncle Ed:	"There are literally hundreds of scriptures in the Bible that talk about the Trinity, thereby refuting Mormonism!"
Elder Smith:	"Oh really, Mr. Brown? Really? Could you show us a few—if Linda has a question about it?"

Linda:	"I would like to know!"
Uncle Ed:	"Ha, I'd be more than happy to! I'll open the Bible for you. In John 10:30, for instance, it says, and these are the words of Jesus Himself: 'I *and* my Father are *one*.' Same being—*one*; Mormonism is destroyed!"
Linda:	"How do you explain that verse, Elders?"
Elder Jones:	"Linda, in John 17:11, where Jesus is praying for His disciples, it reads, 'Holy Father, keep through thine own name those whom thou hast given me, *that they may be one, as we are*.'"
Elder Smith:	"Does this mean, Mr. Brown, that we can all be one God?"
Uncle Ed:	"Wait a minute, I'm not finished yet. Here in John 14:8 and 9 it says, 'Philip saith unto him, Lord, shew us the Father, and it sufficeth us. Jesus saith unto him, Have I been so long time with you, and yet hast thou not known me, Philip? he that hath seen me hath seen the Father; and how sayest thou then, Shew us the Father?' So you see there, boys, Jesus is saying He *was* and *is* the Father."
Elder Jones:	"Well, Mr. Brown, then that means that God must have a body, and that he was born a little baby from a human woman, and that he ate, drank, and died, and now has an exalted flesh-and-bone body in heaven—all the things you claim to be blasphemous and unbiblical!"
Elder Smith:	"'Good goin', companion. But, for Linda's sake, let's look in John, chapter 5, verse 37: 'And the Father himself, which hath sent me, hath borne witness of me. *Ye have neither heard his voice at any time, nor seen his shape*.'"
Linda:	"Okay, if Jesus was God the Father like Uncle Ed believes, then God the Father must have a body, and he must have been born, and the other things."
Elder Smith:	"Good Linda, I'm so proud of you!"
Linda:	"But what does it mean when Jesus says that he is one with God, and he wants his disciples to be one too?"
Elder Jones:	"The oneness means oneness of will. Remember Jesus came not to do his own will, but the Father's, and Jesus wants us to do the Father's will, just as he has done."
Elder Smith:	"Those aren't the only scriptures either, Linda, because in John 14:28 Jesus says: '*I go unto the Father*: for *my*

Father is greater than I.' And in John chapter 20, verse 17, Jesus said unto Mary at His resurrection, 'Touch me not; for I am not yet ascended to my Father: but go to my brethren, and say unto them, *I ascend unto my Father, and your Father; and to my God, and your God.*' So you see...."

Uncle Ed: "Now wait a minute, just wait a minute. It says in the Bible, that 'Even from everlasting to everlasting, thou art God' (Psalm 90:2). That's forever in both directions. So how could your God be God?"

Elder Smith: "Mr. Brown, we already...."

Uncle Ed: "See, you can't!"

Elder Smith: "You see, we already have answered this...."

Uncle Ed: "No, you can't possibly answer this. Show me one verse in the Bible!"

Elder Jones: "Linda and Mr. Brown, Jesus said in John 5:19-20 the following: 'Verily, verily, I say unto you, The Son can do nothing of himself, but *what he seeth the Father do*: for what things soever he doeth, these also doeth the Son likewise. For the Father loveth the Son, and *sheweth him all things that himself doeth*: and he will shew him greater works than these, that ye may marvel."

Elder Smith: "What did Jesus do? He was born of a woman, lived a sinless life, died for the sins of all of us, and ascended into heaven with a flesh-and-bone resurrected body. He was doing what he had seen the Father do before him. Do you understand this, Linda?"

Linda: "I understand that Jesus was only doing what the Father had done. But even if Jesus was the Father, as my uncle said, then God must have a body, and would have done everything Jesus did!"

Elder Smith: "Good Linda, that's right!"

Uncle Ed: "Well, I know certain pagan rites that go on in those Mormon temples that you don't even know about, and I can show you that they...."

Elder Jones: "Mr. Brown...."

Uncle Ed: "Don't interrupt!"

Linda: "Please Uncle Ed, don't *you* interrupt!"

Elder Jones:	"Let's not argue, Mr. Brown. We'll get to that in a moment, but let's stick to the subject at hand and not try to change it."
Uncle Ed:	"No, don't try to evade my questions!"
Elder Smith:	"Mr. Brown, Linda is the one who is supposed to be asking the questions. Linda...."
Uncle Ed:	"Saying that there is an endless stream of gods is of the devil!"
Linda:	"Uncle Ed, please calm down!"
Uncle Ed:	"It's blaspheming the Bible, and God. I can't sit here...."
Elder Jones:	"Since you must not of heard us before, let me explain once more. There are only two possibilities here. If what we're saying to you is true—that Jesus only did what he had seen the Father do—it means that the Father was born upon another earth, lived a sinless life, did the will of *His* Father in Heaven, died, and now has a resurrected body of flesh and bone in heaven."
Uncle Ed:	"Don't try to explain the Bible to me...."
Elder Jones:	"The second possibility is what you have said, the 'three-in-one' theory, that Jesus is God and the fulness of the Godhead bodily, and if the fulness of the Godhead dwelt in Jesus, and Jesus is also the Father, then the Father was born. The Father was born as Jesus, grew up to be a man called Jesus, did the will of Himself, died Jesus, and now has the flesh-and-bone resurrected body that belongs to Jesus. So, Mr. Brown, either way you have it. Ours or yours. God cannot possibly be *only a Spirit*, and God did indeed go through the very same things Jesus did. There is no other possibility."
Uncle Ed:	(Laughing) "Nonsense, the only possibility is that you two are trained deceivers that are trying to dupe my niece into believing...."
Linda:	"Uncle Ed, they're quoting right from the Bible!"
Uncle Ed:	"I don't care!"
Elder Smith:	"Sir, what you care doesn't concern us. We want to know what Linda thinks. Linda?"
Linda:	"I see what you're saying, and it's straight from the Bible. Either way God must be who you say He is. If Jesus said that He was doing only what He saw His

Father do, then what you're saying about God must be true."

"Lucifer's Big Lie" Objection Answered

Uncle Ed: "I still can't believe that men may become gods! That was Lucifer's big lie in the Garden of Eden!"

Elder Jones: "Before we get to that, I want to ask Linda a question. How do you feel about the things we have been showing you about God?"

Linda: "It's right from the Bible. I don't see how anyone could believe any differently. But then again, Elders, I still have other questions that really confuse me—like what he just said. How can men become Gods?"

Elder Jones: "All right, we'll answer that for you. Elder Smith, could you please read the second Article of Faith?"

Elder Smith: "Sure. It says,'We believe that men will be punished for their own sins, and not for Adam's transgression.'"

Uncle Ed: "Okay boys, I'm going to show you right from the Bible how your Mormon doctrine which states that you can become gods is inspired by none other than Lucifer. I showed Linda this scripture the other day. It says in the King James Version, in Genesis 3:3-5, 'But of the fruit of the tree which is in the midst of the garden, God hath said, Ye shall not eat of it, neither shall ye touch it, lest ye die. And the serpent (that's the Devil) said unto the woman, Ye shall not surely die: For God doth know that in the day ye eat thereof, then your eyes shall be opened, and ye shall be as gods, knowing good and evil.' So we see right there, the first one to offer Godhood to man was Satan, and the doctrine that men can become gods is from him."

Linda: "What about this, Elders?"

Elder Jones: "We're pleased that you brought this up, Mr. Brown, because we as missionaries hear it a lot, and the misreading of this passage is the entire basis of the unfounded argument advanced by anti-Mormon critics that Mormons worship the devil."

Uncle Ed: "You said you'd answer it—so answer it if you can."

Elder Jones: "I will if you give me a chance. Just as he has done throughout the centuries, Lucifer mixed falsehood with truth when he talked to Eve. We do know that Lucifer

	lied when he said, 'Ye shall *not* surely die' (Genesis 3:4). But Satan was *not* lying when he told Eve, 'Ye shall be as gods, knowing good and evil'" (Genesis 3:5).
Uncle Ed:	(Laughing) "That's the most ridiculous and blasphemous thing I've ever heard. Of course, I've heard it for a long time from Mormons."
Elder Smith:	"Really, I can prove from the Bible that when Lucifer said, 'Ye shall be as gods, knowing good and evil,' he was stating a true principle."
Uncle Ed:	"And I can prove to you that Mormonism is opposed to the Bible, and that your secret blood oaths are given to Lucifer in your pagan temples, and...."
Linda:	"Please! Let them finish!"
Elder Smith:	"Thanks, Linda. Could you turn the page over and read verse 22 of the third chapter of Genesis?"
Linda:	"Okay. Genesis 3:22?"
Elder Jones:	"That's right."
Linda:	"It says, 'And the LORD God said, Behold the man is become as one of us, to know good and evil: and now, lest he....' Look Uncle Ed, it says right here, 'And *the Lord God said*, Behold,...'"
Uncle Ed:	"Yes, Linda, all right...."
Linda:	"'...The *man is become as one of us, to know good and evil,*' just like the Elders said!"
Elder Smith:	"You see Linda, Satan did lie when he said, 'Ye shall not surely die,' but he was telling the truth when he said, 'Ye shall be *as* gods, knowing good and evil.'"
Elder Jones:	"We hear sometimes from people who've been subjected to anti-Mormon propaganda the false teaching that Latter-day Saints follow Lucifer. They misread that passage and don't even bother to read on to the next page."
Elder Smith:	"God himself refutes that charge against us."
Uncle Ed:	"Oh really, he does really! Just show me one verse— just one verse in the Bible that says that you can become gods?"
Elder Smith:	"We can't show you just one verse."
Uncle Ed:	"Ha. You see, Linda. They can't show you from the Bible!"

Elder Smith: "Wrong, we can't show you *just* one verse, we can show you many verses! In Genesis 1:26 it says that God made Man in his own image, and he gave them dominion over all the earth."

Elder Jones: "Not only that, but in Psalm 82:1 it says that *'God standeth in the congregation of the mighty; he judgeth among the gods,'* and in verse 6 God says, 'I have said, *Ye are gods; and all of you are children of the Most High.'* Jesus quoted this scripture to the Jews in John chapter 10, verse 34."

Elder Smith: "Now in Romans 8, verses 14-17, Paul writes, 'For as many as are led by the Spirit of God, *they are the sons of God.* For ye have not received the spirit of bondage again to fear; but ye have received the Spirit of adoption, whereby we cry, Abba, Father. The Spirit itself beareth witness with our spirit, that *we are the children of God: And if children, then heirs; heirs of God, and joint heirs with Christ*; if so be that we suffer with him, that we may be also *glorified together.'*"

Elder Jones: "Paul says this again in Galatians 4, verses 4-7, which reads, 'But when the fulness of the time was come, God sent forth his Son, made of a woman, made under the law, To redeem them that were under the law, that we might receive the adoption of sons. And because ye are sons, God hath sent forth the Spirit of his Son into your hearts, crying, Abba, Father. Wherefore thou are no more a servant, *but a son; and if a son, then an heir of God through Christ.'* An heir is someone who inherits something, like the firstborn male-child would inherit all that his father had—his land, money, holdings, and titles. In these verses, Paul is teaching very plainly that man can eventually inherit godhood."

Elder Smith: "Peter, in 1st Peter 3:7, says that men and women who are Saints of God are *'heirs together of the grace of life,'* and in Hebrews 1:1-2 it says that 'God, who at sundry times and in divers manners in times past spake unto the fathers by the prophets, Hath in these last days spoken unto us by *his Son, whom he hath appointed heir of all things*, by whom also he made the worlds.' And in verses 4-8 it reads, 'Being made *so much better than the angels, as he hath by inheritance obtained a more excellent name than they.* For unto which of the angels said he at any time, *Thou art my Son, this day have I begotten thee?* And again, I will be to him a Father, and he shall be to me a Son? And again, when he bringeth in the firstbegotten into the world, he saith, And let all the angels of God worship him. And of the angels he saith, who maketh his angels spirits, and his ministers a flame of fire. But unto the Son he saith, Thy throne, O God, is for ever and ever: a sceptre of righteousness is the sceptre of thy kingdom.'"

Uncle Ed: "I know these scriptures better than you do—it's saying that God has given Jesus His throne, nothing about Mormons getting one!"

Elder Smith: "Then you don't believe that if man overcomes like Jesus did, God will grant that he might sit upon Jesus's throne?"

Uncle Ed: (Laughing) "That's blasphemy!"

Elder Smith: "Let's turn to what Jesus himself has to say. In the Book of Revelation, chapter 3 verse 21, it says, 'To him that overcometh *will I grant to sit with me in my throne....*'"

Uncle Ed: "Wait a minute....Now just wait!"

Linda: "Let him read, Uncle!"

Elder Smith: "'...*To him that overcometh will I grant to sit with me in my throne, even as I also overcame,* and am set down with my Father in his throne.'"

Elder Jones: "Linda, do you believe the Bible when it says that if we overcome we shall be granted the privilege of sitting upon Jesus's throne with our Lord?"

Linda: "That's what the Bible says!"

Elder Jones: "According to the Bible, what did Jesus inherit from His Father?"

Uncle Ed: "You're wasting your time, we already...."

Linda: "His throne, his scepter, and His name."

Elder Smith: "Good for you, Linda! Now, what is the name of the Father?"

Linda: "His name is GOD, of course!"

Elder Jones: "Since the Bible tells us that if we overcome, which means to do the will of the Father and keep His commandments like Jesus did, then we shall become the sons of God, and if sons then heirs of God, and

	joint heirs with His Only Begotten Son, Jesus, then, what shall we inherit?"
Uncle Ed:	"Probably a bunch of white salamanders!"
Linda:	(Exasperated) "Please, Uncle Ed! We will inherit all the Son has inherited!"
Elder Jones:	"Could you name some of those things for us, Linda?"
Linda:	"Like you said, we inherit His throne, his scepter, and His name, which is God!"
Elder Smith:	"We're proud of you, Linda!"
Uncle Ed:	"Nonsense!!!"
Elder Jones:	"Linda, in Revelation 21:7, God says, *'He that overcometh shall inherit all things; and I will be his God, and he shall be my son.'*"
Linda:	"That says it pretty clearly."
Uncle Ed:	"Did you know, Linda, that Joseph Smith had over a hundred wives, and he snuck around behind the back...."
Elder Smith:	"Mr. Brown, we'll get to that...."
Uncle Ed:	"No, you won't. You duped, ah, dedicated young men may be sincere, but you don't know what the insider knows about Mormonism!"

"Men Not God's Spirit Children in Pre-existence" Objection Answered

Elder Jones:	"Now, Linda, under this second Article of Faith we also place the doctrine that all are the children of God in the spirit, and that He is our loving Parent."
Uncle Ed:	"That He is a polygamous extraterrestrial, engaging in endless celestial sex with his trillions of goddess wives. What about that? Where in the Bible does it talk about all His goddess wives?"
Elder Smith:	"We'll get to that in a later Article of Faith, but let's see if Linda understands the biblical doctrine of man's pre-existence."
Linda:	"I remember when we talked about this before, and all the scriptures from the Bible that showed how we were the children of our Heavenly Father, and...."
Uncle Ed:	"Linda, boys, here's one scripture that proves you wrong again. In the Bible, in Colossians 1:16 it says that Jesus created everything. Here, it says, 'For by him were all things created, that are in earth, visible and

	invisible, whether they be thrones, or dominions, or principalities, or powers: all things were created by him, and for him.' There, you see—your Mormon Jesus, the spirit brother of Lucifer, cannot be your brother. According to the Bible, He created you, and the angels, and even Lucifer!"
Linda:	"What about that, Elders?"
Elder Jones:	"We do believe that He created all things. He created all *things*, but not all *beings*. To take that to mean literally all things, then Jesus must have created God and Himself!"
Uncle Ed:	"That's absurd!"
Elder Smith:	"Exactly! And not only that, but to say that Jesus created us along with the material universe is to say that the builder of this house created us as well; since we are now part of this house."
Elder Jones:	"We believe that Jesus created man's physical body (Genesis 2:7), but he did not create man's spirit. There are many scriptures that show us that we are the spirit children of God. In Jeremiah 1:5 God says to that prophet, '*Before I formed thee in the belly I knew thee*; and before thou camest forth out of the womb I sanctified thee, and I ordained thee a prophet unto the nations.'"
Uncle Ed:	(Laughing) "Of course God knows us before we are born—not that we existed, because we didn't, but because He knows all things—He can see the future."
Elder Smith:	"There are other scriptures that can't be explained away so easily. Like in Ecclesiastes 12:7 where Solomon says about death, 'Then shall the dust return to the earth as it was: and *the spirit shall return unto God who gave it*.'"
Elder Jones:	"And in Hebrews 12:9 Paul tells us point blank, 'We have had fathers of our flesh which corrected us, and we gave them reverence: shall we not much rather be in subjection unto the *Father of spirits*, and live?'"
Uncle Ed:	"All right, but I'll be damned if you can show me one verse—just one verse—that says that Jesus is your brother!"
Elder Smith:	"We can't show you just one verse, Mr. Brown, we can show you many. Like in Hebrews 1:6, where it reads,

'And again, when he bringeth in the firstbegotten into the world, he saith, And let all the angels of God worship him.' How can you have a *firstbegotten* without a second begotten? The passage shows that Christ was the first of the many spirit children of the Father of Spirits—our Heavenly Father."

Elder Jones: "Paul also tells us in Romans 8:29, 'For whom he did foreknow, he also did predestinate to be conformed to the image of his Son, that he might be the *firstborn among many brethren.*'"

Elder Smith: "And Paul calls the Church in heaven, here in Hebrews 12:23, the 'general assembly and church of the firstborn.'"

Uncle Ed: "You fellas are really ignorant of the Bible."

Linda: "Those 'fellas' were quoting right from the Bible. It looks to me like they know it extremely well."

"Saved by Works" Objection Answered

Elder Jones: "Companion, would you please read the third Article of Faith?"

Elder Smith: "All right. Article three states, 'We believe that through the Atonement of Christ, all mankind may be saved, by obedience to the laws and ordinances of the Gospel.'"

Uncle Ed: "There! You see, Linda? A Mormon believes that he has to save up a bunch of brownie points, by keeping all sorts of laws of the Mormon gospel, and *that's* how he's saved! Not anything to do with Christ's free gift offered at the Cross of Calvary."

Elder Jones: "Linda, do you have any questions on this subject?"

Linda: "Well, my Uncle Ed did show me a scripture. I can't remember which one, but it did say that we shouldn't boast, and it talked about how we're saved by grace. I remember that both of you taught me how we needed to pay tithing and do all sorts of things. This is really confusing to me."

Uncle Ed: "Let me show you boys that scripture. Mormons love to boast how many good things they do, but here Paul warns them, 'For by grace are ye saved through faith;

and not of yourselves: it is the gift of God: Not of works, lest any man should boast.' Now you can look that up in Ephesians 2:8 and 9 if you don't believe me."

Elder Smith: "Oh, we believe you, Mr. Brown, and we also believe the next verse."

Uncle Ed: "What?"

Elder Jones: "Could you read the next verse, Mr. Brown?"

Uncle Ed: "Don't try to change the subject here. Mormons have been boasting for years!"

Elder Smith: "Okay, I'll read the next verse. Paul says in Ephesians 2, verse 10, 'For we are his workmanship, *created in Christ Jesus unto good works*, which *God hath before ordained that we should walk in them*'. It says here that we should walk in good works, and even that God has ordained it."

Elder Jones: "We don't believe that our works alone can save us. We believe that death separates our bodies from our spirits, and Jesus's atonement makes it so that we all will be resurrected from the dead. We believe that sin causes a spiritual death, a separation between ourselves and God. Jesus came to atone for that too. He paid the price for our individual sins. Nephi, a Book of Mormon prophet wrote, in 2nd Nephi 10:24, 'Wherefore, my beloved brethren, reconcile yourselves to the will of god, and not to the will of the devil and the flesh; and remember, after ye are reconciled unto God, that *it is only in and through the grace of God that ye are saved*.' Yes, we know all mankind is saved by grace, but, as Paul says in his letter to the Ephesians you just quoted, we are saved by grace *through faith*."

Elder Smith: "It says in the Epistle of James, chapter one, verse 22, 'Be ye doers of the word, and not hearers only, deceiving your own selves,' and in chapter two, verse 17, James tells us what true faith is. He says, 'Even so faith, if it hath not works, is dead, being alone.' I'll read on. James says, 'Yea, a man may say, Thou hast faith, and I have works: shew me thy faith without thy works, and *I will shew thee my faith by my works*. Thou believest that there is one God; thou doest well; the devils also believe, and tremble, But wilt thou

	know, O vain man, that *faith without works is dead*?' (James 2:18-20)"
Uncle Ed:	"I see you finally quoted from the Book of Mormon. Do you know how many changes there have been in it? And where does it talk about a Melchizedek priesthood in the Book of Mormon, and where do you read anything about a Mother in Heaven, or about secret temple rituals, and about...."
Elder Jones:	"Mr. Brown, we'll get to that, but please don't change the subject. Linda, how do you feel about what we have said?"
Linda:	"Well, it's like you said before. What good is it to accept Jesus as Lord if we don't keep His commandments, because a Lord is one who commands, and we obey."

"Jesus and Lucifer Are Brothers" Objection Answered

Uncle Ed:	"That's just it. The Jesus of Mormonism is not the Jesus of orthodox Christianity! The Jesus of Mormonism is the spirit brother of Lucifer, the Devil!"
Linda:	"Is that true, Elders? How could you believe something like that? Isn't that making Jesus part evil?"
Elder Smith:	"Well, Linda, not exactly. To say that Latter-day Saints believe that Jesus is the spirit brother of Lucifer, without explaining that they believe that *all mankind* are spirit children of God is a half truth similar to the one Satan told Eve in the Garden of Eden—you know, when he lied about not dying, while telling the truth about becoming as gods, knowing good and evil."
Elder Jones:	"That's right, Linda. We believe that we are all the sons and daughters of God—including those that have rebelled against him. In Job 1:6 it reads, 'Now there was a day when the *sons of God came to present themselves before the Lord*, and *Satan came also* among them.'"
Uncle Ed:	"Ah, it just says he was among them, it doesn't say that he was one of them."
Elder Smith:	"Do you believe that Jesus created Satan, Mr. Brown?"
Uncle Ed:	"What are you trying to get at?"
Elder Smith:	"Do you believe that Jesus created Satan?"
Uncle Ed:	"All right, yes I do, he created *all* things, whether in heaven or on earth!"

Elder Smith:	"Then you believe that Jesus created evil?"
Uncle Ed:	"Ah, no ah, Lucifer was once a good angel, but he fell because of pride."
Elder Jones:	"That's right, Mr. Brown. And who are the sons of God mentioned in Job 1:6?" (Long pause)
Linda:	"Uncle Ed?"
Elder Smith:	"They would have to be angels. The sons of God are angels, and Lucifer is an angel, although a fallen one."
Elder Jones:	"That's right. We've seen before that Jesus is called the firstborn and firstbegotten. This can't possibly refer to His physical body, since He is the *Only* Begotten Son of God in the flesh. It must refer to His spirit, He was the firstbegotten spirit."
Elder Smith:	"And what are spirits? The Bible tells us that they are angels. In Psalm 104, verse 4, it speaks of God, 'Who maketh his angels spirits; his ministers a flaming fire.' So these spirits are angels. Some angels sinned against God and rebelled against him."
Elder Jones:	"I have that scripture, Elder. In 2nd Peter 2:4 it says that 'God spared not the angels that sinned, but cast them down to hell, and delivered them into chains of darkness, to be reserved unto judgment.' One of those angels was Lucifer, their leader, who fell from heaven."
Elder Smith:	"You see Linda, angels are spirits. God is the Father of spirits, and Jesus is the firstborn and firstbegotten spirit of God."
Elder Jones:	"That's right, Linda, and Lucifer is a fallen angel, as it says in Isaiah 14:12, 'How thou art fallen from heaven, O Lucifer, son of the morning!'"
Elder Smith:	"Linda, Satan is among the angels that rebelled against God, as we read in Jude 1:6. 'And the angels which kept not their first estate, but left their own habitation, he hath reserved in everlasting chains under darkness unto the judgment of the great day.'"
Elder Jones:	"And in Revelation, chapter 12, verses 7-9, it tells about a war in heaven, and how the Devil and his angels that followed him were cast out. It reads, 'And there was war in heaven: Michael and his angels fought against the dragon; and the dragon fought and his angels, And prevailed not; *neither was their place found any more in heaven. And the great dragon was cast out, that old*

serpent, called the Devil, and Satan, which deceiveth the whole world: he was cast out into the earth, and his angels were cast out with him.'"

Elder Smith: "We don't believe that Lucifer even has the right to be called a son of God any more, because, according to Hebrews 12:8, those who rebel against God are no more worthy to be called His sons."

Elder Jones: "Do you understand what we've been saying, Linda?"

Uncle Ed: "What I understand is that you haven't answered...."

Elder Jones: "Excuse me, but your name isn't Linda!"

Linda: "I've always believed that Lucifer was a fallen angel. That's what they taught me in Sunday School since I can remember, and since he is an angel, he must be a spirit, and if a spirit, then a son of God, although a rebellious one."

Elder Smith: "Good, Linda."

Uncle Ed: "The Jesus of Mormonism is not the Jesus of the Bible."

Linda: "But Uncle Ed. They were quoting straight *from* the Bible."

"Jesus Was Married" Objection Answered

Uncle Ed: "I don't care! The Mormon Jesus was a sinful man, but my Jesus, the Jesus of the Bible, was a *sinless* God!"

Elder Jones: "What do you mean?"

Uncle Ed: "Linda, these boys have never told you this I'm sure, but their early apostles believed and taught that Jesus was a polygamist, and that he fathered a number of children."

Linda: "No, they never told me that. Is that true, Elders?"

Elder Smith: "Yes, Linda, it's true."

Uncle Ed: "You see, Linda? They deliberately hid that from you!"

Linda: "Elders?"

Elder Jones: "Linda, we have met with you about seven times, and each visit was about one hour long. We barely have enough time to share with you the things pertinent to salvation, much less miscellaneous things that have nothing to do with salvation."

Uncle Ed: (Laughing) "Nothing to do? That's absurd! How can a sinful Jesus save you from your sins?"

Elder Smith: "Why do you say he was sinful? Latter-day Saints believe that Christ was without sin."

Uncle Ed: "Not if he was a polygamist, and fathered children!"

Elder Jones:	"If he had just one wife, would he still be a sinful man in your estimation?"
Uncle Ed:	"Not in *my* estimation, but in *yours!*"
Elder Jones:	"Linda, what the Latter-day Saints really believe is what the Bible has to say on the subject. Married couples having children is not a sin. In Genesis chapter one, verses 26 and 27, it says that God created man in his own image, *male and female*, and in verse 28 it reads, 'And God blessed them, and God said unto them, Be fruitful, and multiply, and replenish the earth.' So God ordained marriage, and commanded married couples to have children, and families as something good."
Uncle Ed:	"Yes, but where does it say that Jesus was married! Just show me one verse that tells us Jesus was married!"
Elder Smith:	"Again, we won't give you just one verse, because there are many that point to the fact that Jesus was married. And His being married is commonly accepted by Bible scholars who are acquainted with Jewish law and customs. For instance, under Jewish law, a Rabbi had to be a married man, and Jesus is called Rabbi in John 1:38 and 49; and in John 3:2, and in John 6:25. In fact, Mary Magdalene called Jesus Rabboni in John 20:16. Even those that opposed Jesus called him Rabbi."
Elder Jones:	"Not only that, but at the wedding in Cana, in John chapter two, verses one through 10, Jesus was in charge of supplying the wine at the wedding. That was the responsibility of the bridegroom, according to Jewish customs."
Uncle Ed:	"Nonsense! Jesus was just an invited guest!"
Elder Smith:	"Really? Let's see. In verse three, it reads, 'And when they wanted wine, the mother of Jesus saith unto him, 'They have no wine.' Jesus then commanded the servants to take six waterpots of stone and fill them with water. Then Jesus told the servants to draw out the water and give it to the governor of the feast. Now let's read verses 9 and 10. 'When the ruler of the feast had tasted the water that was made wine, and knew not whence it was: (but the servants which drew the water knew;) the governor of the feast called the *bridegroom*, And saith unto him, Every man at the beginning doth set forth good wine; and when men

have well drunk, then that which is worse: but *thou* hast kept the good wine until now.' And in the very next verse it reads, 'This beginning of miracles did Jesus in Cana of Galilee, and manifested forth his glory; and his disciples believed on him.'"

Elder Jones:	"Linda, who was the bridegroom?"
Linda:	"Jesus!"
Elder Smith:	"Why, Linda?"
Linda:	"Because Jesus supplied the wine, turned water into wine, and the ruler of the feast asked the bridegroom, who was Jesus, why he had kept the best wine until the last part of the wedding feast."
Elder Smith:	"Great Linda!"

"Jesus Was a Polygamist" Objection Answered

Uncle Ed:	"All right, but where does it say that Jesus was a polygamist?"
Elder Jones:	"If Jesus was a polygamist, that shouldn't offend us; so were Abraham and Jacob, King David and King Solomon."
Elder Smith:	"Other scriptures point to the fact that Jesus was married, like in Mark 6:2, where it records that Jesus taught in the synagogue. That was against Jewish law and custom and would never have been tolerated unless he was married."
Elder Jones:	"John, chapter 11 tells how Lazarus died while Jesus was away. Mary sat in her house until Jesus returned and called her out. This is found in verse 28. Under Jewish custom, a woman in mourning stays indoors until her husband calls her out."
Uncle Ed:	"All right, all right, but you still can't show me one verse that says that Jesus was a polygamist!"
Elder Smith:	"Again, Mr. Brown, there are several. According to Luke, in his 24th chapter, certain women came to anoint the body of Jesus, following his crucifixion, with burial spices. In verse 10 Luke says this included Mary Magdalene, Joanna, and the other Mary. Under Jewish custom, it was the widows' responsibility to anoint the body of their dead husbands."

Elder Jones: "Not only that, but in Hebrews 1:8 Paul quotes Psalms 45:6 as applying to Jesus: 'But unto the Son he saith, Thy throne, O God, is for ever and ever: a sceptre of righteousness is the sceptre of thy kingdom.' Let's read in Psalms 45:6 through 9. 'Thy throne, O God, is forever and ever: the sceptre of thy kingdom is a right sceptre. Thou lovest righteousness, and hatest wickedness: therefore God, thy God, hath anointed thee with the oil of gladness above thy fellows. All thy garments smell of myrrh, and aloes, and cassia, out of the ivory palaces, whereby they have made thee glad. *Kings' daughters were among thy honourable women*: upon thy right hand *did stand the queen* in gold of Ophir.' So the passage Paul quotes as referring to Jesus speaks of him having wives."

Uncle Ed: "You're not interpreting that right. Where does it say Jesus had children?"

Elder Smith: "You know of course, Mr. Brown, that Isaiah chapter 53 is the great Messianic prophecy concerning Christ, and in verse 10 of that chapter it reads, 'Yet it pleased the Lord to bruise him; he hath put him to grief: when thou shalt make his soul an offering for sin, *he shall see his seed*, he shall prolong his days.' So Isaiah was prophesying that the Lord would have seed, or descendants."

Elder Jones: "Linda, Jesus was the only sinless one that ever lived or that ever will live. In 2 Nephi 25:20, in the Book of Mormon, the Prophet Nephi says, 'Yea, behold, I say unto you, that as these things are true, and as the Lord God liveth, there is none other name given under heaven save it be this Jesus Christ, of which I have spoken, whereby man can be saved.'"

Uncle Ed: "This has been the most absurd jibberish I've ever heard in my life!"

Elder Smith: "Linda, how do you feel about it?"

Linda: "Well, the Bible teaches that Jesus was married, and the Bible is the inerrant Word of God."

Uncle Ed: "Oh, Mormons don't believe that. They believe that the Bible can't be trusted. That's why they have all those other scriptures."

Linda: "Is that true, Elders?"

| Elder Jones: | "Frankly Linda, no, but we'll discuss that later, under another Article of Faith. Companion, would you please read the fourth Article of Faith?" |

"Satan Transformed as an Angel" Objection Answered

Elder Smith:	"Certainly. It reads, 'We believe that the first principles and ordinances of the Gospel are: first, Faith in the Lord Jesus Christ; second, Repentance; third, Baptism by immersion for the remission of sins; fourth, Laying on of hands for the gift of the Holy Ghost.'"
Uncle Ed:	"Why don't you add, 'We believe in wearing holy underwear 24 hours a day, even during physical intimacy; we believe in blood oaths; we believe in men on the Moon dressing like Quakers; we believe in polygamy....'"
Elder Jones:	"We are discussing now the first principles of the Gospel. Linda, do you have any questions regarding them?"
Linda:	"Well, I don't...."
Uncle Ed:	"We believe that the Mormon Gospel is diametrically opposed to the real gospel. Paul warns us against Mormonism right here in Galatians 1:8. He says, 'But though we, or an angel from heaven, preach any other gospel unto you than that which we have preached unto you, let him be accursed.'"
Elder Smith:	"Oh, so you're saying that Joseph Smith really did see an angel?"
Uncle Ed:	"Not an angel, but Satan. Paul tells us in 2nd Corinthians 11:14 that 'Satan himself is transformed into an angel of Light.'"
Elder Jones:	"Oh, so you're saying that Joseph Smith was deceived by the Devil pretending to be an angel, and that he really did find gold plates, and he did see visions, although those things were Satanically inspired?"
Uncle Ed:	"The Bible right here tells me so!"
Linda:	"But Uncle Ed, you told me yesterday that Joseph Smith lied about seeing angels and finding gold plates, and that...."
Uncle Ed:	"I really think the point here, boys, is not whether Joe Smith saw an angel, but that we should be comparing

the Mormon gospel with the gospel of the Bible to see if they are the same."

Elder Smith: "We couldn't agree with you more, Mr. Brown!"

"No Baptism for the Dead" Objection Answered

Uncle Ed: "Linda, do you remember what we discussed a few days ago about having one chance and one chance only for salvation?"

Linda: "Yes."

Uncle Ed: "All right then, here's the scripture. In Hebrews 9:27 it reads, 'And as it is appointed unto men once to die, but after this the judgment.' There, you see—no second chance to be saved by the Mormon gospel, no baptism for the dead, which was a pagan practice that Paul utterly condemned!"

Linda: "Elders, can you explain this?"

Elder Jones: "We surely can, Linda, but we must agree with your uncle about no second chances. There really is no second chance to be saved promised in the scriptures."

Linda: "What do you mean? I thought you baptized for the dead, and you taught me before that Mormons believe that Jesus even preached to the dead?"

Elder Jones: "Yes, that's true. What I mean...."

Uncle Ed: "You see, Linda, you see—he's trying to cover up what he said before."

Elder Jones: "Not so, Mr. Brown. We have never taught that people will have a second chance to accept the gospel. What we teach is that all men will have a specific opportunity to hear and accept or reject the gospel; if not in this life, then in the life to come."

Elder Smith: "What my companion is saying is that if you hear the gospel in this life and reject it, it will do you no good to hear it in the next life because you've already rejected it. However, millions, if not billions, of God's children have lived and died without ever having the opportunity to hear the gospel even once in this life, and those who have never heard it will have that opportunity in the next life."

Uncle Ed: "Now that is absolutely contrary to the Bible, as I have shown."

Elder Jones: "What do you mean, Mr. Brown?"

Uncle Ed:	(Snickering) "Trying to weasel out of it already, huh? You heard me! It is appointed for man once to die, and then the judgment."
Elder Smith:	"Does that mean that we are judged on whether we're going to heaven or hell right at our time of death?"
Uncle Ed:	"That's what the Bible says."
Elder Jones:	"The Bible also says, Mr. Brown, in Revelation 20:12: 'And I saw the dead, small and great, stand before God; and the books were opened: and another book was opened, which is the book of life: and the dead were judged out of those things which were written in the books; according to their works.'"
Elder Smith:	"Doesn't born-again Christianity teach that the Day of Judgment will take place at the end of the Millennium?"
Uncle Ed:	"Yeah, but that's not the point here. The point here is that there is no preaching to the dead—they've been judged already!"
Elder Jones:	"Then why did Christ preach to them that are dead? We're told in 1st Peter 4:5-6 about people 'who shall give account to him that is ready to judge the quick and the dead. For for this cause *was the gospel preached also to them that are dead*, that they might be judged according to men in the flesh, but live according to God in the spirit.'"
Elder Smith:	"And let's not forget what Peter wrote in 1st Peter 3:18-20, which says, 'Christ also hath once suffered for sins, the just for the unjust, that he might bring us to God, being put to death in the flesh, but quickened by the Spirit: By which also *he went and preached unto the spirits in prison*; Which sometime were disobedient, when once the long-suffering of God waited in the days of Noah....'"
Uncle Ed:	"Oh, I know all about how you Mormons try to misuse those scriptures. But you see, Jesus went to those souls in Hell to show that He had conquered death, and to proclaim he had power over it, and that they were condemned!"
Linda:	"Uncle Ed, that doesn't make sense. It doesn't even say that. It says that Jesus preached the gospel to the spirits in prison, that they might live according to the will

of God in spirit as men do in the flesh. He went to preach the gospel. That's what it says. It doesn't say anything about condemning them."

Uncle Ed: "Linda, I have a few years on you and these boys here, and those years have been spent in deep Bible study."

Elder Jones: "Yet she's right, Mr. Brown. Those verses say nothing about Jesus proclaiming anything but preaching the gospel, just as we teach he did."

Elder Smith: "And baptism for the dead is mentioned in 1st Corinthians 15:29. Paul uses the existence of the practice to convince the Saints at Corinth that there is a literal resurrection of the body. Listen to what he said, 'Else what shall they do which are *baptized for the dead*, if the dead rise not at all? why are they then *baptized for the dead*?' Would Paul use a pagan example, something he utterly disagrees with, to teach a Biblical truth? Of course not. He wasn't condemning the practice, like you said. He was referring to it as an accepted practice, and using it as a doctrinal proof."

Uncle Ed: "Well, I...."

Linda: "No."

"Salamander" Objection Answered

Elder Jones: "Companion, read for us the fifth Article of Faith."

Elder Smith: "My pleasure. It reads, 'We believe that a man must be called of God, by prophecy, and by the laying on of hands by those who are in authority, to preach the Gospel and administer in the ordinances thereof.'"

Elder Jones: "Under this heading, let's discuss the role of the Prophet Joseph Smith. He was the one called by God, by revelation, to be the prophet to open the last dispensation, and...."

Uncle Ed: "Good! Here we have it. Mormonism rests on Joseph Smith. I can prove to you, from the writings of your own apostles, that Joseph Smith was a treasure-seeker who dabbled in witchcraft and the occult. Here I have a copy of a letter by Martin Harris, one of the so-called three witnesses of the Book of Mormon, that proves that Joseph was occultic, and even has an account about your angel Moroni turning into a Salamander!"

Linda: "Elders?"

Elder Smith: "You're not up on your current history, Mr. Brown. That letter was proved to be a forgery, and after that was proved, the man who forged them confessed that he did so to try to make the Church look bad, and for money."

Elder Jones: "Not only that, but he murdered two people in his effort to hide his forgery crimes, but he was caught. He was anti-Mormon."

Linda: "Uncle Ed?"

"Money Digging" Objection Answered

Uncle Ed: "All right! All right, but you can't tell me that Joe wasn't involved in money-digging. Too many people who lived near him can't be wrong."

Elder Smith: "We never said that he wasn't hired, for a few weeks, to dig in search of a treasure believed to be buried in the area. In fact, Joseph Smith, in his own history, says that he was. He worked as a hired hand at one time in a silver mine. Shall we condemn Joseph Smith for honest hard labor?"

Uncle Ed: "No, no, but what about all those affidavits and sworn statements from his neighbors saying he was a drunkard, and a bum, a lazy fellow with a crystal ball. Can you tell me that they are liars too—all sixty-two of them that signed those affidavits?"

Elder Jones: "There's a great contradiction right there, Mr. Brown. Anti-Mormons try to portray Joseph as the laziest no good on earth, but they also say that he spent all his time looking for buried treasure digging up the whole country side, but not finding anything. That's hard work."

Elder Smith: "Don't forget the Bible, Mr. Brown. Were those things they said about Jesus true? After all, they had plenty of witnesses against Him, but we know that they were false witnesses."

Elder Jones: "Not only that, but sixty affidavits were signed in favor of Joseph and his family by other neighbors."

Linda: "How can you explain that, Elders? Some people were for him and others against?"

Elder Smith: "That takes us right back to the Bible, Linda. Not everyone believed in Jesus. In John 7:12 it says that 'There was much murmuring among the people concerning him: for some said, He is a good man: others said, Nay; but he deceiveth the people.'"

Linda: "But what about hunting for treasures?"

Elder Jones: "Linda, you remember that we told you that Joseph received the gold plates from the earth, and he translated them by the Urim and Thummim."

Linda: "Yes, I remember that."

Elder Jones: "We know that rumors are bad enough among friends, but rumors are typically circulated among enemies. People heard that Joseph found gold plates in a hill, and translated them by some sort of revelatory instrument. Pretty soon, as gossip would have it, the story disintegrated into tales of buried treasure and crystal balls."

Elder Smith: "Some believed Joseph was a prophet, and some believed not. Those that disbelieved were ready to think the worst. And, as rumor would have it, the worst was given them—not by Joseph, but by gossip and false witnesses."

Elder Jones: "That's right, Linda. Back in ancient times, people who didn't believe that Jesus was sent from God swore to things that weren't true either, because they were ready to believe in false rumors and gossip."

"Varying First Vision Accounts" Objection Answered

Uncle Ed: "Okay, here's something that will really prove Joseph Smith to be a false prophet. The Mormon Church is based upon the first vision, but in one version Joseph says that Jesus only appears to him, but in a later version Joseph says that God the Father *and* Jesus appear to him! Here Joseph is lying in one or in both accounts."

Linda: "Is this true, Elders?"

Elder Smith: "Linda, it's true that there are several accounts of his first vision written by Joseph Smith. They were written years apart, and there are some differences between them. But by way of comparison, there are differing accounts in the Bible about the resurrection of Jesus. In Luke 24:4 it says that two angels appeared at the empty tomb to the women, while in Matthew 28:2 it mentions only one angel appearing to the women."

Linda:	"How can you explain that, Uncle Ed?"
Uncle Ed:	"It doesn't say that there was only one angel—Matthew just doesn't mention the other one, while Luke does."
Elder Jones:	"Exactly, Mr. Brown, and that holds true for Joseph Smith's accounts of his first vision also. In one account, the shorter one, Joseph relates his conversation with Jesus in his first vision, but at another time Joseph gives more details—like the appearance of the Father, other angels, and more details of the conversations he had with Jesus."
Linda:	"There's no contradiction at all—just stories told twice. Some things are always left out, and other things added."
Elder Smith:	"Sharp, Linda."
Uncle Ed:	"Joseph Smith couldn't have been a prophet. He broke God's laws because he was a polygamist!"
Elder Jones:	"We'll get to that in connection with our thirteenth Article of Faith, Mr. Brown."

"Glasslooker" Objection Answered

Uncle Ed:	"All right, what about Joseph being convicted of being a glasslooker? I have copies of court records, and...."
Elder Smith:	"Mr. Brown, weren't we going to stick to the Bible?"
Uncle Ed:	"I am. How could god call a convicted criminal?"
Elder Jones:	"God called Jesus, His son, who was a convicted criminal according to the supreme court of his land."
Elder Smith:	"Regarding the so-called 1826 trial of Joseph Smith you just alluded to, you should know that the so-called eye witness accounts, all from anti-Mormon sources, are extremely contradictory; at least two of them say Joseph was acquitted...."

"Joseph Smith Not Needed" Objection Answered

Elder Jones:	"Linda, do you have any more questions on Joseph Smith?"
Linda:	"A question that still lingers in my mind is one my Uncle asked me. If we have Jesus, why do we need Joseph Smith? I didn't know what to say."
Elder Smith:	"That's like asking, if we have Jesus, why do we need Peter or Paul or Isaiah or Moses? Or if we have Jesus, why do we need John the Baptist?"

Linda:	"Huh?"
Elder Jones:	"I think what my companion is trying to say, Linda, is that we need everything Jesus says that we need. Joseph Smith is a modern John the Baptist."
Linda:	"What do you mean?"
Elder Jones:	"We know that Jesus came in the meridian of time, and God sent a prophet, John the Baptist, to prepare His way. And we know that Jesus will come again, in all his glory. Doesn't it make sense that God would follow the pattern he previously established and send another forerunner, another prophet to prepare the way for the second coming of His Son?"
Linda:	"Yes, it fits."
Elder Smith:	"Well Linda, Joseph the Seer is that prophet."
Uncle Ed:	(Laughing) "I don't believe this. Jesus warned us against Joseph Smith when he said, 'Beware of false prophets which come to you in sheep's clothing, but inwardly they are ravening wolves'" (Matthew 7:15).
Elder Jones:	"Yes, but Jesus wasn't condemning all who claimed to be prophets. We know that, according to Acts 5, Judas of Galilee and Theudas were claiming to be prophets at the same time as John the Baptist. We know Judas and Theudas were false prophets, but that doesn't mean that John was a false prophet, nor were the apostles of Jesus false prophets."
Uncle Ed:	"Ah, but wait—the world accepts John the Baptist and the Apostles as true prophets, but not Joseph Smith. He was a false prophet!"
Elder Smith:	"Mr. Brown, the 'world' at the time of John and the Apostles regarded all of them as false prophets, just as anti-Mormon adversaries today claim Joseph and the modern LDS Apostles are false prophets. Jesus called His disciples out of the world, and he said in Matthew 23, verse 34, 'Wherefore, behold, I send unto you prophets, and wise men, and scribes: and some of them ye shall kill and crucify; and some of them shall ye scourge in your synagogues, and persecute them from city to city.'"
Elder Jones:	"Not only that, Mr. Brown, Jesus told the Pharisees that they built beautiful shrines and monuments to the prophets, but if those very same prophets were alive in

their day, they would kill them." (See Matthew
23:29-37.)

Linda: "Elders, I don't have any more questions about this—
maybe we should get on to the next subject."

"Apostles Not Needed Today" Objection Answered

Elder Smith: "Good idea, Linda. Let me see, the sixth Article of Faith
reads, 'We believe in the same organization that existed
in the Primitive Church, namely, apostles, prophets,
pastors, teachers, evangelists, and so forth.'"

Linda: "My uncle told me that we have the Bible, so we don't
need apostles today."

Elder Jones: "Again Linda, we need what Jesus says we need."

Uncle Ed: "Where in the Bible does it say that we need to have
apostles today?"

Linda: "Elders?"

Elder Smith: "Well, Linda, let me ask you this: What is the Church?"

Linda: "It's the body of Christ—the assembly of believers."

Elder Smith: "Good. Now, are there believers today? Is there a body
of Christ?"

Linda: "Yes, of course!"

Elder Smith: "Well then, the Church, or body of Christ, must exist
today, just as it existed 2,000 years ago."

Linda: "Right!"

Elder Jones: "I see where you're going, companion. Now Linda, we
know that the Church must exist today as it did 2,000
years ago, because there are many believers. But what
does Paul say about the Church? In Ephesians 2, verses
19 and 20, Paul writes, 'Now therefore ye are no more
strangers and foreigners, but fellowcitizens with the
saints, and of the household of God; And are *built upon
the foundation of the apostles and prophets*, Jesus
Christ himself being the chief corner stone.'"

Elder Smith: "So we see, Linda, if the body of Christ, or the Church,
exists today, it must have a foundation of apostles and
prophets."

Linda: "That really makes sense."

Uncle Ed: "Yeah, nonsense."

"Christ to Come in 1891" Objection Answered

Elder Jones: "Companion, would you read...."

Elder Smith: "Read the next Article of Faith, right? Article seven reads, 'We believe in the gift of tongues, prophecy, revelation, visions, healing, interpretation of tongues, and so forth.'"

Elder Jones: "Under this heading, let's put prophecies and priesthood."

Uncle Ed: "Ah I'm glad you mentioned prophecies, because Joseph Smith uttered lots of false prophecies. Joseph Smith declared that Jesus was going to return in 1891, when he was 85 years old. Well, Jesus didn't come. Conclusion: Joseph was a false prophet!"

Linda: "Is that true, Elders? Did he really say that?"

Elder Smith: "Not exactly, Linda. If you're curious about it, let's read what Joseph really had to say."

Elder Jones: "I have that, Elder. I'll read it. Your Uncle is referring to the Doctrine and Covenants, section 130, verses 14 through 17. Let me read what Joseph Smith recorded. He wrote, 'I was once praying very earnestly to know the time of the coming of the Son of Man, when I heard a voice repeat the following: Joseph, my son, if thou livest until thou art eighty-five years old, thou shalt see the face of the Son of Man; therefore let this suffice, and trouble me no more on this matter.'"

Uncle Ed: "There. You see Linda, false prophecy."

Elder Jones: "I'm not through with my quote. He said...."

Uncle Ed: "This other false prophecy has to do with the Civil War, and...."

Linda: "Uncle Ed, please! Elder, go ahead."

Elder Jones: "The very next verses read, 'I was left thus, without being able to decide whether this coming referred to the beginning of the millennium or to some previous appearing, or whether I should die and thus see his face. I believe the coming of the Son of Man will not be any sooner than that time.'"

Elder Smith: "You know, Linda, in Joseph Smith's day millions of Christian people proclaimed and believed that Jesus was going to return in 1844. Joseph apparently knew the Lord wouldn't come at that time."

Elder Jones:	"Joseph didn't know if the Lord would return when he was 85, or if he would die and meet him, or if the Lord would make some preliminary appearance prior to His coming in glory. Either way, we don't know what would have happened, because Joseph was martyred at 38 years of age."
Linda:	"Uncle Ed, why didn't you show me the next verses? Why didn't you explain this to me?"
Uncle Ed:	"Linda, it would have only confused you more than these young men have already done!"

"Mormons Distrust the Bible" Objection Answered

Elder Jones:	"Companion, let's move on."
Elder Smith:	"Way ahead of you. The eighth Article of Faith reads, 'We believe the Bible to be the word of God as far as it is translated correctly; we also believe the Book of Mormon to be the word of God.'"
Uncle Ed:	"Aha, there you go. See Linda, they don't trust the Bible!"
Linda:	"Then why do they use it all the time?"
Uncle Ed:	"To make people think they're Christian. But you just heard them—as far as it is translated correctly. That means if they come across verses that disagree with Mormonism, which almost all Biblical verses do, they just say the Bible isn't translated correctly!"
Elder Jones:	"Could you give us an example of that, Mr. Brown?"
Uncle Ed:	"Of what?"
Elder Jones:	"Of what you just said. Have we challenged the translation of any Biblical scriptures here today that we've discussed?"
Uncle Ed:	"You haven't explained one to my satisfaction!"
Elder Smith:	"Neither did the Savior satisfy those that opposed him!"
Linda:	"But what does it mean, 'as far as translated correctly'?"
Elder Jones:	"It means, Linda, that Latter-day Saints believe the Bible as written by the original authors, in Hebrew and Greek, is inerrant. But we occasionally find some verses in which the meaning has become somewhat obscured in the translation."
Uncle Ed:	"You see Linda, they told you. They don't trust the Bible."

Linda: "But that's not what they said, Uncle Ed. Don't you remember Pastor Johnson telling us in Sunday School how he studied Greek and Hebrew for years at seminary because these original languages helped him find clearer meanings in the Bible than could be found in English, and how we had word study workshops, and...."

"Changes in the Book of Mormon" Objection Answered

Uncle Ed: "All right Linda, but the foundation of Mormonism doesn't rest on the Bible; it rests on the Book of Mormon. How can you boys explain the 4,000 changes in the Book of Mormon?"

Elder Smith: "How can you explain the hundreds of thousands of changes made in the English Bibles? They occur because translators are constantly revising the Word of God to make it more readable and up-to-date."

Elder Jones: "Not only that, but the first draft of the Book of Mormon had relatively few periods and punctuation marks, limited capitalization and no columns. These had to be added later. And the typesetter made hundreds of spelling mistakes and typesetting errors in the first edition."

"Revelation Has Ceased" Objection Answered

Uncle Ed: "Well, I can prove from the Bible that revelation has ceased. Revelation 22, verse 18, says that 'If any man shall add unto these things, God shall add unto him the plagues that are written in this book.'"

Elder Smith: "Let's read the next verse. 'And if any man shall take away from the words of *the book of this prophecy*, God shall take away his part out of the book of life.' When John wrote what he calls 'this book,' he was referring to the Book of Revelation and not the New Testament, because the New Testament didn't exist at the time. It wasn't compiled until hundreds of years later."

Elder Jones: "Not only that, but John wrote his gospel and his epistles, the Gospel of John and 1st John, 2nd John and 3rd John, *after* he had written the Book of Revelation. Holding your view, we should remove them from the New Testament."

Elder Smith:	"Linda, was there anything in the Book of Mormon that you don't accept? How do you feel about it?"

"Solomon Spaulding Authorship" Objection Answered

Linda:	"I felt really good about it, but my uncle said that Joseph Smith copied the book from some Solomon.... something?"
Elder Jones:	"Solomon Spaulding?"
Linda:	"Yes, that's right!"
Elder Smith:	"Mr. Brown, you should know better than a lot of people that the Spaulding Theory on the origins of the Book of Mormon, advanced by anti-Mormons, was proven false many years ago. Even most anti-Mormon writers have long since given it up. You should too."
Uncle Ed:	"There is absolutely no evidence for the Book of Mormon. Archaeology has not found one coin, not one city mentioned in the Book!"
Elder Jones:	"Mr. Brown, we can sit here and argue archaeology until next week, and there is considerable archaeological evidence for the Book of Mormon. But the real evidence for the Book of Mormon is found between it's covers. The Book of Mormon promises that those who read it with real intent, and pray to God whether the things it contains are true or not, will be given their own personal revelation that it is truly the word of God. Millions of people have applied that promise and found that it is true."

"Burning in the Bosom Is Satanic" Objection Answered

Uncle Ed:	"Oh, I know all about your 'burning-in-the-bosom,' but that is a Satanic feeling that is subjective and totally unreliable!"
Elder Smith:	"Oh really, Mr. Brown? It seemed to work for the disciples of Jesus!"
Uncle Ed:	"What do you mean?"
Elder Smith:	"You said the burning in the bosom was unreliable, subjective, and even Satanic?"
Uncle Ed:	"That's right!"

Elder Smith:	"In Luke chapter 24, verses 13-32, the resurrected Jesus appeared to two disciples on the road to Emmaus. They didn't recognize Jesus, but they walked and talked with Him, and then they invited Him to eat with them. I'll read verses 31 and 32: 'And their eyes were opened, and they knew him; and he vanished out of their sight. And they said one to another, *Did not our heart burn within us*, while he talked with us by the way, and while he opened to us the scriptures?'"
Elder Jones:	"Was that burning in their bosoms Satanically inspired, Mr. Brown?"
Uncle Ed:	"No, of course not. But that has nothing to do with anything anyhow."
Elder Jones:	"That burning in the bosom is a very real, tangible manifestation of the presence of the Holy Ghost. Those anti-Mormon adversaries who deny its existence apparently have never experienced it, or else they wouldn't challenge it. But there are millions of LDS converts and members who have experienced it regularly, and they know that burning in the bosom truly exists, and they know how to be guided by it."

"Fulness of the Gospel" Objection Answered

Uncle Ed:	"The Book of Mormon claims to contain the fulness of the Mormon gospel, but where can one read about a Heavenly Mother, or secret temple rites in the book?"
Linda:	"I don't remember reading anything like that in the Book of Mormon!"
Elder Smith:	"What is the gospel, Linda?"
Linda:	"The gospel is the good news that Jesus is the Son of God, that He died for us, that God raised Him from the dead, and that Jesus has given men certain principles and ordinances to live so they can partake in full of Christ's atonement."
Elder Smith:	"Good memory, Linda. And that's exactly what the Book of Mormon teaches in its fulness! There are some teachings on other subjects which aren't contained in the Book of Mormon, but the basic principles of the gospel—that Jesus is the Christ, that He died for all mankind, and that we come to Him through faith, repentance, baptism, and obedience to the guidance

we receive through the promptings of the Holy Ghost, are taught clearly and fully. And that's why the scriptures say that the Book of Mormon contains the fulness of the everlasting gospel."

"Heavenly Mother" Objection Answered

Elder Smith: "The ninth Article of Faith reads, 'We believe all that God has revealed, all that He does now reveal, and we believe that He will yet reveal many great and important things pertaining to the Kingdom of God.'"

Elder Jones: "In this category, let's include what the scriptures call the mysteries of God."

Uncle Ed: "You're trying to evade the issue. Jesus never taught any secret rites, much less those of your pagan temples. And what about your belief that there's a Heavenly Mother? Of course, it's not in the Bible, but the mystery is that you can't find it in Mormon scriptures as well. So why believe it?"

Linda: "Why isn't that in the Bible, Elders?"

Elder Smith: "It is in the Bible! It says in Genesis, chapter 1, verses 26-27, that 'God said, Let us make man in our image, after our likeness: and let them have dominion over the fish of the sea, and over the fowl of the air, and over the cattle, and over all the earth, and over every creeping thing that creepeth upon the earth. So God created man in his own image, in the image of God created he him; *male and female created he them.*'"

Uncle Ed: "So what does that prove?"

Elder Jones: "It proves that man *and* woman, male *and* female, were created in the image of God."

Uncle Ed: (Snickering) "Huh! God is neither male nor female!"

Linda: "Then why does everyone, and why did Jesus, call God our Heavenly Father? And wasn't Jesus God—wasn't He male?"

Uncle Ed: "Linda, you're talking about things you don't understand!"

Elder Smith: "Linda, we know that God is the Father of our spirits, and if a Father of our spirits exists, then a mother must also!"

Linda: "I can see that now!"

"Temple Ceremonies Are Secret" Objection Answered

Uncle Ed:	"What I can see is secret pagan temple rituals with blood oaths and lives being offered up to Lucifer!"
Elder Jones:	"What do you mean, Mr. Brown?"
Uncle Ed:	"You know what I mean! Your pagan temple rites!"
Elder Smith:	"Why do you call them pagan, Mr. Brown?"
Uncle Ed:	"Because you offer your souls to Lucifer, and have secret passwords and such. Why don't you tell Linda what goes on in there?"
Linda:	"I'd like to hear it from you, Elders."
Elder Jones:	"Linda, if Jesus were to tell you, 'I am the Christ, but tell this to no man,' what would you do?"
Linda:	"I would obey him, of course!"
Elder Smith:	"In that same manner, Linda, Latter-day Saints promise to keep the sacraments of the temple sacred. That is why we don't discuss the temple ceremony in detail outside of the temple."
Uncle Ed:	"Jesus would never instruct anyone not to tell others that he is the Christ—that's absurd!"
Elder Jones:	"Then the Bible is absurd, because in Matthew, chapter 16, verse 20, it says,'Then charged he his disciples that they should tell no man that he was Jesus the Christ.'"(See also Matthew 8:4; 17:9; Mark 7:36; 8:26,30; 9:9; Luke 5:14; 8:56; 9:21).
Elder Smith:	"But let me bear you this testimony, Linda. Though we don't discuss details of our temple service outside of the temple, I bear you my solemn witness that the temple ceremony is fully God-centered, and the covenants Latter-day Saints make there are that they will live lives of the highest moral caliber. And I bear you witness that the idea that Mormons make pledges or offer up their lives to Satan in the temple is totally false. It's a lie started and perpetrated by anti-Mormon adversaries. They have tried to circulate falsehoods on this subject because they know Latter-day Saints won't discuss the temple ceremony in depth to refute these claims. What they say about Satan is directly opposite to what really occurs in the temple, and I have no doubt but that they will bring the judgments of God upon themselves for continually circulating such a lie."

"No Mention of Temple Rites in Bible" Objection Answered

Uncle Ed: "What I meant to say is that the Bible and Jesus are contrary to secrecy. Jesus said, in John 18:20, 'I spake openly to the world; I ever taught in the synagogue, and in the temple, wither the Jews always resort; and in secret have I said nothing.' There, it is said, no secret rites—no Mormon temples, at least from the Bible."

Elder Smith: "Why do you quote John 18:20, Mr. Brown? Those were Jesus's words *before* His resurrection. We know that Jesus taught His most sacred teachings, the temple rites called the mysteries of God in the scriptures, to His disciples *after* His resurrection, during His post-resurrection forty-day ministry."

Uncle Ed: "Ha, Jesus was just reiterating what he had taught before. He said nothing about secret temple rites!"

Elder Jones: "But Mr. Brown, Jesus said in John 16:12, '*I have yet many things to say unto you, but ye cannot bear them now.*' This was right before He offered His great intercessory prayer, Mr. Brown. Right after that He was arrested and crucified. Just when did Jesus teach His disciples those 'many things' which they then could not yet bear? Remember, He made that statement to them at the *completion* of His mortal ministry."

Linda: "He must have taught them higher truths during His forty-day ministry—*after* He was resurrected."

Uncle Ed: (Angrily) "Linda! Now look boys, just show me one verse, just one verse from the Bible that says Jesus taught secret rites and oaths."

Elder Smith: "Again, Mr. Brown, we won't show you just one verse— we can show you many verses. There are many scriptures that speak of Jesus teaching mysteries, or secret things. There's Matthew 13:11, 1st Corinthians 4:1, 13:2, and 14:2, there's Mark 4:11, also Revelation 1:20, as well as...."

Elder Jones: "Perhaps we need to read one, Elder. Linda and her uncle may not be familiar with these scriptures."

Elder Smith: "You're right, Elder, I'm sorry. Let's see. Perhaps the words of Paul best explain this. In 1st Corinthians 2:7, Paul writes, 'But we speak the *wisdom of God in a mystery, even the hidden wisdom*, which God ordained before the world unto our glory.' And in 1st Corinthians

	4:1, Paul says, 'Let a man so account of us, as of the ministers of Christ, and *stewards of the mysteries of God.*"
Uncle Ed:	"Ha, you don't know what you're trying to say. What does that prove?"
Elder Jones:	"It proves a lot, Mr. Brown. Because in 2nd Corinthians 12:2-4, Paul writes, 'I knew a man in Christ above fourteen years ago, (whether in the body, I cannot tell; or whether out of the body I cannot tell: God knoweth;) such an one caught up to the third heaven. And I knew such a man, (whether in the body, or out of the body, I cannot tell: God knoweth;) How that he was caught up into paradise, and heard *unspeakable words, which it is not lawful for a man to utter.*"
Uncle Ed:	"That doesn't prove anything. All Paul is saying is that Jesus showed him a vision, and that what Jesus showed him was not lawful for him to speak of. Nothing about secret oaths...."
Linda:	"But Uncle Ed, didn't you say before that Jesus would never say anything in secret?"
Uncle Ed:	"Well ah, ah, eh, don't confuse me. Now look boys, where in the Bible does it talk about getting a new name, and secret handshakes and signs. All of that is from Lucifer!"
Linda:	"Where does it talk abut those things, Elders?"
Elder Smith:	"Okay, Linda, in the Book of Revelation we read, here in chapter 2, verse 17, 'To him that overcometh will I give to eat of the hidden manna, and I will give him a white stone, and in the stone *a new name written, which no man knoweth saving he that receiveth it.*"
Uncle Ed:	"That doesn't prove anything!"
Linda:	"Well, if it doesn't mean a person can receive a new name, what does it mean, Uncle Ed?"
Uncle Ed:	"Ah, it means, ah well, (angrily) I don't know what it means, but it sure doesn't mean what you're saying it means!"
Elder Smith:	"Well Mr. Brown, it definitely speaks of a new name being given. But of course you're entitled to your own opinion."
Uncle Ed:	"And you'll be damned for yours...."
Linda:	"Uncle Ed...."

"Swear Not At All" Objection Answered

Uncle Ed:	"No, I've tried to be patient with you boys, but you've done nothing but avoid the issues. Now just tell me where it says we must offer up oaths in secret temple rites. You can't, because Jesus Himself said, 'I say unto you, Swear not at all; neither by heaven, for it is God's throne: Nor by the earth; for it is his footstool: neither by Jerusalem; for it is the city of the great King. Neither shalt thou swear by thy head, because thou canst not make one hair white or black. But let your communication be Yea, yea; Nay, nay: for whatsoever is more than these cometh of evil.' And you can find that, boys, in the Bible in Matthew 5:34-37!"
Linda:	"How can you explain that, Elders? Doesn't that say not to swear any oaths at all?"
Elder Jones:	"Let us ask both of you a question. Should we follow God's example?"
Linda:	"Of course!"
Uncle Ed:	"What are you getting at?"
Elder Jones:	"I'm getting at this—that we should follow God's example, and in Psalm 110:4 we read, '*The LORD hath sworn*, and will not repent, Thou art a priest for ever after the order of Melchizedek' and in Jeremiah 44:26 it says, '*I have sworn by my great name, saith the LORD*,' and in Psalm....'"
Uncle Ed:	"All right, God can give oaths, but we can't!"
Elder Smith:	"Exactly, Mr. Brown."
Linda:	"But what did Jesus mean?"
Elder Jones:	"What he meant, Linda, was that many people were dishonest in his day, just as they are today. Dishonesty became so bad that people began to swear by God's throne, or by the hairs of their head. Jesus wanted them to seal their agreements and promises by simply saying yea or nay, or, in other words, by just being honest."
Uncle Ed:	"But how about those bloody oaths where you promise to have your throat cut and all the rest if you tell what goes on inside your temples?"
Linda:	"Is that *true*, Elders?"
Elder Smith:	"No Linda, that is not true. We make no promises to have any harm come to us if we reveal the mysteries of God. But I will say that rather than reveal the

	mysteries of God, those sacred things Jesus has entrusted me with, I would allow my life to be taken."
Elder Jones:	"I second that, Elder!"

"Bloody Oaths" Objection Answered

Uncle Ed:	"How can you call yourselves Christians? Your oaths are still bloody, no matter what you do or don't promise."
Elder Smith:	"Why do you say bloody, Mr. Brown? There is no blood shedding in the temple, nor any other violent things such as you have described."
Uncle Ed:	"Saying or promising to have my throat cut—that's gruesome, and definitely not of Jesus!"
Elder Jones:	"Do you believe in the Bible, Mr. Brown?"
Uncle Ed:	"Of course I do, and I don't attach any 'as far as it is translated correctly' onto that."
Elder Jones:	"Good. And if Jesus told you to do something, would you do it?"
Uncle Ed:	"Of course."
Elder Jones:	"Good. Let's read Jesus's words in the 5th chapter of Matthew, verses 29 and 30. Jesus said, 'And if thy right eye offend thee, pluck it out, and cast it from thee: for it is profitable for thee that one of thy members should perish, and not that thy whole body should be cast into hell. And if thy right hand offend thee, cut it off, and cast it from thee: for it is profitable for thee that one of thy members should perish, and not that thy whole body should be cast into hell.' Has your right hand or right eye ever offended you, Mr. Brown?"
Uncle Ed:	"What you're getting at is absurd—Jesus was only using symbolical language!"
Elder Smith:	"Exactly Mr. Brown!"
Linda:	"Oh, I see what you mean, Elders."

"No Temples After Jesus's Day" Objection Answered

Uncle Ed:	"Well, I don't see, and I can't see worshipping Jesus in Mormon temples. There were going to be no more temples after Jesus was here, and that was 2,000 years ago."

Elder Jones:	"Oh, really Mr. Brown? Then why does Jesus tell John, in Revelation 7:15, 'Therefore are they before the throne of God, and *serve him day and night in his temple*: and he that sitteth on the throne shall dwell among them?'"
Linda:	"Uncle Ed?" (Pause)

"Garden of Eden in America" Objection Answered

Elder Jones:	"Elder?"
Elder Smith:	"Right. Our tenth Article of Faith reads, 'We believe in the literal gathering of Israel and in the restoration of the Ten Tribes; that Zion (the New Jerusalem) will be built upon the American continent; that Christ will reign personally upon the earth; and, that the earth will be renewed and receive its paradisiacal glory.'"
Uncle Ed:	"Here's yet another strange belief, Linda, that proves them wrong once again. They believe that the Garden of Eden was here in America, (laughing) in Missouri in fact, and that Jesus isn't coming back to Jerusalem, but to Salt Lake City."
Linda:	"Elders?"
Elder Jones:	"Linda, we do not believe that Jesus is coming back to Salt Lake City, because right here in Doctrine and Covenants 45:48 it says that the Lord will return and set his foot on the Mount of Olives in Jerusalem."
Linda:	"Okay, but what about the Garden of Eden? I thought it would be in the Middle East somewhere."
Uncle Ed:	"That's right Linda. In fact, Genesis chapter two identifies the lands of Assyria and Ethiopia, and the river Euphrates—they're all in the Middle East, far away from Missouri."
Elder Smith:	"Let's take a closer look. Here in Genesis 2:10 it says, 'A river went out of Eden to water the garden; and from thence it was parted, and became into four heads.' According to verse 13, one of these subsidiaries encircled Ethiopia; another subsidiary of that same river encircled Assyria, according to verse 14."
Uncle Ed:	"So?"
Elder Jones:	"So, Mr. Brown, Ethiopia and Assyria are on two separate continents, father apart than New York and Chicago. They're divided by thousands of miles of

	ocean and desert and mountains, with no river joining the two...."
Uncle Ed:	"If God said there was once a river there, then there was."
Elder Smith:	"But a river can't cross over mountain ranges and through the Red Sea."
Linda:	"What about the names, Elders? I mean, Ethiopia is still in Africa, and Assyria is still in the Middle East."
Elder Jones:	"Exactly Linda, but we know that there is a Portland in Maine, and a Portland in Oregon—three thousand miles away."
Elder Smith:	"There is a London, England, and another London in Ontario, Canada, almost seven thousand miles away. Linda, when Noah and the ancient peoples civilized the Middle East, they named places and rivers after their old homes here in America."
Elder Jones:	"And remember that in Genesis, the river of Eden broke into four heads, or subsidiaries, and that fits very well into the geography of the Mississippi River Valley."
Uncle Ed:	"You can't prove that the Garden of Eden was in Missouri."
Elder Smith:	"You're right, we can't, any more than you can prove it was in the Middle East. And none of us here today can prove to anyone that there even was a Garden of Eden to begin with. But Latter-day Saints believe it because a prophet of God declared it. We believe in the inspired words of God's prophets, whether it be Moses or Joseph the Seer."
Elder Jones:	"Have we answered that question for you, Linda?"
Linda:	"Uh-huh."

"Mountain Meadows" Objection Answered

Elder Smith:	"All right. The eleventh Article of Faith reads, 'We claim the privilege of worshipping Almighty God according to the dictates of our own conscience, and allow all men the same privilege, let them worship how, where, or what they may.'"
Uncle Ed:	"Ah, but that's not true. Brigham Young had people killed who tried to leave Mormonism and come back to Biblical Christianity. Remember me telling you about the Mountain Meadows Massacre, Linda?"

Linda: "Yes, I couldn't believe it. How could Brigham Young order the killing of over a hundred innocent people?"

Elder Jones: "The fact is that he never did, Linda. At that time, the enemies of the Saints in Utah, the anti-Mormons, were trying to make it appear that the Mormon's were rebelling against the U.S. Government, which was a falsehood. The President, his name was Buchanan, sent a large army to crush the so-called rebellion. When the Army arrived in the Utah territory, they discovered that the anti-Mormons had lied to them. It went down in history as 'Buchanan's Blunder.' Some of the Saints colonized southern Utah, which was virtually cut off from the rest of the world. Anyway, wagon trains to California would pass through southern Utah on their way west. One such wagon train was passing through from Arkansas and Missouri. Most of them were pioneer families heading for California, but they hired some rough riders as guides and to protect them from the Indians. These riders called themselves the Missouri Wildcats, and they were men who had taken part in the anti-Mormon persecutions in Missouri, where many hundreds of the Saints were driven from their homes, raped and murdered. As they passed through southern Utah, they shot several Indians to death just for sport, and poisoned the springs so neither the Mormons nor the Indians would have any water to drink. In a desert area like Southern Utah, that in and of itself was like committing murder. The Indians came to the Mormons living there, whom they considered their allies, and demanded that they join in killing the members of the wagon train in retaliation. The Indians said if the Mormons didn't help them kill the bad whites in the wagon train that they would kill the Mormons. A handful of the Mormons agreed to help the Indians. A messenger was sent to Brigham Young, who was in Salt Lake City two hundred and fifty miles away, riding as fast as he could on horseback, to ask what should be done. Brigham Young instructed the messenger that the settlers were to protect the wagon train at all costs. But by the time the rider got back to southern Utah, the massacre had already occurred. All the wagon-train adults were killed by the Indians and the few Mormons who were with them, but the Mormon settlers were able to get the Indians to spare the lives of the young children. They were placed in orphanages and foster homes."

Linda: "What happened to the few Mormons that helped the Indians kill those people?"

Elder Smith: "They were excommunicated from the Church. Their leader was tried according to the laws of the land and was eventually executed."

Uncle Ed: "John D. Lee, their leader, was the captain of the Danites, the Avenging Angels, Brigham's hit squad."

Elder Jones: "Hardly, Mr. Brown. He lied about the event. He told everyone he tried to get the Indians not to do it, but in fact, he killed men and women himself. When Brigham Young found out the truth he excommunicated Lee. Lee then became a 'Christian' and wrote an anti-Mormon book, but his upcoming anti-Mormon career was cut short because he was tried by the law and executed for his murders."

Elder Smith: "Anti-Mormons have tried to use the Mountain Meadow massacre as so-called 'evidence' to support the falsehood they spread that Brigham Young killed people, or ordered other men to do it, that tried to leave Mormonism."

Uncle Ed: "That's true."

Elder Smith: "Well, I don't think so, because the people killed at Mountain Meadows were never Mormons to begin with, and their deaths were the exact opposite of the instructions Brigham gave."

"Blood Atonement" Objection Answered

Uncle Ed: "Ah, but I have statements here from Brigham Young himself about blood atonement—that there are certain sins that Jesus's blood cannot atone for. A man's own blood must be shed."

Linda: "Is this true, Elders?"

Elder Smith: "Do you believe in capital punishment, Mr. Brown?"

Uncle Ed: "Now you're trying to change the subject."

Elder Jones: "No he's not, Mr. Brown. All he is trying to say is that Brigham Young taught that a murderer should be put

	to death, and most 'born-again' Christians would agree with this."
Elder Smith:	"Linda, I've seen those quotes from anti-Mormon books that supposedly quote Brigham Young advocating killing people, but once you see them in context, you find that what he was doing was advocating capital punishment."
Uncle Ed:	"But it's in black and white."
Elder Jones:	"So is this, Mr. Brown. In Luke 19:27 Jesus told His disciples, 'But those mine enemies, which would not that I should reign over them, bring hither, and slay them before me.' Was Jesus advocating killing people there, Mr. Brown?"
Uncle Ed:	"Let me see that...(pause)...ha, no, no. Jesus here is giving a parable about a King. It's just figurative."
Elder Smith:	"Exactly, Mr. Brown. And so are the statements of Brigham Young. He was advocating a legal procedure, not telling men to commit murder."
Elder Jones:	"Do you have any more questions on this point, Linda?"
Linda:	"No."

"Secret Government Takeover Plans" Objection Answered

Elder Smith:	"All right, the twelfth Article of Faith reads, 'We believe in being subject to kings, presidents, rulers, and magistrates, in obeying, honoring, and sustaining the law.'"
Uncle Ed:	"That's a bunch of malarky."
Linda:	"Elders, my uncle told me that your Church has secret plans to take over the U.S. and then the world, and that you store guns and ammunition with your year's supply of food. Why do you do that?"
Elder Jones:	"Linda, Mormons do not have secret plans to take over the government, and I challenge Mr. Brown to submit even a shred of evidence to show that we do, knowing full well that he can't because no such plans exist."
Uncle Ed:	"Well, I know a former member of the hierarchy of your Church, a Minister I.M. Phoney, and he told me on strict report that the Mormon Church has plans to take over the U.S. government. That's why there are so many Mormons in government."

Elder Smith: "Mr. Ira Millhouse Phoney was a ward clerk at one time I believe, and an Elder for a short while. Definitely not one whom you would say is a member of the LDS hierarchy or general Church leadership."

Uncle Ed: "Okay, you say he was an Elder. There you go—hierarchy."

Linda: "But Uncle, these are both Elders, and they're both my age. You wouldn't consider them part of the Church's general leadership hierarchy, would you?"

Uncle Ed: "I just wouldn't consider them Christian."

Elder Jones: "Mr. Brown, just because there are a substantial number of Latter-day Saints in government service does not mean that there is an LDS conspiracy to take over the U.S. Government, any more than the fact that there are a lot of Lutherans and Baptists in government service means that those churches have a plot to take government control. The reason why there are so many Mormons in government service may be because of the great love we have for this country and our strong desire to serve it. Mormons are a very patriotic people."

Elder Smith: "You know Hitler rose to power because he lied to the German people. He told them that the Jews were trying to take over. They weren't; he did."

Uncle Ed: (Angrily) "What? Are you calling me a Hitler?"

Elder Jones: "All we are saying, Mr. Brown and Linda, is that anti-Mormon adversaries claim that Latter-day Saints have treasonous plans against the U.S. Government, but this is a fictitious claim which is absolutely without merit or factual basis. There's a long history of Mormon loyalty to the nation dating back to pioneer times. When the U.S. Government asked the Church for 500 men to fight in the war with Mexico, the Saints gave the men requested, even though the government had looked the other way while the Mormons were raped, brutalized, and killed by their enemies. During all of America's wars, with the exception of the Revolutionary war, of course, Utah, which is mostly Latter-day Saints, has given a higher percentage of soldiers to the armed services than any other state. The Saints have given and given. During the Civil War, the Confederacy came to Brigham Young and offered the Saints statehood and other rights (something they were denied by the Union), if they would only support the South. Brigham Young refused and said, 'We shall stand by the Union.' This took place shortly after the 'Union' had sent an Army to kill them, and during a time that carpet-baggers were controlling Utah and treating the Saints like slaves."

Elder Smith: "In other words, Linda, Mr. Phoney's witness against the Mormons is no more valid than the testimony of those false witnesses that accused Jesus of treason, and of those false witnesses that accused the loyal Moses of treason when he wanted only to take Israel to the desert to worship."

Linda: "Uncle Ed, what evidence, and I mean *real* evidence, do you have that the Mormon Church is disloyal to the U.S. Government, and planning to take it over?"

"Polygamy" Objection Answered

Uncle Ed: "The best evidence that I have, Linda, is polygamy. The Mormon Church practiced polygamy, an abomination before God and His Holy Word, for over fifty years, in direct violation of the Constitution of the United States. They only gave it up when the government threatened to take their money away."

Elder Jones: "I'm afraid you have your chronology confused, Mr. Brown. The amendment to the Constitution you are referring to did not come until the late 1860's, and was not finally declared constitutional until the Supreme Court rendered it so in the late 1880's. Very shortly thereafter, the LDS Church gave up the practice of plural marriage."

Elder Smith: "Not only that, but the government disenfranchised the Church many years before the Saints ended the practice of plural marriage. To say that the Church ended plural marriage because the government 'threatened' to disenfranchise them is historically inaccurate in the extreme."

Uncle Ed: "I don't care. Polygamy is an abomination before God, a devil-centered sensual, evil practice that God has never and would never sanction nor command. Joseph

	Smith and Brigham Young were nothing more than charlatans and seducers in the first degree, and Joseph Smith got what he deserved because of it."
Linda:	"Elders, I can understand about the other things, but this polygamy—how could that be of God? I just can't see it!"
Elder Jones:	"Elder, this leads us to our last Article of faith."
Elder Smith:	"Right, the thirteenth Article of Faith reads, 'We believe in being honest, true, chaste, benevolent, virtuous, and in doing good to all men; indeed, we may say that we follow the admonition of Paul—We believe all things, we hope all things, we have endured many things, and hope to be able to endure all things. If there is anything virtuous, lovely, or of good report or praiseworthy, we seek after these things.'"
Uncle Ed:	"There sure isn't anything praiseworthy in seeking after many wives (laughing)."
Elder Jones:	"You say that Joseph and Brigham were evil men because of plural marriage, Mr. Brown?"
Uncle Ed:	"No, I believe they were just plain evil men, and one thing they did to reveal that they were evil was to practice polygamy."
Elder Smith:	"Were Abraham, and Jacob, and King David evil men, Mr. Brown?"
Uncle Ed:	"They needed salvation."
Elder Smith:	"Very true, but were they evil men like you say Joseph and Brigham were?"
Uncle Ed:	(Laughing) "Of course not—they were men of God."
Elder Smith:	"Yet they practiced polygamy, and, according to you, that makes them evil men."
Linda:	"What? They practiced polygamy? You never told me that, Uncle."
Uncle Ed:	"Well, so, they were sinners like you and I. The difference between Abraham and Joseph Smith is that Abraham looked to his God to forgive his sins, while Joe Smith looked to his God to justify his sins."
Elder Smith:	"So you are saying that when Abraham, Jacob, and David practiced polygamy they were sinning?"
Uncle Ed:	"Absolutely! God allows sin. It doesn't mean he approves of it."

Elder Jones:	"Let's turn to the scriptures. Why didn't God command Abraham, or Jacob, or David, or Solomon not to marry all these women?"
Uncle Ed:	"Ha! Can you show me where He does command them to practice polygamy?"
Elder Jones:	"All right, here in 2nd Samuel 12, verses 7 and 8, the Lord says to David, 'Thus saith the Lord God of Israel, I anointed thee king over Israel, and I delivered thee out of the hand of Saul; and *I gave thee* thy master's house, and thy master's *wives* into thy bosom.'"
Uncle Ed:	"Ah, but that doesn't prove a thing. You're forgetting that David was a fallen king."
Elder Smith:	"Mr. Brown, even you should know that the Lord called David the apple of his eye, and blessed him all the time he had many wives, and chastized him only when he had committed adultery with Uriah's wife."
Uncle Ed:	"No, wrong. You don't know what you're talking about."
Linda:	"But Uncle Ed, the Lord himself said that he gave David's wives to him."
Uncle Ed:	"Quiet, Linda. Now look boys, polygamy is of the devil and Joseph Smith is a false prophet! Heaven has no room for polygamous gods!"
Elder Jones:	"Mr. Brown, Paul says in Galatians 3:7 that Christians are 'the children of Abraham,' in other words, children of a polygamist. Paradise itself is called Abraham's bosom. (Luke 16:22) All born-again Christians want to enter the New Jerusalem, but they might be offended, because written on the twelve gates are the names of the twelve sons of Jacob, a polygamist, and many of them were polygamists themselves. (Revelation 21:14) Christians the world over wish to worship Jesus, a descendant of Judah, who was a polygamist, and David, who was a polygamist, and Solomon, probably the world's greatest polygamist. (Revelation 22:16) I'm afraid, Mr. Brown, that whether it be in Abraham's bosom, or in the New Jerusalem, or before Jesus who is a descendant of David, the polygamists Joseph and Brigham will feel right at home. But you, Mr. Brown, may feel a bit uncomfortable."
Linda:	"Elder Jones, that was fantastic."

Uncle Ed:	(Extremely angry) "I've had enough of these insults. Both of you kids have persistently lied, blasphemed, interrupted, disrupted, and corrupted. I'll have no more of it!"
Elder Smith:	"If you want no more, that's your choice, Mr. Brown. We didn't ask to have this discussion with you in the first place. It was your request. What we're concerned about, Linda, is how *you* feel about the things we've shared with you today. Do you believe what we have explained is true?"
Linda:	"No, I don't *believe* it is."
Uncle Ed:	(Contentfully) "Well, I think that's all, boys. Thank you for stopping by."
Linda:	"Wait Uncle Ed, let me finish. Like I said, I don't just *believe* it's true—I *know* its true!"
Uncle Ed:	(Shocked) "What? Now wait just one damned minute!"
Linda:	"Elders, can we go ahead with my baptism as soon as possible?"
Elder Jones:	"We certainly can, Linda."
Uncle Ed:	(Extremely angry) "Now listen, you boys, get out. Get out. I'm in charge of Linda's spiritual welfare, and I can see that you've brainwashed her!"
Elder Smith:	"We've answered all of her questions, and...."
Uncle Ed:	"You've answered nothing. All you have done is evade issue after issue. You haven't answered one question—not one. Now get out! I deliver both of you over to the buffetings of Satan, and to the eternal flames of hell!"
Linda:	"Uncle, you don't have the right to throw these Elders out. You are my guest. Remember, this is *my* apartment."
Uncle Ed:	"Linda, if you insist in proceeding with your baptism into this cult then I shall be forced to break all ties with you and deliver you likewise."
Linda:	"Uncle Ed, when you have calmed down you may visit again, but my decision is final."
Uncle Ed:	(Gets up and starts out the door.) "Linda, you're letting them split up the family. I can tell you that your parents will probably disown you."
Linda:	"I hope that my parents' love for me is greater than all of their prejudices."

Uncle Ed:	"Linda. please. I have other things to show you about Mormonism."
Linda:	"I have seen enough, Uncle Ed. The Elders have answered my questions and fully supported their answers from the Bible, while all you've done is criticize them. Time after time they showed me what you and your anti-Mormon people have charged is untrue. I'm sorry, I'm going to become a Latter-day Saint."
Uncle Ed:	"I'm sorry for you Linda, because you're going to hell! You haven't seen the last of me, boys." (Slams the door.)
Elder Jones:	"I'm afraid that *will* be true."
Elder Smith:	"We're sorry about all of this, Linda."
Linda:	"Oh, I'm not, Elders. I'm not sorry a bit, because now my prayers have been answered. Now I know the truth."
Elder Jones:	"Companion. Would you offer a closing prayer?"
Elder Smith:	"You bet! Heavenly Father, we thank thee for Linda, and for her testimony in the face of opposition, and we pray that she may be a strength to her family and that...."(fade).

* * * * * * * * * * * * * *

Please remember the points brought up in this dialogue. Contending with anti-Mormon adversaries is futile. They are not seeking truth and light, but attempting to ensnare and entrap.

However, sincere seekers of truth need to have their questions answered. Telling them "not to worry," or "just have faith" may imply to investigators that anti-Mormon allegations could be true, or that perhaps you cannot answer them.

How can you tell if a person is a sincere investigator rather than an anti-Mormon antagonist? That is simple: bear your testimony at the *beginning* of the discussion. Anti-Mormons may "play the part" of a sincere investigator at the beginning, but they will *not* want to hear your testimony. They will want to contend against the Spirit manifested in your testimony.

Remember, teach with the Spirit and the scriptures, and if the Spirit leaves, follow His example. Remember prayer, and remember also that truth will prevail.

Endnotes

1. Who's On The Lord's Side?

1. "Announcing the God Makers", Letter From J. Edward Decker Jr. to Pastors, p. 1.

2. *Here They Come...30,000 of Them,* (Tucson, Arizona: Calvary Missionary Press, N.D.), p. 3.

3. J. Edward Decker, Jr., "Mormonism", *Christian Life Magazine,* (April, 1979), p. 2.

4. Michael D'Antonio, *Group Aids Those Exiting Fundamentalist Religions.* The Sacramento Bee, August 19, 1982, p. 13.

2. Satan's Counter-mission: Ancient and Modern Parallels

1. *Mormonism: Christian or Cult?*, Saints Alive Tract, p. 1.

2. Joseph Klausner, *From Jesus to Paul,* (New York: The Macmillan Company, 1943), p. 297.

3. Herbert Danby, *The Jew and Christianity,* (London: The Sheldon Press, 1927), pp. 8, 20.

4. Justin, "Dialogue with Trypho", *The Ante-Nicene Fathers,* (Grand Rapids, Michigan: Wm. B. Eerdmans Publishing Company, 1885), vol. 1, pp. 203, 210, 198-199.

5. *Ibid.*

6. Adolf Von Harnack, *The Mission and Expansion of Christianity in the First Three Centuries,* (New York: Harper & Brothers, 1961), pp. 57-58.

7. Daniel J. Lasker, *Jewish Philosophical Polemics Against Christianity in the Middle Ages,* (New York: KTAV, 1977), p. 1.

8. Joseph Kausner, *Jesus of Nazareth,* (New York: Macmillan, 1959), pp. 18-19.

9. Pinchas Lapide, *Isrealis, Jews, and Jesus,* (Garden City, New York: Doubleday, 1979), p. 88.

10. *Ibid.*, p. 94.

11. R. Travers Herford, *Christianity in Talmud and Midrash,* (London: Williams & Norgate, 1903), p. 44.

12. Lapide, *op. cit.* p. 89.

13. *Ibid.*, p. 90.

14. Lasker, *op. cit.*, p. 5.

15. David Berger (Trans.), *The Jewish-Christian Debate in the High Middle Ages,* (Philadelphia: Jewish Publication Society of America, 1979), p. 3.

16. *Ibid.*, p. 4-6.

17. G. R. S. Mead, *Did Jesus Live 100 B. C.?,* (New Hyde Park, New York: University Books, 1968), p. 241.

18. Gustaf Dalman, *Jesus Christ in Talmud, Midrash, Zohar, and Liturgy of the Synagogue,* (New York: Arno, 1973), p. 11.

19. *Ibid.*, p. 8.

20. W. H. C. Frend, *Martyrdom and Persecution in the Early Church,* (Oxford: Basil Blackwell, 1965), p. 185.

21. *Ibid.*, p. 219.

22. *Ibid.*

23. *Ibid.*

24. *Ibid.*, p. 179.

25. *Journal of Jewish Studies,* (Autumn 1978), vol. 29, no. 2, p. 165.

26. Berger, *op. cit.*, p. 169.

27. Frend, *op. cit.*, p. 330.

28. Decker & Hunt, *The God Makers* (Eugene, Oregon: Harvest House Publishers, 1984) p. 143.

29. Fuller, Reginald H. *The Foundations of New Testament Christology* (New York: Charles Scribners's Sons, 1965), p. 90.

30. Workman, Herbert B. *Persecution in the Early Church* (Cincinnati: Jennings & Graham, 1906), p. 139.

31. Decker & Hunt, *op. cit.*, p. 259.
32. Ibid.
33. Williams, John, *The Holy Spirit, Lord & Life-Giver* (Neptune, New Jersey: Loizeaux Brothers, 1980), p. 286.

34. Decker & Hunt, *op. cit.* p. 98.
35. Berger, *op. cit.*, p. 64.

3. Man Can Attain Godhood: Ancient Evidence for Modern Mormon Doctrine

1. Decker & Hunt, *op. cit.*, p. 29.
2. *Ibid.*, p. 30.
3. *Ibid.*, p. 31.
4. Jerome, *The Homilies of Saint Jerome*, (Washington, D. C.: The Catholic University of America Press, 1964), pp. 106-107.
5. *Ibid.* p. 353.
6. *The Ante-Nicene Fathers, op. cit.*, vol. 3, p. 608.
7. G. L. Prestige, *God in Patristic Thought*, (London: 1956), p. 73.
8. *Ibid.*
9. Henry Bettenson, *The Early Christian Fathers*, (London: Oxford University Press, 1956), pp. 16-17.
10. *Ibid.*, p. 94.
11. *Ibid.*
12. *Ibid.*, pp. 95-96.
13. *Ibid.*, p. 106.
14. *Ibid.*, p. 243-244.
15. *Ibid.*, p. 324.
16. *Ibid.*
17. Lewis A. Hart, *A Jewish Reply to Christian Evangelists*, (New York: Bloch Publishing Company, 1906), p. 207.

18. Hislop, *op. cit.*, p. 16.
19. *Ibid.*, p. 197.
20. Richard P. McBrian, *Catholicism*, (Minneapolis: Winston Press, 1980), p. 347.
21. William J. Hill, *The Three-Personed God*, (Washington, D.C.: The Catholic University of America Press, 1982), p. 27.
22. *New Testament Theology*, (Grand Rapids, Michigan: Zondervan, 1967), vol. 1, p. 84.
23. *Ibid.*
24. James L. Barker, *Apostasy from the Divine Church*, (Salt Lake City, Utah: 1960), p. 44.
25. *Ibid.*
26. Bettenson, *op. cit.*, pp. 322-23.
27. *Ibid.*, p. 330.
28. *Ibid.*, p. 336.
29. *The Ante-Nicene Fathers, op. cit.*, vol. 3, p. 597.
30. *Ibid.*, vol. 3, p. 604.
31. *Ibid.*, vol. 3, pp. 612-613.
32. *Ibid.*, vol. 3, p. 603.

4. Early Christian Temple Rites: Ancient and Modern Parallels

1. D. S. Russel, *The Method and Message of Jewish Apocalyptic—200 B. C.-A. D. 100*, (Philadelphia: The Westminster Press, 1964), p. 107.
2. *Ibid.*, pp. 107-109.
3. Dr. E. S. Drower, *The Secret Adam*, p. xiv.
4. *Ibid.*, p. 66.
5. *Ibid.*, p. 24.
6. Dr. Johann L. Mosheim, *Historical Commentaries on the State of Christianity*, (New York: S. Converse, 1854), vol. 1, p. 127.

7. *Ibid.*, 1:373.
8. *Ibid.*, 1:77.
9. *Ibid.*, 1:391.
10. *Ibid.*, 2:472.
11. Tertullian, *Apologetical Works*, (Washington D. C.: The Catholic University of American Press, 1962), pp. 335-336.
12. *Ibid.*, p. 336.
13. *Ibid.*
14. Origen, *op. cit.*, p. 339.
15. *Ibid.*, p. 398.
16. Tertullian, *op. cit.*, p. 339.

17. *Ibid.*, p. 338.

18. Henry Bettenson, *The Early Christian Fathers* (London: Oxford University Press, 1956), p. 347.

19. Edwin Hatch, *The Influence of Greek Ideas on Christianity*, (New York: Harper & Row, 1957), p. 336.

20. R. P. C. Hanson, *Tradition in the Early Church*, (London: SCM Press, 1962), p. 32.

21. *Ibid.*, p. 182.

22. *Ibid.*, pp. 182-183.

23. Cyril, *The Works of Saint Cyril of Jerusalem*, (Washington D. C.: The Catholic University of America Press, 1969), vol. 1, pp. 79-80.

24. Dr. Hugh Nibley, *Since Cumorah*, (Salt Lake City, Utah: Deseret Book Company, 1976), p. 120.

25. *Ibid.*, pp. 118-119.

26. William H. Kelly, *Presidency and Priesthood*, (Lamoni, Iowa: Herald Publishing House, 1908), p. 80.

27. Decker & Hunt, *The God Makers* (Eugene, Oregon: Harvest House Publishers, 1984), p. 142.

28. *Ibid.*, p. 194.

29. *Ibid.*, p. 141.

30. Herbert B. Workman, *Persecution In the Early Church* (Cincinnati: Jennings & Graham, 1906), p. 157.

31. Robert Starling, *Errors, Distortions, and Misrepresentations in the Movie "The God Makers"*, (1984), p. 8.

32. Nibley, *op. cit.*, pp. 109-110.

33. Morton Smith, *The Secret Gospel*, (New York: Harper & Row, Publishers, 1973), pp. 73-74.

34. Joachim Jeremias, *The Eucharistic Words of Jesus*, (New York; Charles Scribner's Sons, 1966), p. 125.

35. *Ibid.*, pp. 130-131.

36. Charles W. Heckthorn, *The Secret Societies of all Ages and Countries*, (New Hyde Park, New York: University Books, 1965), p. 107.

37. William Kingsland, *The Gnosis or Ancient Wisdom in the Christian Scripture*, (London: 1937), p. 75.

38. Hugh Nibley, *The Message of the Joseph Smith Papyri*, (Salt Lake City, Utah: Deseret Book Company, 1975), p. 282.

39. Cyril, *op. cit.*, pp. 161-164, 171-172.

40. *Ibid.*, p. 195.

41. Nibley, *op. cit.*, p. 281.

42. *Ibid.*, p. 282.

43. Cyril, *op. cit.*, p. 197.

44. Nibley, *op. cit.*, p. 282.

45. *Ibid.*

46. Cyril, *op. cit.*, p. 194.

47. Heckthorn, *op. cit.*, pp. 98-99.

48. John J. Gunther, *St. Paul's Opponents and Their Background*, (Leiden: E. J. Brill, 1973) p. 290.

49. *Ibid.*, p. 293.

50. *Ibid.*, p. 296.

51. *Ibid.*

52. Andre Dupont-Sommer, *The Jewish Sect of Qumran and the Essenes*, (New York: The Macmillian Company, 1956), p. 49.

53. Edmund F. Sutcliffe, *The Monks of Qumran*, (Westminster, Maryland: The Newman Press, 1960), p. 124.

54. Diane and R. Scott Pike, *The Wilderness Revolt*, p. 75.

55. Howlett, *The Essenes and Christianity*, (New York: Harper & Brothers, 1957), pp. 134, 136, 142-143.

56. Martin A. Larson, *The Essene-Christian Faith*, (New York: Philosophical Library, 1980), p. 189.

57. *Ibid.*, p. 229.

58. Geza Vermes, *The Dead Seas Scrolls*, (Cleveland, Ohio; William Collins & World Publishing Co., 1977), p. 4.

59. Decker & Hunt, *op. cit.*, p. 121.

60. *Origins*, (London: Watts, 1909), p. 4.

61. Rev. C.P. Lyford, *The Mormon Problem* (New York: Hunt & Eaton, 1886) p. 81.

62. James L. Barker, *Apostasy from the Divine Church* (Salt Lake City, Utah: 1960) p. 65.

63. Joseph A. Seiss, *The Apocalypse*, (New York: Charles C. Cook, 1906), pp. 192-193.

64. *Ibid.*

65. J. Dwight Pentecost, *Things to Come*, (Grand Rapids, Michigan: Zondervan, 1958), p. 313.

66. Rev. L. T. Nichols, *Bible Chronology From Adam to Eternity*, (Rochester, New York: 1911), pp. 27-28.

67. Seiss, *op. cit.*, p. 190.

68. *Ibid.*, pp. 186-190.

69. Parley P. Pratt, *Key to Theology*, (Salt Lake City, Utah; Deseret Book Company, 1948), p. 80.

70. Joseph Fielding Smith, *Teachings of the Prophet Joseph Smith*, (Salt Lake City, Utah: Deseret Book, 1979) p. 364.

5. Gainsayer Missionary Strategies

1. Decker & Hunt, *The God Makers* (Eugene, Oregon: Harvest House Publishers, 1984) p. 18.

2. Origen, "Against Celsum", *The Ante-Nicene Fathers*, Book 1, *op. cit.*, p. 395.

6. "The God Makers" Film: An Example of Extreme Anti-Mormon Propaganda

1. NCCJ, *Programs in Pluralism*, March-April, 1984, Number 2, p. 3.

2. "Mormonism", reprint of J. Edward Decker, Jr., in Christian Life Magazine, April, 1979, p. 1.

3. Flo Conway, and Jim Siegelman, *Holy Terror: The Fundamentalist War on Freedoms in Religion, Politics, and our Private Lives*, (Garden City, New York: Doubleday & Company, 1982), p. ii.

4. *Ibid.*

5. *Ibid.*

6. Decker & Hunt, *The God Makers* (Eugene, Oregon: Harvest House Publishers, 1984) pp. 1, 10, 14-15, 19.

7. Conway & Siegelman, *op. cit.*, p. 4.

8. *Ibid.*, pp. 4-6, 15.

7. Responses to Other Anti-Mormon Distortions and Misrepresentations

1. *The Washington Christian News*, (October, 1979), vol. 3, No. 7, 1980, p. 8.

2. Joseph Fielding Smith, *Teachings of the Prophet Joseph Smith* (comp.) (Salt Lake City, Utah: Deseret Book, 1979) p. 119.

3. *Ibid.*, p. 327.

4. *Ibid.*, p. 290.

5. *Journal of Discourses*, vol. 1, p. 273.

6. *Journal of Discourses*, vol. 14, p. 113.

7. *Journal of Discourses*, vol. 14, p. 226.

8. *Journal of Discourses*, vol. 1, p. 239.

9. *Journal of Discourses*, vol. 12, p. 227.

10. *Journal of Discourses*, vol. 1, p. 238.

11. Joseph Fielding Smith, *Doctrines of Salvation*, (Salt Lake City, Utah: Bookcraft, 1956), vol. 3, p. 191.

12. James Montgomery Boice, *Does Inerrancy Matter?*, (Oakland, California: International Council on Biblical Inerrancy, 1979), p. 12.

13. *Ibid.*

14. Decker & Hunt, *The God Makers* (Eugene, Oregon: Harvest House Publishers, 1984), p. 199.

15. Henry Chadwick, (Trans.), *Origen: Against Celsum*, (Cambridge: At the University Press, 1965). p. 38.

16. *Journal of Discourses*, vol. 1, p. 50.

17. *Journal of Discourses*, vol. 1, p. 51.

18. *Journal of Discourses*, vol. 18, p. 290.

19. Bruce R. McConkie, *Doctrinal New Testament Commentary*, (Salt Lake City, Utah: Bookcraft, 1966), vol. 3, p. 822.

20. Bruce R. McConkie, *Doctrinal New Testament Commentary*, vol. 1, p. 82.

21. Lactantius, *The Divine Institutes*, (The Fathers of the Church, Washington D. C.: The Catholic University of America Press, 1964), vol. 49, p. 139.

22. James L. Barker, *Apostasy from the Divine Church* (Salt Lake City, Utah, 1960) p. 49.

23. Arno C. Gaebelein, *Gabriel and Michael*, (Wheaton, Illinois: Van Kamper Press, 1945), p. 7.

24. *Ibid.*, p. 92.

25. Archibald Robertson, *The Origins of Christianity*, (New York: International Publishers, 1954), p. 175.

26. Marcel Simon, *Jewish Sects at the Time of Jesus*, (Philadelphia: Fortress Press, 1971), p. 117.

27. *Ibid.*, p. 118.

28. Raphael Patai, *The Hebrew Goddess*, (New York: KTAV Publishing, 1967), p. 139.

29. *Ibid.*

30. R. V. Sellers, *Two Ancient Christologies*, (London: S. P. C. K., 1954), pp. 20-21.

31. *The Ante-Nicene Fathers*, vol. 3, p. 614.

32. Joseph Fielding Smith, *Teachings of the Prophet Joseph Smith, op. cit.*, p. 375.

33. Ogden Kraut, *Jesus Was Married*, (1969), p. 21.

34. *Ibid.*, p. 136.

35. *Ibid.*, p. 137.

36. *Ibid.*

37. Kraut, *op. cit.*, p. 24.

38. *Ibid.*, p. 90.

39. *Ibid.*, p. 92.

40. "Trend and Differentials in Births to Unmarried Women," *Vital and Health Statistics*, (Series, 21, No. 38, U. S.: 1970-76; U. S. Department of Health and Human Services, May 1980), p. 51.

41. *Ibid.*, (March 1978), Series 21, No. 29, p. 29.

42. Robert Starling, *Errors, Distortions, and Misrepresentations in the Movie 'The God Makers,'*, (1984), p. 9.

43. Dr. Joe J. Christensen, "Our Religion and Mental Health," *The Improvement Era*, (1984), p. 9.

44. Decker & Hunt, *op. cit.*, p. 40.

45. *Journal of Discourses*, vol. 18, p. 231.

46. *LDS Bible Dictionary*, p. 617.

47. *Ibid.*, p. 697.

48. Roland H. Bainton, *Here I Stand*, (New York: Abingson-Cokesbury Press, 1950), p. 331.

49. *LDS Bible Dictionary, op. cit.*, p. 617.

50. Form Letter from Saints Alive to Pastors, p. 1.

51. Alexander Hislop, *The Two Babylons*, (Neptune, New Jersey: Loizeaux Brothers, 1916), p. 201.

52. Decker & Hunt, *op. cit.*, p. 209.

53. Friedrich Rest, *Our Christian Symbols*, (Philidelphia: The Christian Education Press, 1954), p. 1.

Index

237